The Angel out of the House

VICTORIAN LITERATURE AND CULTURE SERIES

Karen Chase, Jerome J. McGann, and Herbert Tucker, Editors

The Angel out of the House

Philanthropy and Gender in Nineteenth-Century England

Dorice Williams Elliott

UNIVERSITY PRESS OF VIRGINIA

CHARLOTTESVILLE AND LONDON

The University Press of Virginia
© 2002 by the Rector and Visitors of the University of Virginia
Printed in the United States of America on acid-free paper

First published 2002

9 8 7 6 5 4 3 2 1

LIBRARY OF CONGRESS CATALOGING-IN-PUBLICATION DATA
Elliott, Dorice Williams, 1951–
    The angel out of the house : philanthropy and gender in
nineteenth-century England / Dorice Williams Elliott.
        p.   cm.— (Victorian literature and culture series)
Includes bibliographical references and index.
    ISBN 0–8139-2088-4 (cloth : alk. paper)
    1. Women in charitable work—England—History—19th century.
    2. Women philanthropists—England—History—19th century.
    3. Women in literature.   4. Charity in literature.   I. Title.   II. Series.
        HV541 .E44 2002
        361.7′082′094209034—dc21

                                                                2001005108

For Bob

Contents

Acknowledgments

THIS PROJECT WOULD NOT have happened without the insight and direction provided by Mary Poovey and Frances Ferguson, who oversaw it in its first incarnation as a dissertation. Thanks should go to many other professors and fellow graduate students at Johns Hopkins, especially Judy Walkowitz, Cynthia Rogers, and William Weaver. Members of the Folger Library's colloquium on Women in the Eighteenth Century offered valuable feedback on drafts of several chapters. Special thanks go to Sue Lanser, Vin Carretta, and Cathy Temple. I am also grateful to my colleagues at the University of Kansas. Pete Casagrande supplied helpful suggestions on the entire manuscript, while Byron Caminero-Santangelo, Joe Harrington, Katie Conrad, Dick Hardin, George Worth, and Max Sutton also read portions and gave thoughtful criticism, as did members of the Hall Center for the Humanities British Seminar. I also appreciate the advice and support of Jim Hartman, Tom Lorenz, and Marta Caminero-Santangelo.

Much of the work of the later stages of this project was supported by the University of Kansas General Research Fund, and travel grants for research in the British Library were furnished by the Johns Hopkins University English Department Bollman Fund and the Women's Studies Ford Foundation travel fund.

For assistance in preparing the manuscript, I would like to thank Pam LeRow, Paula Courtney, and Lynn Porter, as well as Donna Bonnel, Ann Thonen, Lori Whitten, and Dodie Coker. I also want to express thanks to Cathie Brettschneider at the University Press of Virginia for her patience and encouragement, to Ellen Satrom and Toni Mortimer for their careful attention and skillful editing, and to the series editors for the Victorian Literature and Culture Series.

For astute criticism of the manuscript and much-needed emotional support, I thank my colleague and friend Anna Neill. My deepest thanks go to my family. My parents, Tess and Maxine Williams, have been unfailingly supportive, and my children, Brooke, Jane, and Colin Elliott, have been cheerful and understanding about the countless hours required to finish this book. To my husband, Bob Elliott, I owe an "unrepayable debt" for his great personal sacrifice and the many ways, intellectual, emotional, and material, that he contributed. This book could not have been written without him.

A version of chapter 2 was published as "Sarah Scott's *Millenium Hall* and Female Philanthropy," *Studies in English Literature, 1500–1900* 35, no. 3 (1995): 535–53, by The Johns Hopkins University Press. Chapter 3 appears as "'The Care of the Poor Is Her Profession': Hannah More and Women's Philanthropic Work," *Nineteenth-Century Contexts* 19, no. 2 (1995): 179–204, and is reproduced with permission from Taylor and Francis Ltd. Chapter 5, "The Marriage of Classes in Elizabeth Gaskell's *North and South,*" appeared in *Nineteenth-Century Literature* 49 (June 1994): 21–49, and is reprinted with permission of the University of California Press.

The Angel out of the House

Introduction

THE 1893 INTERNATIONAL EXHIBITION, held in Chicago and dedicated to showcasing the achievements of the nineteenth century, featured a new and unique section devoted to "women's work." The contribution of Great Britain to this new department of the exhibition focused on women's philanthropy and was organized, at the invitation of a Royal Commission, by the well-known philanthropist Baroness Angela Burdett-Coutts. The exhibit included a published report, a collection of "Congress Papers" by "Eminent Writers" entitled *Woman's Mission*. In her preface to the report, the baroness writes: "It is fitting that the close of the nineteenth century should focus and illustrate in a definite form the share which women have taken in its development, of which, in my humble judgment, the truest and noblest, because the most natural, part, is to be found in philanthropic work." Reflecting on the previous sixty years of British history, Burdett-Coutts credits women's philanthropy, women's "most natural" work, with raising the moral tone of the nation and significantly contributing to the amelioration of the social ills industrialization caused. The papers that make up *Woman's Mission* stress the benevolent and sympathetic, but also efficient and professional, nature of the philanthropies they describe. "No feature of the single-handed work of women is more striking," writes Burdett-Coutts, "than the wisdom and discretion with which it is generally conducted. Inspired by a large-hearted benevolence, and warm sympathy with the poor and suffering, the majority of women workers in philanthropy have not allowed their feelings to obscure their judgment. They recognize that—'The truly generous is the truly wise'" (285).

Published two years earlier, a popular satire by an anonymous clergyman gives a different view of nineteenth-century women philanthropists. *My District Visitors* (1891) represents women who participate in parish charity work as either officious and overbearing or naive and gullible. Of Kerenhappuch Blyte, "Spinster and Prophetess," the clergyman writes, "To set her down amongst our peace-loving denizens would be equivalent to introducing the hawk to the wood-pigeon"; her self-authored tracts and hectoring visits frighten not only the poor but the clergyman as well (16). Dolly Beniment, by constrast, is young, sexually attractive, and credulous; although a "most indefatigable visitor," she is so trusting and indiscriminate with her charity that the clergyman has to spend much of his time undoing what she has done (32). The third visitor, Mistress Agatha Comfort, is likewise taken advantage of by the poor because of her generosity and old-fashioned assumptions about the respect and deference due her as the lady of the manor. Despite their enthusiasm and well-meaning intentions, the parson's visitors either offend or are hoodwinked by the poor, and they require constant and careful supervision by the more judicious clergyman to keep them from doing more harm than good. Whether a domineering old maid, a pretty but silly young woman, or a patronizing Lady Bountiful, a philanthropic woman seems able to succeed only at "making herself an object of derision" (77).

The figure of the philanthropic woman had long evoked such contradictory perceptions. Perhaps the most famous parodies of the strong-minded woman philanthropist were the "telescopic philanthropist," Mrs. Jellyby, and the "cast-iron Lady Bountiful," Mrs. Pardiggle, in Charles Dickens's *Bleak House* (1853), but many others appeared in print as well throughout the nineteenth century.[1] An unsigned 1859 article in *Fraser's Magazine,* for example, worried about the supposedly inevitable defeminization of women who became involved in philanthropic work. Entitled "A Fear for the Future, That Women Will Cease to Be Womanly," the article describes a group of typical modern young women at a ball:

> There are plenty of good-looking young ladies, whose toilette is
> not the most carefully arranged in the world. . . . They are in-
> fluential members of society; they are presiding influences of
> sundry Committees and Female Associations for the Alteration
> of This, the Abolition of That, or the Advancement of the
> Other. They write pamphlets, and issue manifestoes; they speak
> at crowded meetings, and take an ardent part in important con-
> troversies. They are not really young women—they are Public
> Persons. (246)

The article writer's description explicitly raises the threat that women's
philanthropy will jeopardize the separation between the domestic and
public spheres that seemed to Victorians to be the foundation of social order. Paying attention to public affairs, the writer concludes, leads
young women to neglect feminine duties, such as proper attention to
their "toilette." Women in his generation, the writer maintains, "were
women, the helpmates, consolers, and adornments of our homes." To the
younger generation, made unwomanly by their interest and participation
in public activities related to philanthropy, he gives this warning about
the consequences of their unfeminine behavior: "Any of my sons, I am
quite sure, would as soon think of making love to Lord Brougham or the
statue of Mr. Canning, as of uttering a word of anything sentimental to
these ladies" (246–47).

Another contemporary (male) writer, however, directly counters such
attacks on philanthropic women. "A vast amount of practical work has
been recently done by women in ways hitherto unattempted," wrote
J. H. Howson in 1860. "New enterprises have been bravely undertaken
by them, and patiently and successfully pursued." He explains that "during the last ten years a palpable change has taken place amongst us, both
in feeling and practice": "There is less prejudice than there was. This is
very evident to any one who has carefully noticed the books and pamphlets which have been published during this period, in description, and
in justification, of the work of women."[2] In praising the work philanthropic women have accomplished, Howson notes that written representations have worked not only to describe but to justify women's work
outside their homes.

Clearly, for a mid-Victorian audience proud of what Anna Jameson called its "awakened public conscience," philanthropic work, and the widespread participation in it of middle- and upper-class women, was a crucial public issue.[3] Philanthropy was crucial because it was the era's chief method of dealing with the social ills created by the rapid rise of industrial capitalism as well as by the age-old problems of poverty, illness, and misfortune. Although many men were involved in the direction of charities, visiting systems, and other philanthropic projects, the voluntary efforts of middle-class women were the mainstay of most philanthropic endeavors, as Baroness Burdett-Coutts documents retrospectively in *Woman's Mission*. Vital as their work may have been, however, contemporary representations—whether parodic such as Dickens's, admonitory such as that of the unnamed writer in *Fraser's Magazine,* or laudatory such as Howson's—reveal the tensions and anxieties inherent in the figure of the philanthropic woman.

Middle-class women's volunteer philanthropic work was centrally concerned with two social and ideological issues—the appropriate role of women and relations between the classes. On the one hand, women's charitable work was promoted as a laudable and natural extension of the idealized domestic sphere assigned to women. By relieving and educating the poor, often in their own homes, women's charity was supposed to ease conflict between the classes and foster social harmony. On the other hand, however, because philanthropy was the "sphere of independent labour most accessible to ambitious women," it also gave rise to apprehensions about the defeminization of women and the destruction of the happy home life they were expected to superintend.[4] Moreover, women's philanthropic efforts—especially the "wrong" kind of philanthropic efforts—could work to increase friction between working-class people and "their betters." Dickens's Mrs. Pardiggle, for instance, ostensibly aims to break down class barriers by helping the poor in their own homes; instead, she creates resentment and hostility, symbolized by her voluminous skirts that both protect her person from any physical contact with the people she visits and also knock down "little chairs" that are "quite a great way off." It is not surprising that the brickmaker whose cottage she visits responds to her intrusion with annoyance: "I wants it done, and over. I wants a end of these liberties took with my place. I wants an end of being drawed like a badger. Now you're a-going to poll-pry and question according to custom—I know what you're a-going to be up to. Well! You haven't got no occasion to be up to it."[5] Similarly, the unnamed parson of *My District Visitors* has a working-class woman express the resentment many of the poor were feared to harbor: "I reckon these Districk Visitors is a goin' to set us all to the rightabouts. . . . I 'spose poor folks was made to be axed questions on" (78–79). Visitors such as these, of course, would not contribute to more harmonious class relations.

Because philanthropic work involved women in relations among the classes, it also inevitably brought them into contact—and conflict—with a (relatively) new class of male professionals whose claim to authority came from their supposed expertise in diagnosing and treating society's problems. Doctors and clergymen, of course, had long engaged in personal dealings with the poor and disadvantaged, but by the nineteenth century many other men—political economists, journalists, statisticians, and bureaucrats, as well as parliamentary reformers and well-known novelists such as Dickens and Disraeli—were making careers out of observing, reporting, and analyzing the conditions of life among the lower orders. The satires of "professional" female philanthropists and ignorant or overbearing charitable visitors reveal these male professionals' anxieties about competition for authority in a newly conceived social sphere. Such writers revealed they were uneasy about the challenge that systematized female philanthropy posed not only to accepted gender roles and class relations but also to their own position as experts on social relations.

Considering how controversial women's philanthropic work was for nineteenth-century writers and observers, it is surprising how many historians and literary critics, including feminists, have written off women's philanthropic work as do-gooding or patriarchal collusion without recognizing the crucial role it played in redefining both gender and class roles in eighteenth- and nineteenth-century Britain.[6] Although eighteenth- and nineteenth-century philanthropy did work to reinforce some dominant cultural ideas and practices, the fact that women's participation in philanthropy could provoke such varied representations gives an inkling of the inherent challenge that women's practice of philanthropy posed to the domestic ideology of separate spheres and to the ideal of harmonious class relations, despite the common assumption that it was merely an extension of women's domestic role. It is not coincidental, for instance, that by the end of *Bleak House* Dickens has Mrs. Jellyby turn from philanthropy to women's suffrage.

While women's charitable activities could arouse anxieties and spark ridicule, most people in mid-nineteenth-century England believed that women should and would participate in philanthropic work.[7] As a number of historians and critics who have studied the history of women and their roles have observed, women's philanthropy seemed to be a natural extension of their domestic role. Very few, however, have offered any explanation of why this assumption came to be made. Charity is not a "natural" extension of women's domestic role; rather, the connection between charitable and domestic work, like many other assumptions about gender roles, is the result of specific historical factors and cultural representations. It is the aim of this study to document the cultural work that such representations of women performing philanthropic deeds accomplished in eighteenth- and nineteenth-century Britain.

By employing the term "cultural work" in connection with literary representations, I assert that literary works function along with other kinds of discourses in shaping the ideas, attitudes, and ideologies that organize human relations. Novels in particular, because they construct imaginary worlds peopled with invented characters, provide the ground on which ideological problems can be imaginatively staged and resolved. Thus novels, however realistic they may seem, not only reflect certain ideas or perceived realities but work to shape what people think and perceive as real. The novels and other texts that I discuss portray middle- and upper-class women taking an active part in endeavors that were perceived to have important social, economic, and political consequences, and in doing so they also helped to produce and authorize women's desires to participate in such endeavors.

Women's Ambitious Desires and Domestic Ideology

According to the eighteenth- and nineteenth-century bourgeois ideology of separate spheres for men and women, women's desires centered in the home. Although the Eve-like image of women as sexually voracious, inherent in the Christian creation story and prevalent in the medieval and early modern periods, was largely replaced by the chaste, modest "angel" by the end of the eighteenth century, even this model of pure, virtuous womanhood defined women as inherently sexual. Marlene Legates, for instance, suggests that the eighteenth-century preoccupation with female chastity was a "response to an underlying conviction of female sexuality"; virtuous women's much-praised self-regulation assumed that underneath there were lascivious desires that needed to be regulated.[8] Even if a woman's unruly desires were carefully controlled and properly channeled into marriage and motherhood, her position as the guardian and nurturer of the home was predicated on her sexual reproductive function.

As late as the early twentieth century, Sigmund Freud re-inscribed sexuality as the sole determiner of women's nature. In his discussion of fantasies, Freud ascribed both "ambitious" and "erotic" desires to men, but he maintained that women have only "erotic" desires. Within the term "erotic," of course, Freud would include not only overtly sexual but romantic and motherly desires, which, by extension or displacement, could even include spiritual or altruistic longings. All such emotions are similar in that they are traceable to women's reproductive function— their capacity to bear and nurture children. Men, by contrast, are only partly defined by their reproductive role as inseminators; Freud attributes to them another whole realm of desires not directly related to their sexuality—the realm of conquest and aspiration that he terms "ambitious."[9]

Nancy K. Miller has disputed Freud's analysis, arguing that the "implausibilities" in literary works by women signal their hidden ambitious desires.[10] Like Freud, however, Miller assumes that such desires are innate. I argue, by contrast, that women's ambitious desires for activity outside the domestic sphere were generated in part by representations of women's philanthropic work. My contention is based in part on René Girard's theory of desire in *Deceit, Desire, and the Novel*. Girard maintains that desire is fundamentally imitative and contagious; one's desires are not spontaneous but rather arise from an awareness that someone else desires the chosen object.[11]

While theorists of the concept of desire, including psychologists and philosophers, have debated whether desires are inherent and natural or culturally constructed and imbedded in language (or some combination of the two), Girard's theory of mimetic desire works especially well in describing the competitive, individualistic society that followed the Industrial Revolution, beginning roughly in the later eighteenth century.[12]

In a historical situation in which social hierarchies are unstable, explains Girard's follower Paisley Livingston, not only are specific desires likely to be mimetic but mimesis as a way of desiring is pervasive.[13] In other words, a competitive capitalist society is fueled by people's desires for what other people have and desire.

Girard assigns literary representations a key role in generating mimetic desires because they can serve as the model of desires to be imitated. Gustave Flaubert's Emma Bovary, Girard suggests, "desires through the romantic heroines who fill her imagination," while Don Quixote desires to experience the exploits of the heroic Amadis.[14] Although he wrote in the second half of the twentieth century, Girard's examples still repeat Freud's split between male and female desires; Don Quixote has both ambitious and erotic desires, while Emma Bovary's are all erotic. It is interesting, however, that an eighteenth-century rewriting of Cervantes's *Don Quixote,* Charlotte Lennox's *The Female Quixote* (1752), already uses women's philanthropy to undermine that distinction. Arabella, the heroine, tries to fashion her life (and her wardrobe) after antiquated tales of romance, but her activities include regular visits to the poor and performing other charitable works as well as seeking a heroic lover.[15] Unlike Emma Bovary, then, Lennox's heroine exhibits both erotic and ambitious desires derived directly from literary representations.

While not all desires are generated so directly, especially by literary works, Girard's model suggests that eighteenth- and nineteenth-century women may have begun to develop ambitious desires through seeing them represented. These desires could be generated even before actual opportunities to fulfill them were readily available. Although many women may never have read a novel that featured a philanthropic heroine or heard a charity sermon praising women's contributions to charitable institutions, such representations contributed to the array of cultural possibilities people came to accept as natural and desirable. Texts that represented women whose desires were neither exclusively erotic nor entirely contained within the domestic sphere made women's ambitious desires seem possible and even reasonable.

This project builds on the work of previous literary-historical critics such as Nancy Armstrong and Mary Poovey, who have demonstrated that ideas about and prescriptions for women, their desires, and their appropriate roles were foundational in the formation of a middle-class subjectivity in the later eighteenth and early nineteenth centuries.[16] Domestic ideology, promulgated in large part through conduct books and sentimental novels, depicted a female subject whose value was defined by her exemplary internal qualities rather than by the showy exterior such texts associated with a corrupted aristocracy. As guardians of a domestic sphere that was increasingly portrayed as the repository of society's best values, women were accorded not only the management of the crucial activities of the home but also the power of their influence. Thus, women were accorded a new kind of cultural authority because of their role within a recently valorized domestic space, but it came at the cost of having their desires and activities more strictly confined within that space.

While earlier feminist scholars focused primarily on women's oppression by and resistance to patriarchal authority, these more recent accounts of the new power that domestic ideology afforded to women, in conjunction with historical examinations of the economic conditions many women faced, go a long way toward explaining why most women did not rebel against or actively resist what seem to twentieth-century feminists to have been intolerable limitations and constraints.[17] Women of all sorts, including noted early feminists such as Mary Wollstonecraft, participated in and benefited from the organization of social relationships that assigned different roles and desires to men and women.[18] Yet despite the fact that domestic ideology's gendered division of labor had achieved almost universal acceptance in nineteenth-century Britain, its ideals could not accommodate all women. Single women, whether never married or widowed, posed a problem for an ideology that confined all women's activities and desires to a home, husband, and family. Philanthropy was domestic ideology's primary answer to the "problem" of the single woman who had no obvious family duties; it was arguably a domestic activity, but it did not require a woman to be married. Because philanthropy allowed women to perform useful activities defined as domestic without channeling all their desires into marriage, it not only offered unmarried women an alternative to marriage but also proved that women could be defined by something other than their sexuality, or their ability to reproduce. Therefore, including women's philanthropic work under the umbrella of domestic ideology both reinforced and posed a fundamental challenge to that ideology's most basic premise. Rather than resisting the sexual division of labor, philanthropic representations extended it beyond the home to include social and eventually national institutions, thereby reinforcing the notion that men and women were essentially different. At the same time, however, by encouraging women's ambitious desires, such representations contested the idea, which was still being repeated by Freud at the end of the nineteenth century, that women's desires were fundamentally dissimilar to men's.

By focusing on a contradiction or tension within what by the mid-nineteenth century seemed a hegemonic ideology, I am able to identify one of the factors that enabled a change in the way the category of woman was defined between the beginning of the eighteenth century and the end of the nineteenth. One of the problems with studies that focus on women's oppression is that once the power of the oppressor is established and elaborated, it is difficult to explain where change comes from, or how individuals believed they could resist. Similarly, if, like many Foucauldians, one focuses on totalizing discourses that assimilate even open resistance, it becomes nearly impossible to explain how change occurs. By concentrating not on resistance but on an internal contradiction within domestic ideology, I am able to show how even women who heartily embraced its ideals (unconsciously or not) challenged and helped to change them.

Thus this book is not merely a thematic study of women and philanthropic work, several of which have been published, but rather it is an exploration of the ideological impact of philanthropy through its representation in literary and nonliterary works, primarily by women authors. I am indebted to two important historical studies of nineteenth-century women's philanthropic work: F. K. Prochaska's *Women and Philanthropy in Nineteenth-Century England* and Anne Summers's "A Home from Home—Women's Philanthropic Work in the Nineteenth Century."[19] Prochaska documents women's participation in a variety of philanthropic undertakings and gives consideration to both the causes and effects of such activity in the lives and experiences of women from many ranks of society. Summers pays attention to the ideological implications of women's charitable work in the context of the nineteenth-century rethinking of the causes and proper treatment of poverty. Both also recognize that women's philanthropy played an important role in other women's issues, including employment, education, and suffrage. While such historical studies are essential to a complete understanding of the impact of women's philanthropy in eighteenth- and nineteenth-century Britain, this book takes up an equally significant aspect of this issue. Rather than analyzing the impact philanthropic work had on the lives of women, I consider how representations of women doing philanthropic work changed the way people conceived of the nature of women, regardless of whether any particular woman engaged in philanthropy.

Domestic ideology, of course, defined women as wives and mothers — emotional, nurturing, kind, and sympathetic. It was women's association with these qualities that supposedly justified their taking on the duty of caring for the poor and unfortunate; by depicting the needy as children, middle- and upper-class women could be represented as mothers to those beneath them on the social scale and as wives to public men who used philanthropy to address political and social problems. As the theory and practice of philanthropy changed, however, becoming at first more businesslike, later more professionalized, and finally bureaucratized, it became more difficult to naturalize women's "mothering" and "wifely" participation in philanthropic work. Nonetheless, by recasting the terms of domestic ideology, women could defend their participation in activities that were further and further removed from the domestic sphere that ideology prescribed. Using the terms of domestic ideology to elude its restrictions also limited what philanthropy could accomplish for women. As long as middle- and upper-class women were content to live with the legal, political, and economic inequality that domestic ideology justified, philanthropic volunteer work could only be a partial fulfillment of the desires that philanthropic representations helped to produce.

While philanthropy might open new avenues and opportunities for middle- and upper-class women, whatever gains they attained by manipulating the terms of gender were made at the expense of both men and women of the lower classes who were infantalized and kept in a subordinate position by philanthropic work. Thus philanthropy cannot be said to have offered new opportunities for all or even the majority of actual women in eighteenth- and nineteenth-century Britain; nonetheless, by helping to rewrite the defining terms of the category of woman, specifically by acknowledging their ambitious desires, philanthropy did help to remove some of the limitations that the gendered division of labor placed on women in the nineteenth century.

To understand how representations of upper- and middle-class women performing acts of charity contributed to a redefinition of the category of woman, it is first necessary to trace some changes in the understanding of charity, philanthropy, and their roles that occurred during the eighteenth century in Britain. This account will unavoidably oversimplify complex historical processes and interactions, but to explain how significant changes in the understanding and practice of philanthropy occurred I also need to give a brief summary of the gradual yet critical changes in the organization and structure of eighteenth-century society at large. The changes I summarize are important to the study of philanthropy because they gradually redefined virtue so that sympathy, marked by the performance of charitable acts, became an important manifestation both of individual character and class status.

To explicate the role of philanthropy in relation to eighteenth-century notions of sympathy and virtue, I also need to clarify my use of the terms "charity" and "philanthropy." Although in twentieth-century usage, the term "philanthropy" often refers to large donations to any kind of nonprofit institution, in the eighteenth century "philanthropy" and "charity" could be used interchangeably with the general sense of having love for one's fellow beings or with the particular meaning of practical efforts to aid those in need.[20] However, the term "charity" was more often used to signify traditional, Christian, and localized or individual efforts to aid the poor and needy, while "philanthropy" referred more to secular, institutionalized, or at least systematized charitable endeavors. "Charity" was also sometimes used to refer to the emotion of benevolence that motivated the practice, termed "philanthropy." By the nineteenth century, "charity" and "philanthropy" are most often used synonymously, although some nineteenth- and even twentieth-century texts still reflect the slightly different sense earlier conveyed by the two terms. Like most historians of voluntary efforts for the relief of the needy, I frequently use terms such as "philanthropic" and "charitable" interchangeably. Part of what I document, however, is a shift in the way voluntary relief activities were conceived from the eighteenth to the nineteenth centuries, and, since the use of these terms reflects this transition, my usage follows that of the texts I discuss.

Sympathy, Sentiment, and Eighteenth-Century Philanthropy

One of the foremost philanthropists of the eighteenth-century Age of Benevolence was a London bookseller named Thomas Guy.[21] Guy, the son of a lighterman and coalmonger, began his apprenticeship in 1660, the year Charles II was restored to the throne, and he set up business for himself in 1668 with two hundred pounds as capital.[22] A noted contemporary praised Guy's "probity, skill, and zeal," although he also made a large portion of his money from the dubious practice of selling and reselling unlicensed Dutch Bibles that had been seized by the king's printers—and he was rumored to have engaged directly in "Bible-running" from the continent on a large scale.[23] After a stint as university printer for Oxford in the late seventeenth century and fourteen years as a member of Parliament, Guy devoted most of his time and resources to philanthropic projects—and to speculative investments.

Guy invested heavily in the South Sea Venture—he is said to have owned 45,500 shares of the original South Sea stock. As the stocks gradually rose, Guy began to sell out (first at three hundred pounds per share and finally at six hundred pounds per share), which earned him a fortune—unlike most of his fellow investors, who lost huge sums in the "Bubble." In addition to the charities he was already supporting and managing—an almshouse, a library, a town hall, numerous poor relatives, debtors, distressed families, young men setting up in business, Protestant refugees from Catholic Europe, and poor members and widows of the Stationers' Company (of which he was a long-standing member)—Guy used the money from his South Sea investments to finance the building of Guy's Hospital (adjacent to Saint Thomas's Hospital, to which he had already contributed heavily and on whose board of directors he served). His will, in which he left his still huge fortune to a large number of charitable causes, was published and went through at least four editions.[24]

Although he lived early in the century, Guy had a career emblematic of the economy of charity in the 1700s. Unlike the majority of large donors in previous eras, Guy was neither an aristocratic landowner nor a great overseas merchant. He was an upwardly mobile tradesman who made most of his fortune through entrepreneurial ventures, some of which were ethically questionable, and speculative investments. At the same time, however, he established a reputation for rectitude, generosity, and distinguished citizenship both through his major donations to charitable projects and his extensive service on the boards of governors for numerous philanthropic institutions. Although some of Guy's charities, particularly Guy's Hospital, were funded and endowed entirely with his own money, a number of the causes he worked for were financed by subscriptions solicited from many smaller donors, a relatively new method of philanthropic fund-raising.

Over the course of the eighteenth century, many members of the middle ranks of society such as Thomas Guy became involved in both the financing and managing of charities. Some made large donations from fortunes gained through shrewd business practices and investments, as Guy did. In addition, soliciting charitable subscriptions from numerous smaller donors became more and more common as a method of financing all sorts of philanthropic projects; the system of charitable subscription is commonly viewed as the hallmark of eighteenth-century philanthropy.[25] Modeled on joint-stock ventures such as the South Sea Venture, soliciting subscriptions for charity was like selling stock, and it seemed a logical step for philanthropists who had gained their fortunes through joint-stock investments. Most of the subscription charities were also managed like commercial enterprises, with a director, a body of governors, and weekly committees—and some turned out to be as fraudulent as the South Sea Bubble.[26] The language of the marketplace was even employed by clergymen promoting charitable activity; one clergyman found "spiritual significance in joint-stock companies" and declared that money invested in charity would bring "a dividend in the improved happiness and morality of the poor."[27] In fact, claims the historian David Owen, "properly administered charities can almost be thought of as instruments of mercantilist policy" because they would ensure a stable workforce and hence "safeguard national power."[28] Thus what contemporaries saw as progressive philanthropic endeavors were both modeled on and contributed to successful economic ventures and were an integral part of what William Wilberforce would later call the "commercial spirit" of the age.[29]

Prior to the eighteenth century, the two major motivations to charitable activity had been Christian doctrine and the tradition of aristocratic paternalism. For members both of the established church and dissenters, almsgiving was an essential part of Christianity, a duty and a means to salvation. Whether it took the form of donating large sums to build hospitals and almshouses or giving money to individual beggars or paupers, almsgiving was an essentially religious exercise. In Christian terms, such a gift was made, explains Betsy Rodgers, "for the sake of giving: the act was beneficial in itself and not in its results." [30] Under the long-standing system of aristocratic paternalism, which included poor law relief, those who lived and worked on or near the estates of landed proprietors were regarded as entitled to maintenance and care in case of accident, illness, infirmity, or other kinds of distress. The bonds between landholders and their "dependents" were reciprocal, and they were reinforced by the rituals of deference, as a number of historians have established.[31] Thus paternalistic acts of charity—visiting the sick among the poor; donating clothing, food, or bedding to the needy; and founding and teaching in charity schools—were part of the wealthier classes' duties to those who supplied their income. Poverty, explains Donna T. Andrew, was seen as "God's gracious method of allowing men to win salvation in the exercise of their mutual ties of obligation and gratitude," while charity was "the rent annexed [by God] to the use of property." [32] Both religious and paternalistic incentives continued to be powerful motivations for charitable activity throughout the eighteenth and nineteenth centuries, but alongside eighteenth-century innovations in financing and managing charity emerged another discourse that provided new arguments for participating in charitable enterprises—the secular discourse of sympathy.

The discourse of sympathy arose as part of more general changes in eighteenth-century Britain. As a broad generalization, it is accurate to say that eighteenth-century and early-nineteenth-century Britain saw a gradual transition from an agrarian, paternalistic, aristocratically ruled society to an individualistic market economy driven by the demands of industrial capitalism. Skillful exploitation of new market forces elevated Thomas Guy, for instance, from a tradesman to a wealthy and powerful political and social figure. The transition from an agrarian to a market economy and its precise historical significance have of course been studied intensively by countless historians, political theorists, economists, literary critics, and scholars from numerous other disciplines. What many of these accounts document is a shift away from genealogy and the possession of inherited landholdings as the sole measure of worth and standing to a new estimate of a person's worth based on individual qualities.[33] While family position and the ownership of inherited land continued to exert an enormous influence on social, political, and economic relations well beyond the nineteenth century, even the wealthiest aristocrats came more and more to be judged by new standards of virtue that rejected what was portrayed as profligacy and extravagance in favor of thrift, tastefulness, and, most crucial for this project, sympathy.

Sympathy was a key component of a complex of values that served as a new form of, or, as J. G. A. Pocock suggests, a substitute for, virtue.[34] In the sixteenth and early seventeenth centuries, virtue had been grounded in and guaranteed by the ownership of (nonmovable) property. Pocock describes how early-eighteenth-century commerce and government depended on a neoteric system of national, as well as local, credit. Some worried, however, about the imaginary nature of credit; relying on credit was trusting the nation's economic affairs to unpredictable forces that could be equated with the vagaries of human passions. Like a person who relied on passion rather than reason, the nation's economy, they feared, might succumb to hysterical forces.[35] The antidote to an economic and political system based on passion run wild was politeness and refinement. A number of thinkers, including the Earl of Shaftesbury, Francis Hutcheson, and David Hume, argued that the politeness and refinement that were to guarantee stability and hold society together were based in sympathy, or the general capacity for fellow feeling. John Mullan shows how Hume's early work, the *Treatise of Human Nature,* theorizes sympathy as the socializing of the passions. Like many other eighteenth-century thinkers, Hume's later work relies on a notion of sympathy as innate general benevolence. In his earlier work, however, Hume presented sympathy as the transfer of passions from one person to another. This capacity allowed one person not only to imagine but to feel the passions of another; thus sympathy was a condition of the social feelings of benevolence or humanity.[36]

For Adam Smith, in his *Theory of Moral Sentiments,* sympathy becomes an even more complicated regulator of passions that have to be governed to ensure social, political, and economic order. For Smith, sympathy is not simply the ability to feel another's passions, but rather it is the capacity to imagine one's own reactions to the situation that initially elicited the passion; sympathy involves becoming a spectator to one's own emotions as well as putting oneself in another's place.[37] Because a person can perform this act of imagination, he can also imagine how another spectator would view his own passionate reactions to situations.[38] Thus this internal spectator, which is part of the dynamic of sympathy, serves as a restraining force on the passions. Sympathy as an important moral guide and regulator of human relationships develops, according to Smith, through the experience of interacting with others, either through social converse or reading.[39] Thus the "man of feeling," whose sympathy had been developed through social interactions in polite society and literature, could replace—or at least join—the propertied "man of virtue" as a member of the ruling class.[40]

As this brief explanation of the historical significance of sympathy as a new signifier of virtue makes clear, the early-eighteenth-century notion of sympathy had everything to do with status and power, or what we might call class negotiations. Sympathy had a double valence: it was a quality located within an individual that validated his worth, his fitness to engage in private conversation and in public activities, and his creditworthiness (in both moral and economic senses) by stimulating and regulating his passions; but for the man trying to establish his credibility as a citizen and man of business, sympathy also needed to be publicly manifested in acts of fellow feeling—such as charity. Thus sympathy tied personal virtue to public benefit, both by regulating behavior and motivating benevolent actions that were increasingly viewed as solutions to social and political problems.

Sympathy as a private virtue, then, was the ability to imagine and share in the passions—or what were increasingly termed sentiments— of others. Sympathy with the sentiments of others was exhibited most prominently in novels of sentiment, which were in vogue in the 1760s in particular. In sentimental novels, a virtuous character in distress is pitted against a predatory aristocrat who personifies the supposed evils of a ruling class whose passions are unregulated by sympathy.[41] In such novels, a character's "sensibility" is the sign of his or her virtuous fellow feeling, or sympathy. Sensibility was understood as a special susceptibility to feelings and sensations, often manifested physically through sighs, tears, and illness; although such symptoms might seem painful, sensibility was also represented as an exquisite pleasure, one that could even have the force of sexual pleasure.[42] Another indication of a character's sensibility, of course, is the performance of acts of charity for individuals in distress; such charitable acts are both caused by and give rise to exquisite sensations.[43] Although novels of sensibility have been repeatedly denigrated by later critics for these excessive displays of feeling, virtually all eighteenth-century sentimental novels extol not only the possession of the sympathetic emotions that characterized sensibility but also their regulation by considerations of honor and virtue, or what Adam Smith would call the inner spectator. Ungoverned sensibility was rarely portrayed as virtuous, even in the most sentimental novels. Thus sentimental novels both taught and valorized sympathy, comprising both sensibility and its regulation, as a virtue that validated a "modern" commercial society.

If sentimental novels were one manifestation of commercial society's new "reign of virtue," then philanthropy was another. While some recent critics have questioned the connection between portrayals of sentimental benevolence and actual philanthropic activity, contemporaries saw the two as causally related.[44] Charitable sermons and prospectuses frequently employed scenes of distress that would have been at home in any sentimental novel, with the express purpose of motivating audiences to donate time and money to philanthropic causes by playing on their "sensibilities." "Our Heart smites us, and our Flesh creeps, when Spectacles of Misery present themselves to us," preached Henry Layng in a sermon for Northampton County Infirmary in 1746; "It is sufficient to appeal to every Man's Breast, whether he does not feel a strong Sympathy, an unaccountable Disturbance, at the Appearance of a miserable Object, nay, even at the hearing of a tragical Story, wherein he is no way concern'd; nay, when he is apprized that the whole Representation is a Fiction, yet will it extort a Sigh, a Tear, even against the Bent of our Wills, and the Assistance of our Reason." Layng specifically connects the sympathetic feelings generated by "tragical Stor[ies]" with charity: "such a Commiseration and Charity is [sic] so deeply implanted in our Nature, that we cannot see any in Affliction and Misery, and not endeavour their Relief, without doing Violence to ourselves." "Now," Layng concludes, "under what Circumstances does any Charity bid so fair as the present [Northampton County Infirmary] to be universal? Wherein each Person may be reliev'd at so small a Part of the Expence, which his Case would necessarily require in a *separate* and *private* Way; and where the Increase of Numbers in the *Collective* Body will still more and more lessen the Expence of each *associated* Individual." [45]

Along with most other philanthropic writers, Layng represents the sympathy and benevolence of the person of sensibility, stimulated by real or fictional scenes of distress, as leading almost inescapably to a desire to perform charitable acts. His purpose in calling on the vocabulary of the novel of sentiment is, on the one hand, to inculcate the virtue of sympathy in his listeners and readers; on the other hand, he also aims to raise subscriptions for a philanthropic institution based on the model of business enterprise. By contributing to his project, his listeners will manifest their inner virtue with a material demonstration of their outward fellow feeling.

Besides exhibiting the refined sympathies of those who contributed to philanthropic institutions, eighteenth-century representations of philanthropy gave it an important new role in the management of society. Speaking of the recently established Asylum for Female Orphans in 1768, for example, Thomas Francklin claimed that "this useful charity, whilst it relieves *private* distress, promote[s] *public* happiness." [46] The notion that relieving "*private* distress" through organized, businesslike charity was an effective and necessary way of promoting "*public* happiness" had become current in England only in the second half of the seventeenth century. Because traditional notions of charity were tied both to conceptions of property and paternalistic social relations, the new versions of property and rights articulated by seventeenth-century philosophers such as Hugo Grotius, Samuel Pufendorf, and John Locke resulted in new ways of thinking about charity as well.[47] As property became more "mobile," to use Pocock's term, charitable giving could be represented as a hereditary duty entailed on the "steward" of property and as the voluntary benevolence a sympathetic heart would produce. When social relationships were represented as contractual rather than paternal, then charity became the citizen's duty to society rather than the landlord's obligation to his dependents. With large numbers of the laboring population displaced by enclosure and other economic stresses, relieving distress through charity often became, in practice as well as in theory, a matter of voluntarily promoting general public good rather than fulfilling obligations to God by providing expected support and services to those on one's estate or in the parish.[48]

Charitable acts, especially those undertaken as associated or joint charities, were increasingly seen as potential solutions to specific social concerns sparked by fears of lower-class unrest.[49] Charitable institutions, it was believed, would yield practical benefits not only to distressed individuals but to the contributors and the public interest as well.[50]

The Gender of Sympathy

So far this discussion has assumed that the person who benefited from the redefinition of virtue as sympathy was an upwardly mobile man such as the philanthropist Thomas Guy. While it was ideologically crucial to claim sympathy and sentiment for a new version of public man in the early eighteenth century, however, such claims were complicated by the traditional association of emotion with women. The tension between representations of the "man of feeling" and the "natural" sensibility of women is mirrored in twentieth-century accounts of eighteenth-century sympathy, sentiment, and sensibility. Robert Markley, for instance, allies himself with G. S. Rousseau and John Mullan in characterizing sentimentality as "a masculinist complex of strategies designed to relegate women to the status of perpetual victims, constrained by their hypersensitivity and emotionalism to passive suffering and sociopolitical docility."[51] By ignoring the active role that women's traditional association with emotion authorized them to take both in the writing of sentimental fiction and in new versions of philanthropy, such accounts in effect participate in the eighteenth-century project of rendering women "perpetual victims."

Nancy Armstrong, by contrast, attributes a new kind of power to women because of their "natural" identification with sympathy and related domestic virtues. In making these claims, however, she is forced to write off the "man of feeling" as "anomalous." Like Markley, Armstrong glosses over the tensions inherent in an ideology of sympathy that was advocated as advantageous to women and men, both inside and outside the home. Although she recognizes that women's "acknowledged aptitude for performing acts of charity first enabled [them] to move out of the house and into the political arena," Armstrong's reading cannot provide an account of how this happened.[52] On the contrary, her description of the revaluation of women's role in the eighteenth century through their position within the home logically precludes women from having a role outside the domestic sphere.

Unlike Markley and Armstrong, G. J. Barker-Benfield recognizes that both men and women (particularly those of the middle ranks) stood to gain from the eighteenth-century valorization of sympathy, although sometimes in contradictory ways. In *The Culture of Sensibility,* Barker-Benfield maintains that both the home and public spaces became more heterosocial in the eighteenth century—that a culture of reform, based in values such as the controlled susceptibility to the sentiment of sympathy, sought to displace an earlier male culture of rakes and taverns that cut across class lines to allow men to inhabit public spaces and confined women within their homes. The "culture of sensibility," explains Barker-Benfield, worked both to liberate women "from their internalized and brutally enforced limitations" and to reform men. However, as men and women began to inhabit the same spaces (that is, as men spent more time in the home and women were gradually admitted to more public places) and to emulate similar behaviors (sensitivity to feelings and general benevolence), it became necessary to make clearer distinctions between what made men men and women women.[53]

Sensibility posed a dilemma for men, claims Barker-Benfield, because they were caught between an older definition of manhood characterized by disorder and violence and a newer version that was more "decent" but also less discernable from what was defined as "feminine." Barker-Benfield implies that men's participation in philanthropic associations was one way to reconcile this dilemma. By joining together to raise subscriptions for charitable purposes, men of business could distinguish themselves from an older corrupt male culture, demonstrate their sympathy and public spirit, and bond together with other men of sympathy in groups that resembled old-styled clubs without duplicating the perceived excesses of such male assemblies; in addition, participating in philanthropic associations could be an effective way of making business contacts or of establishing a reputation that would enhance a man's business affairs.[54] Thus joining philanthropic causes was a suitably masculine way for a man to exhibit his sympathetic nature. Barker-Benfield's contention that participation in philanthropic institutions could resolve men's difficulties with being both sympathetic and masculine helps to explain why women were largely excluded from such participation throughout much of the eighteenth century, despite their traditional association with sympathy and charity. It also demonstrates that the process of making public spaces heterosocial was never simple, but rather it was fraught with conflicting claims.[55] Because it blurred gender distinctions and stereotypes, however, sensibility did open possibilities for women to participate in what could be considered public activities that were normally restricted to men.

Women and Philanthropy

Women, of course, did participate in eighteenth-century philanthropy, both in informal expressions of charity and eventually in the new businesslike institutions. Women's charitable endeavors were also represented in eighteenth-century novels. Most scholars, however, have paid little attention to the implications of eighteenth-century women's philanthropy. The majority of literary analyses of sympathy only briefly mention the way in which actual philanthropic practices also manifested this cultural virtue or they focus only on philanthropies instituted and directed by men. Historians of philanthropy have tended not to be concerned with the implications of philanthropy for gender or with recording women's philanthropic efforts.[56] The historian Donna T. Andrew does note the names of many women on subscription lists and identifies the charities to which they were most likely to contribute.[57] Published philanthropic writings, especially charity sermons, provide further evidence of eighteenth-century women's participation in philanthropy by explicitly addressing women and soliciting their donations.[58] Focusing primarily on women's financial contributions to philanthropic organizations, however, tends to obscure the kind of charitable contribution that consisted of time and personal energy rather than money. This less historically visible kind of charity, as Andrew mentions, became more and more significant to society's understanding of philanthropy as the century progressed[59]— and it was also the kind of charity that women had been practicing for centuries.

For the purpose of this study, I do not document how many and which women participated in philanthropy, although research of this nature is both interesting and valuable, but rather I explain why women's philanthropic activities became increasingly more visible and what this augmented visibility meant for definitions of women's nature and role. I examine how women's role in philanthropy came to seem even more important than it had in earlier centuries despite changes in the understanding and practice of philanthropy that would seem to make women's participation less welcome and defensible, such as the eighteenth-century turn toward philanthropic institutions financed and managed like business concerns and conceived of as interventions in political and social problems. Each of the succeeding chapters considers the ways in which both historical precedents for women's philanthropy and practical considerations that seemed to necessitate their participation fostered women's continued involvement in philanthropy of both old and new varieties.

Among the historical precedents for women's involvement in charitable activities was what is commonly labeled the Lady Bountiful tradition. "The lady of the manor's duty of personally attending the poor and sick," writes Jessica Gerard, "had been established since the Middle Ages." "Landowners' wives," she continues, who were "responsible for the largely self-sufficient household economy," were also expected to apportion some food and money for the poor, and to provide first aid and medicines."[60] The charitable duties of wives and daughters of the landed classes were mentioned in diaries from as early as the sixteenth century, and they were depicted or assumed with regularity in numerous conduct books, personal memoirs, and literary works from the eighteenth century on. Samuel Richardson gives evidence of his heroine's virtue in *Clarissa,* for instance, by mentioning that a portion of her time was set aside for charitable activities among the poor and distressed in the villages connected to her family's property, while a London lady in Charlotte Lennox's *Female Quixote* remarks to her cousin that "I know you Country Ladies . . . are very fond of visiting your sick Neighbours."[61] By performing these charitable duties, upper-class women were supposed to reinforce the reciprocal obligations of a paternal hierarchical society by conferring obligations on the poor that would be reciprocated with gratitude and deference. Such charitable activities not only continued but increased throughout the eighteenth and into the nineteenth centuries. As the endowments and bequests of wealthy landowners were supplemented with the subscriptions of numerous smaller donations from less wealthy members of the middle ranks in the eighteenth century, so the charitable largesse of landed women was augmented by middle-class women visitors who were often represented as having advice and education, rather than gifts, to offer the needy. In short, the large role that wealthy women had long played through face-to-face contacts with the poor made it seem natural not only that country women should continue the tradition but also that women of education and refinement, even if they were less wealthy than the traditional Lady Bountiful and not connected to large estates and country villages, could contribute to the work of new philanthropic projects.

Another historical precedent for women's philanthropic work was religious. Not only did Scripture enjoin women, like men, to emulate Christ through charitable almsgiving but Catholicism had left a legacy of Sisters of Charity, whose primary occupation was practical philanthropy. While England had no sanctioned religious sisterhoods after the dissolution of the monasteries under Henry VIII, the existence of European sisterhoods kept alive the idea of women living together for the purpose of performing acts of charity, and proposals for secular or Anglican sisterhoods appeared in seventeenth-, eighteenth-, and nineteenth-century England. One of the most famous of these was Mary Astell's *A Serious Proposal to the Ladies* of 1694. An earnest advocate of women's education, Astell proposed founding a "Monastery, or if you will . . . a Religious Retirement," which would serve the double purpose of being "not only a Retreat from the World for those who desire that advantage, but likewise, an Institution and previous discipline, to fit us to do the greatest good" in the world. As she describes it:

> For a stated portion of [their time] being daily paid to GOD in Prayers and Praises, the rest shall be imploy'd in innocent, charitable, and useful Business; either in study in learning themselves or in instructing others, for it is design'd that part of their Employment be the education of those of their own Sex; or else in spiritual and corporal Works of Mercy, relieving the Poor, healing the Sick, mingling Charity to the Soul with that they express to the Body, instructing the Ignorant, counselling the Doubtful,

comforting the Afflicted, and correcting those that err and do amiss.[62]

Although Astell's proposal was never implemented, largely because it raised fears of popery, its arguments about the suitability of charitable work for women were influential throughout the eighteenth century. Astell's ideas served as a model for a few smaller scale women's retreats dedicated to the performance of charity and for fictional accounts of such institutions, including Sarah Scott's *Millenium Hall,* the subject of the first chapter in this study.

The traditional association of sympathy with women was related to these historical precedents for women's philanthropic activity. Eighteenth-century philanthropists often relied on this association, in conjunction with religious precedents for women's charity, to urge women's participation in philanthropy. For instance, in his 1768 charity sermon Thomas Francklin assured his listeners that, "In behalf of Objects like these [female orphans], I need not, I am satisfied, address myself to those who are of the same sex with themselves: your sympathetic hearts, untaught and uninstructed, will dictate all that can be said, and all that can be done: as women you will pity them, as mothers you will feel for them, as Christians you will, I doubt not, contribute to relieve and support them." [63] Women's hearts, Francklin assumes, need not be taught or instructed in sympathy (presumably, as men's must be), because sympathy is already natural to women; considered as mothers, the connection is even stronger. Apparently, these women's belief in Christian doctrine will translate this natural sympathy into charitable action.

Along with these traditional precedents for women's participation in philanthropy were pressing practical considerations. As I have already pointed out, charitable works were often proposed as an appropriate occupation for unmarried women who lacked obvious domestic obligations. In addition, many women, both married and unmarried, had money at their disposal, whether their own or their husbands', that promoters of philanthropic organizations needed. And, as I argue in chapter 1, the men who managed some kinds of philanthropic institutions, especially those whose objects were distressed women and children, began to believe that they needed middle- and upper-class women's domestic skills to appropriately administer their charities. In some cases, moreover, such as asylums for penitent prostitutes, the charitable services of educated, refined—and chaste—women were perceived as necessary to combat the "problem" of ungoverned lower-class female sexuality.

The historical and practical precedents I have just described, as well as the textual analogies and representations I discuss in the chapters that follow, contributed to the process of naturalizing women's philanthropic work as part of their domestic role. Since philanthropic work allowed eighteenth- and nineteenth-century Englishwomen of the middle and upper classes to participate in activities that took place outside their homes, its representation helped to produce the ambitious desires that led to their participation not only in charitable endeavors but also in other activities that took them beyond the strictly defined domestic sphere, including professional writing. Portrayals of women visiting and aiding the poor also played a large part in determining the ways that people in eighteenth- and nineteenth-century England thought about relations among social classes. Thus the novels, sermons, conduct books, and lectures I will discuss formed a discourse that had important effects from the mid-eighteenth century to the mid-nineteenth century, effects that continue to have an impact on us in the beginning of the twenty-first century.

Each of the following chapters deals with a historical moment in which changes in the understanding and practice of philanthropy coincided with and contributed to redefinitions of the appropriate roles women should play and of how relations among different social classes should be conducted. Although the texts, most of them literary works, span a period of more than one hundred years, they all make use of the metaphor drawn from the ideology of separate spheres that I have mentioned: they all represent women's charitable dealings with the poor and unfortunate as analogous to their role in the home as mothers and wives. At the same time, however, these writers also employ the vocabulary of the philanthropic institutions that originally arose out of commercial men's need to authorize their power and moral authority by contesting women's exclusive association with sympathy. In different ways and in the face of various historical conditions, then, all these writers use the conjunction of the terms of domestic and philanthropic discourse to project women into a space that can be construed as both private and public.

The opening chapter examines the first novel to portray in detail women administering extensive charitable projects. Sarah Scott's 1762 utopian novel *Millenium Hall* addresses a problem that the novel of sensibility poses for women, especially if they are not married: how to retain the newfound power the emergent domestic ideology of separate spheres supposedly granted to women but without becoming passive victims defined only by their erotic desires. Using the conventions of both sentimental novels and philanthropic discourse, Scott imagines a literal place where single women can "mother" the poor and distressed without actually becoming mothers. Thus Scott's novel capitalizes on the terms of domestic ideology to represent ambitious desires not otherwise permissible or possible to domestic women, although to do so it must purge them of any sexual desires.

While Scott was able to use philanthropy to represent an alternative to a threatening patriarchal home for unmarried women, the famous Evangelical Hannah More's widely read conduct books, tracts, and novel worked to generalize the "mothering" of the poor to all women of the middle and upper ranks, whether married or single. By the end of the eighteenth century, the French Revolution had triggered a reaction against the kind of Rousseauian sensibility that could assign equal worth to the middle ranks but also to the unruly lower classes as well. The second chapter explains how More included rational women's philanthropy in the Evangelical project of reform so as to convert philanthropy into a public duty equivalent to men's political endeavors. Propounding a new kind of paternalism adapted to a market society, More's texts engage the domestic analogy to rewrite the public market as a larger version of the domestic sphere. Her many published works exemplify the contradictions written into women's practice of philanthropy: although More's writings reinforced and promulgated women's domestic role, by advocating the same rational desires and behaviors for women philanthropists that later political economists would recommend for men in the business world, she helped to ensure that middle- and upper-class women would play a central role in social and economic relations.

As effective as More's strategy of representing women's philanthropy as analagous to their domestic duties was for gaining gradual acceptance of women's participation in all kinds of charitable work, women writers following her lead in the 1820s and 1830s faced a new challenge when philanthropy came under attack as a solution to social problems. The political economists, led by Jeremy Bentham and his followers, who argued for the passage of the New Poor Law in 1834, urged that all assistance to the poor and needy, if not eliminated, must be reconciled with the "laws" of laissez-faire political economy. The third chapter explores the efforts of three women writers to reclaim a role for women's philanthropy in new urban environments that most assumed were impervious to the efforts of charitable women. Borrowing her fictional form from Hannah More, Harriet Martineau took on a secular version of the role of philanthropist-teacher in educating the poor and those who would help them in her *Illustrations of Political Economy*. Although she envisions a world run strictly according to political economy's laws, Martineau nonetheless manages to preserve a version of philanthropic paternalism that includes women as volunteers and as writers such as herself. Faced with the daunting prospect of a factory environment dominated by unregulated laissez-faire capitalism, the novelists Frances Trollope and Charlotte Elizabeth Tonna also manage to retain a role for philanthropic women in their vision of a system of reformed and government-regulated factories by retooling traditional rural paternalism for an urban setting. Although these three writers see the importance of bringing the domestic into the commercial and public world of the factory, however, none of them is able to represent her heroine functioning within it.

Even though political economy posed a theoretical challenge to women's participation in managing the lower classes through their role as philanthropists, by the middle of the nineteenth century thousands—perhaps hundreds of thousands—of women were engaged in some kind of philanthropic volunteer work.[64] Hannah More's prescription for women's domestic role, which included philanthropic work as its "natural" extension, had in essence become the norm for middle-class women. At the same time, however, a new class of male professionals had begun to claim the social territory that philanthropic women had so successfully inhabited. Hence a struggle arose between male professionals, who wanted to characterize women volunteers as amateurs, and women philanthropists, who strove to use their experience in charitable work with the poor to argue for increased training, education, and even paid employment for women. Chapter 4 traces the anxieties that some women philanthropists provoked in their attempts to claim authority in a newly defined social sphere. I examine two published lectures on "professionalizing" women's philanthropy, written by the well-known writer and philanthropist Anna Jameson, in conjunction with the response of a group of male professionals published under the title *Lectures to Ladies on Practical Subjects*. I demonstrate how Jameson's attempt to use the analogy of women's wifely role in philanthropy to provide a vocation for "redundant women" provoked embattled professional men to turn her domestic metaphor against itself by representing marriage as a hierarchical relation in which women are necessary and valued but always subordinate helpmeets.

By contrast, Elizabeth Gaskell's highly successful social-problem novel *North and South,* the subject of chapter 5, takes the wifely domestic metaphor into the scene of conflicted labor relations. Gaskell's womanly visitor vies with both male professional experts and capitalist entrepreneurs for access to the social sphere. Unlike the earlier heroines of Trollope and Tonna, Gaskell's Margaret Hale succeeds at mediating a strike and defusing a violent labor crisis, and her more egalitarian marriage to a capitalist seems to promise equal opportunities for productive work. Even Gaskell's ideal visitor, however, is hampered by the (always potentially unruly) sexual desires that link her to working-class men and that require supervision by a middle-class husband.

The decade of the 1850s, when Jameson and Gaskell were representing philanthropic women entering and assuming authority in the social sphere, also saw the rise of historical women philanthropists to public prominence—most notably Florence Nightingale. Many novelists capitalized on this increased attention to and acceptance of the possibilities of female philanthropy, and both literary and nonliterary representations of heroic female philanthropists abounded during the 1860s. This figure, the subject of the sixth chapter, became so common during the period that the "philanthropic heroine" could be said to rival the traditional "romantic heroine" as a literary convention. The philanthropic heroine of many popular novels differed from the traditional romantic heroine not only because her devotion to philanthropic works carried her into the social sphere beyond the home but also because she had ambitious desires that were at least as strong as her erotic ones. While representations of female philanthropists as heroines might implicitly endorse women's ambitious desires, however, they are by no means without anxiety about what unleashing those desires might mean. The many philanthropic heroine novels published during the 1860s thus seek to educate their readers in how to reconcile and discipline both their ambitious and erotic desires.

Written in the late 1860s and published in 1871–72, George Eliot's *Middlemarch* can be read as a reaction to and critique of these philanthropic heroine novels. In chapter 7, I demonstrate how Eliot's novel dramatizes the appeal to women of the philanthropic heroine who is defined by her ambitious, as well as her erotic, desires. Because of the legal, economic, and social limitations for women that domestic ideology both sanctioned and enforced, however, Eliot can satisfy her heroine's ambitious desires only by displacing them onto a feminized male dilettante who eventually becomes Dorothea's husband. The emotionally disappointing ending of Eliot's masterpiece can thus be read as a lament for the failure of philanthropy to fulfill the desires its representations have aroused.

My reading of *Middlemarch* suggests that by the last third of the century philanthropy began to seem, especially to those beginning to characterize themselves as feminists, an inadequate vehicle for representing women's ambitious desires. Female characters could now more plausibly be represented as professional social workers, artists, and so forth. Also, as women gained more access to other public discourses, there was less need to rely on the novel as the primary outlet for women's social investigations and criticisms. Hence, although novels and other kinds of literature continued to portray women performing charitable acts, the figure of the philanthropic heroine receded as a popular convention.

This does not, however, negate the cultural work accomplished by the representations I have been describing. In the beginning of this chapter, I assert that representations of women's philanthropy were crucial in redefining gender roles in eighteenth- and nineteenth-century Britain, and by the time that Eliot began writing *Middlemarch,* those redefinitions were already partially accomplished. Domestic ideology, with all its limitations, of course continued—and still continues—to exert a powerful influence on the way gender differences were defined and gender roles were assigned, but by the 1870s it was clear to many that women could and did have desires and needs that could not be met within the strictures of the traditional domestic sphere. By this time, for instance, avowed feminists were organizing campaigns for legal reforms, new educational opportunities began to be available to women of all classes, and more forms of employment were opened to women. Eventually women's legal and political status would also undergo major change. All these important (if still tentative) revisions of the traditional terms of gender were sparked, at least in part, by earlier representations of women participating in the varied activities of philanthropy.

"An Assured Asylum against Every Evil"

Sarah Scott's *Millenium Hall* and Mid-Eighteenth-Century Philanthropic Institutions for Women

IN 1766 NEWTON OGLE, deputy clerk of the closet to His Majesty George III, summarized the achievements of mid-eighteenth-century English philanthropists in a charity sermon delivered before the assembled governors of the Magdalen Charity: "Houses of Charity have been opened for every Malady incident to Man. The Aged, the Maimed, the Sick, the Foundling, the Woman Labouring of Child, even those polluted by the foul Effects of their own Vices, have justly been admitted to a Share of our Bounty." [1] The "Houses of Charity" that Ogle lauds were charitable subscription societies modeled after joint stock corporations.[2] Although in previous centuries rich benefactors had often founded hospitals and almshouses to receive the sick and aged poor, these new societies were formed to meet a variety of specific social needs, many of them the result of increasing urbanization. Thus the institutions subscription societies founded would, it was hoped, have important economic and political, as well as humanitarian, effects.[3]

Based as they were on commercial and political principles, the modern philanthropic ventures Ogle praises were usually organized, supervised, and managed by men; in the numerous prospectuses for and reports of midcentury philanthropic societies, names of women occasionally appear as subscribers but never as directors or governors.[4] Although women of the landed classes continued to play their traditional role in rural charitable activities by distributing largesse and advice to their poorer neighbors and tenants, tending to the sick, founding and teaching in charity schools, and, in some cases, leaving large benefactions in their wills, the developing ideology of domesticity threatened to make their active participation in newer businesslike charities seem inappropriate and improper.[5] Excluded from the leadership of these new charitable projects, women faced the potential loss of the opportunities that philanthropy had offered them—occasions not only for useful public activity but also for an alternative vocation to marriage, as the celebrated Mary Astell had proposed in her *A Serious Proposal to the Ladies* in 1694 (1 : 36). Thus when Sarah Scott came to write her novel about women and charitable activity, some sixty years after Astell's *Serious Proposal,* she faced the problem of reclaiming women's traditional prerogatives from a new kind of philanthropic practice that threatened to exclude them.

Scott's *Millenium Hall,* published in 1762 and her most successful novel, imaginatively resolves the problem of integrating the upper-class Englishwoman's traditional charitable role as Lady Bountiful with the principles of public, businesslike philanthropic institutions by utilizing both the discourses of philanthropy and of sensibility. While *Millenium Hall* has been read as a typical example of the novel of sensibility, its contribution to midcentury discussions of philanthropy has received less attention.[6] Like novels of sensibility, many of the houses of charity promoted in philanthropic prospectuses and charity sermons aimed to rescue victimized single women, teach them to be proper domestic women, and restore them to their appropriate place in the home—ideally, by finding them husbands. *Millenium Hall,* with its utopian female community dedicated to charitable works, offers a feminized version of these male-run philanthropic institutions as a solution to the "problem" of unmarried and sexualized women as well as to the larger social problems such women symbolized. In so doing, Scott's novel helped to establish philanthropy as a defining characteristic of the domestic woman and to generate women's ambitious desires to contribute to the resolution of social, political, and economic questions. To authorize these ambitious desires, however, *Millenium Hall* must renounce its heroines' sexuality.

Sarah Scott was well aware of the predicament of the victimized woman in mid-eighteenth-century England. Although she had been married briefly, her father and brothers had "removed her" from the marriage after less than a year. Her family feared for her reputation, as letters between her sister, the famous bluestocking Elizabeth Montagu, and various correspondents indicate.[7] Scott's reputation was apparently salvaged when her husband returned half of her marriage portion; although her means were now modest, she had enough to retire to the country to live with her friend Lady Barbara Montagu and devote herself to charitable projects. *Millenium Hall* was evidently based in part on her life with Lady "Bab" in Batheaston.[8]

The problem that Scott addresses in *Millenium Hall* is one that many unmarried women confronted in the face of domestic ideology's prescription for women. While recent critics, especially Nancy Armstrong, have written convincingly about the role of a new domestic ideology in the eighteenth century, such accounts have not taken unmarried women into consideration.[9] Like the eighteenth-century texts they discuss, their focus on the domestic woman as (sexualized) wife and mother implicitly casts unmarried women as misfits or "monsters." Similarly, readings of *Millenium Hall* as a lesbian novel also reenact domestic ideology's definition of women by their sexuality.[10] Scott's project in *Millenium Hall,* I contend, was precisely to contest the view that women could be defined only by their sexuality. For her, the problem was neither how to get her heroines married off nor how to represent an alternative sexuality, but rather her point was to show that a woman who was not married could define herself as something other than an "old maid" or a "fallen woman." Scott's fictional solution to this problem is to use philanthropy as a vehicle for redefining both the sexualized female victim and the independent woman. Philanthropy was crucial to this project because it was a discourse that linked the masculine world of business and politics to the feminized world of domesticity. By writing a novel about women doing philanthropy, Scott purges the novel of its sexualized sentimental overtones; by casting it in the form of a philanthropic tract, she strips philanthropy of its specifically masculine component and makes it hospitable to nonsexualized women.

Because the ideological work that Scott's novel attempts had not yet received social recognition, however, Scott had to hide her identity by posing as an anonymous male author; there was as yet no precedent for a woman to participate in philanthropic discourse, even in novel form. It was certainly not uncommon for writers of either gender to publish anonymously in the mid-eighteenth century, and Scott may have withheld her name partly because publishing a novel could compromise her social standing, or for a variety of other reasons.[11] However, although many women wrote novels during this period, they were not writing philanthropic pamphlets, prospectuses, sermons, or public letters. Thus Scott's suppression of her female identity in favor of an anonymous male, in imitation of Jonas Hanway and others, would have given her philanthropic recommendations a weight they would not have had were she known to be a woman writing. Scott's novel, in fact, seems to have been the first published text authored by a woman that dealt seriously with the subject of philanthropic institutions.[12]

Attributed to "A Gentleman on his Travels," *Millenium Hall* is narrated by a wealthy merchant who comes across a country estate in a remote location in Cornwall that is owned and inhabited by a group of six single women (one of whom conveniently turns out to be the narrator's cousin). The narrator, along with his foppish young companion, Lamont, is charmed with the ladies and their estate, especially with the extensive philanthropic system the women have established, and he gives their home the fictitious name of Millenium Hall to avoid offending "that modesty which has induced them to conceal their virtues in retirement." Interspersed with the novel's descriptions of the ladies' various charities are a series of inset narratives in which Mrs. Maynard, the narrator's cousin, tells the story of each of the ladies, with most emphasis on the interlocking tales of the two devoted friends, Mrs. Morgan and Miss Mancel. Each of the inset narratives is like a miniature sentimental novel; each of the women has been a woman in distress whose virtue has been tried. As a result of the men's experiences at Millenium Hall, the rake Lamont is reformed and undergoes a religious conversion, while the narrator vows to "imitate [the ladies] on a smaller scale" on his own estate.[13]

Millenium Hall is written in the form of a long letter addressed to a bookseller in London; the narrator gives the bookseller permission and encouragement to publish the letter as an example "which may teach those virtues that are not easily learnt by precept and shew the facility of what, in mere speculation, might appear surrounded with a discouraging impracticability" (2). By framing her story in this way, Scott links her novel to a common form that philanthropic discourse assumed in the eighteenth century—the public letter.[14] Uniting the sentimental novel with philanthropic discourse in this framework enabled Scott to rewrite both genres; *Millenium Hall* transforms the sexualized victim of both discourses into a desexualized agent of charity.[15]

Philanthropic Discourse and Unmarried Female Victims

When Saunders Welch published his "thoughts upon the subject of providing for prostitutes" in 1758, he noted that it was a subject "which at present seems to engross the attention of . . . many worthy minds." "Prostitutes," Welch reports, "swarm in the streets of this metropolis"; a stranger would think "that the whole town was one general stew." The consequences, Welch declares, are "a general depravity of morals, a constant supply of sharpers and robbers to infest our streets, and a chain of other evils, which naturally flow from minds depraved by lust and enervated by debauchery."[16]

As Welch's comments indicate, midcentury perceptions that the number of prostitutes was increasing were tied to more general concerns about the disorder and social chaos that seemed to pervade England. Welch's contemporaries worried about the regular influx of displaced rural laborers and soldiers into London.[17] Particularly during the wars of the 1740s and 1750s, there was concern about the ill health and moral depravity of the laboring classes as well as about the economic conditions that were thought to contribute to the idleness and extravagance of the nation's workforce.[18] Thus, at a time when a strong and growing populace seemed the key to both national prosperity and security, many feared that the venereal diseases that the prostitutes spread to their customers would not only enervate men and make them less fit to function as soldiers and citizens but would also infect innocent wives and the children they bore. Since sexual debauchery, even without the risk of venereal diseases, was believed to render women infertile, prostitution also robbed the nation of productive mothers.[19] Regarded as idle, prostitutes were thought to lure men into lives of idleness, depravity, and extravagance, turning productive workers into thieves and young men of the middle and upper ranks into rakes. With prostitutes to meet every man's taste readily available, some feared there would be no incentive for men to marry at all.[20] If, as Donna T. Andrew claims, the major social aims of philanthropists in the middle of the century were to increase the population and to improve society's morals, the prostitute was a convenient figure on which to pin both concerns.[21]

While the prostitute could be used to figure these widespread anxieties about social dislocation and crime, her supposed opposite, the domestic woman, was represented as the reservoir of morality and stability. This domestic ideal, which pictured women as modest, chaste, and devoted only to the interests of their families, was an integral part of the bourgeois ideology that gradually displaced the older aristocratic model of society during the eighteenth century.[22] Domestic ideology, on the one hand, defined itself against an image of a woman that emphasized her vanity and voracious sexual desire; the domestic woman, on the other hand, exercised charm only with her virtue and her desires all conformed to the will of her husband or father. Although, as Armstrong suggests, this domestic ideal furthered the interests of the developing middle classes, it was held up to women of all classes.[23] A domestic woman was by definition one whose sexuality was channeled into marriage; curbing her own and men's desires, she became the repository of a social morality that countered anxieties about general moral laxness and shifting economic and social conditions. Fears about social problems could thus be translated into concerns about women's ungoverned sexuality, which could be assuaged by reassurances about the naturally tractable nature of the domestic woman.

The fact that so many of the new philanthropic ventures that originated in the middle of the century had somehow to do with women's sexuality or its consequences demonstrates how fears about social problems were often translated into gendered terms.[24] The Foundling Hospital, for instance, which was still being discussed and debated at midcentury, provided for the offspring of women's (presumably illicit) sexual relations; the Lock Hospital treated women for venereal diseases; Magdalen asylums reclaimed penitent prostitutes; the Asylum for Female Orphans aimed to prevent prostitution; and even the Lying-In Hospital and the Lying-In Charity were intended to foster marriage and legitimate childbearing among poor women.[25] Those who promoted such ventures invariably pointed out not only how the institution would benefit the unfortunate female victim but also how it would solve the social problems the female victims seemed to incarnate. Plans for female asylums were frequently published jointly with treatises on crime or on the inadequacy of the poor laws.[26] Hanway, for instance, links prostitution to social concerns: "was there nothing more in view than political prudence, with regard to the increase of the species, and the good order of the state, there is the utmost reason to check the progress of this baneful vice."[27] In his charity sermon for the London Magdalen Asylum, Ogle compares the vice that is associated with the prostitute to a "raging sea" and suggests that the asylum will prevent such "Overflowings as might end in general Ruin." Treating the problems that come from wayward female sexuality has "now become necessary," he declares, "and should be made to accompany our Increase of Empire, Wealth, and Luxury" because such "Increase" produces "great Inequalities" that necessarily, in his view, "open new Veins of Vice."[28]

The "Veins of Vice" that troubled Ogle were not only the laboring classes' perceived lax morality and unruliness, represented in the figure of the prostitute and her unlicensed sexuality, but also their seeming lack of productivity. In his sermon Ogle expresses fears that the poor of his time have acquired "an Aversion from Labor" and will be "either tempted to recur to unlawful Means to gratify their Wants, or must patiently submit to that Misery which is the Consequence of their Irregularities."[29] With prostitutes regarded as idle and extravagant, in contrast to domestic women, who were noted for their frugality and industry, another female figure, however, could also stand in for the fear that the poor were unproductive—the "old maid." Since, according to domestic ideology, a woman's virtue and value were defined in relation to her reproductive capacities, a single adult woman was by definition a misfit or a burden; she was unproductive. In fact, both the terms "old maid" and "spinster" picked up their pejorative connotations in the eighteenth century, when unmarried women, whose desires were not channeled into marriage and motherhood and who were not producers of population, posed a challenge to domestic ideology's ability to contain anxieties about changing social conditions.[30]

The anxiety the figure of the spinster aroused was almost as strong as that provoked by the prostitute, and it was generally less sympathetic, as the numerous biting satires about "old maids" produced during the period attest. Arthur Murphy's 1761 play "The Old Maid," for instance, portrays the humiliation of a forty-three-year-old woman who has rejected many suitors in hopes of procuring the kind of husband her vanity leads her to believe she deserves. Murphy implies that the "old maid," like the prostitute, is driven by (what for her are ludicrous) sexual desires; she breaks off what her contemporaries would call a more prudent engagement with a wealthy but older man in order (she thinks) to marry a more attractive younger man. Murphy's play wastes no sympathy on his "old maid." In the end she is refused by both suitors and vilified by her brother and his beautiful wife, who, presumably along with the audience, find her predicament hilarious. Like most other "old maid" satires, Murphy's play blames the woman's vanity and her ungoverned desires, not her economic situation, for her embarrassing fate.[31]

The figure of the "old maid" attracted such opprobrium because, like the poor, she was both too dependent and too independent. Without adequate economic resources, unmarried women of almost all classes could drain the finances of their families or, in the case of spinsters of the lower classes, the parish ratepayers. If women were of age and not married, however, they were legally independent. Similarly, the laboring classes were also economically at risk and a burden because they were dependent on the resources of "their betters"; Ogle recognized that it was often the lot of the poor to "patiently submit to . . . Misery." As the poor seemed to become more numerous and more destitute than ever before, the problems of dealing with poverty became more troublesome and received more attention, as the concern devoted to reforming the poor laws suggests. The laboring classes were also, though, as another philanthropic writer worried, more independent than ever before; the English common people, writes Josiah Tucker, "have been growing up into Freedom for several Generations back, and are now become entirely independent, and Masters of themselves and their own Actions"—no longer subject to "discipline."[32] Domestic ideology, however, made it possible to displace such concerns onto the figure of the "old maid" or the prostitute, both of whose situations, like that of the poor, combined economic dependence with a threatening legal independence.

In the mid-eighteenth century, then, anxieties about social disruption could be transformed into fears about women's sexuality and independence. Domestic ideology also provided a solution to such "problems"— return sexualized women to the domestic sphere where their desires could be properly governed. This, of course, was the goal of the many philanthropic institutions founded to aid female victims. "Many persons," claims Hanway, "from prostitutes, have been made joyful mothers of children" as a result of the efforts of philanthropists.[33] Most descriptions of female asylums represent the institution as a family. A female asylum, proposes J. Massie, "may be conducted with as much Regularity, good Order, and Harmony, as appear in a well-regulated private Family."[34] By reincorporating unruly and independent women first into a family-like institution and eventually into an actual family, female asylums enabled philanthropists to "imitate their Maker, in a work of *creation* as well as *redemption;* that is, in making *bad* women into *good* ones."[35] "Good" women, of course, were domestic women.

Although what fictional single women such as Murphy's spinster most fear is the opprobrium of being labeled an "old maid," the real hardships that most single women of any class had to face were economic. Widows were the most common recipients of poor relief,[36] while never-married women even of the middle and upper classes frequently had to choose between living as dependents, treated often little better than common servants, or descending into poverty.[37] Domestic ideology made "bad" women into "good" domestic ones by providing a proper place for their desires; paradoxically, however, not every woman could fill that place. Women who did not have the means to marry were thus by definition "bad"—they were either prostitutes, who were too sexualized, or "old maids," who were too dependent and too independent.

Millenium Hall and Unmarried Female Victims

Philanthropic discourse, as we have seen, portrayed the sexualized prostitute as a victim who needed to be reclaimed. Similarly, the sentimental novel portrayed all female victims as inherently sexual. As in philanthropic representations, the primary evil that threatens women in these novels is seduction and thus eventually, according to eighteenth-century narratives, either death or a descent from pampered lover to castoff mistress to bedraggled prostitute.[38] This choice of fates is clearly spelled out, for instance, in Samuel Richardson's *Clarissa,* in which the innocent heroine's attempted seduction occurs in a brothel, where the assembled prostitutes gather round as if to receive her into their company; even though she resists seduction and her tormentor turns to rape to accomplish his desires, the now sexualized heroine has to die to prove her true virtue and avoid being cast as a "fallen woman."[39] Either marriage or death, according to domestic ideology and the novels of sensibility that promoted it, are the only honorable fates available to the sexualized woman victim.

Although *Millenium Hall,* like most sentimental novels, tells the stories of women in distress, Scott does not portray these victims as primarily sexual. The six ladies who live at Millenium Hall and superintend a variety of philanthropic projects have all survived attacks on their virtue (or their reputation) and have created for themselves a new position within a transformed domestic ideology. The ladies of Millenium Hall are not, and will not become, wives or mothers; instead of graciously presiding over a home and family, they establish and manage a philanthropic community; instead of channeling their desires toward husbands and children, they live in harmony with other women. In creating this new position for women, predictably, *Millenium Hall* also offers alternative symbolic solutions to the social problems that domestic ideology was supposed to address. Philanthropy provides Scott with the terms for such alternative solutions, but to make it serve her ends she must rewrite philanthropy; whereas philanthropic discourse had emphasized the sexualization of women, Scott uses philanthropy to de-emphasize this sexuality.

Domesticating the sexualized prostitute and the independent "old maid," as I have discussed, supplied a symbolic resolution to the problems posed by the perceived increase of poverty, unruliness, nonproductivity, and independence among the laboring classes. According to domestic ideology, however, the domestic woman herself was defined by her sexuality.[40] Domestic ideology's insistence on women's purity and passivity signaled a belief in their essentially sexual nature that was as strong, however well-disguised, as the aristocratic ideology it was supposed to supplant. Nature's "kind provision," preached William Hazeland in 1760, has "appropriat[ed] the term of virtue in women to this single point in honour"—their chastity. Virtuous women exist to marry and bear children, Hazeland assumes, and society "owes no less than its very being and continuance to this prolific union." "Let us see your matrons faithful and exemplary, and your maidens virtuous and discreet," entreats Hazeland; "leave then the rest to nature: She will never fail to bind the connubial tye as frequently as the utmost wants of society can require." For Hazeland, as for many others, women's sexuality is at the base of all social relationships; it need not be flaunted. His sermon represents virtue itself as sexual; it has "winning graces" and a "powerful attraction."[41] Although the prostitute's open sexuality was supposed to be the reverse of the domestic woman's purity and the spinster's independence the reverse of her passivity, the domestic woman was also defined by her active reproductive capacity.

Unlike such accounts, which addressed social problems in the potentially equally problematic terms of female sexuality, Scott's novel answers fears about both women and the poor by stressing the qualities of cleanliness and industriousness. Since philanthropic discourse cast the philanthropic institution as a family in order to reclaim sexualized victims, philanthropic writers always insisted on the need for cleanliness, regularity, and industry as the antidotes to wayward desires.[42] Although they are not literally mothers and wives, the Millenium Hall ladies can impose these domestic virtues on their "children"—those they relieve through their charities. Instilling cleanliness, which answers fears about women's immorality, thus serves also to counteract uneasiness about the immorality and unruliness of the poor; industriousness, which answers concerns about women's dependence, also allays anxieties about the poor's lack of productivity. In this way, philanthropy provided Scott with a tactic for relating domesticity to social problems without reproducing the problematic sexualization of the philanthropic tracts and the sentimental novels.

The first charities, for instance, that Mrs. Morgan and Miss Mancel take up when they decide to retire to Millenium Hall are charity schools and almshouses. These were the traditional and most conventional routes of eighteenth-century charitable endeavor and ones that were already associated with women. What the narrator first notices about the ladies' schools is that the pupils are "perfectly clean" and always busy (150). The narrator uses the word "clean" every time he brings up the subject of the poor who are served by Millenium Hall. This preoccupation with cleanliness—an "article of unspeakable Moment," as one charity sermon puts it[43]—is a key element in the philanthropic goals of restoring both the health and morals of the nation's working population. If the poor are clean, they are understood to be deserving, and the charity bestowed on them can be expected to achieve its desired goal.

Along with cleanliness, all the charities in *Millenium Hall* also promote industry. Even the aged are not allowed to rest in idleness. For instance, the first of the charities that the narrator observes at Millenium Hall is a group of "the neatest cottages I ever saw" (12). The cottages are inhabited by elderly women whose job is to raise the younger children of over-crowded poor families (14). Like the Lying-In charities in London, such a system promotes the growth of population by making it more feasible economically for the poor to have large families. The ladies' system, however, is even more efficient than the London charities, because it extends the charity beyond childbirth to the raising of the children. It also provides employment for elderly women, who otherwise, we are told, through "no shame" of their own, must live on the edge of starva-tion (12). "If we are not idle," reports one of the old women, "that is all they desire, except that we should be cleanly too" (14). Similarly, in the ladies' carpet and rug manufacture, higher wages are paid to the children and the aged, "in proportion to the work they do, than to those who are more capable, as a proper encouragement and reward for industry in those seasons of life in which it is so uncommon" (201–2). The success of this charity is evident to the narrator because he sees the signs of in-dustry and cleanliness, joined with cheerfulness, in the appearance of the poor: "Several hundreds of people of all ages, from six years old to four score" work in the various parts of this manufacture, "all busy, singing and whistling, with the appearance of general cheerfulness, and their neat dress shewed them in a condition of proper plenty" (201).

Millenium Hall's insistence on the poor's industry, as well as their cleanliness, enlists domestic virtues as the solution not only to general social disorder but also to a specific political problem. The carpet and rug manufacture, the narrator is told, was initially established because the neighborhood "was then burdened with poor and so over stocked with hands that only a small part of them could find work" (201). According to the original poor laws enacted under Queen Elizabeth, the parish was legally obligated to provide work for the unemployed, as well as a free technical education to the children of the poor, and to relieve the "lame, impotent, old, blind, and such other among them being poor and not able to work." [44] As economic and social conditions changed, however, it became increasingly difficult for the parish to provide relief for the grow-ing number of unemployed or underemployed poor. A renewed wave of enclosures, a series of wars that left many widows and orphans as well as unemployed soldiers, and other changing economic conditions had forced major migrations of the poor to cities and towns, or to other rural areas where there was more wasteland, resulting in the problem of widespread "vagrancy." Legislation intended to moderate the migration of the poor, such as the 1662 Act of Settlement that enabled parishes to relocate any poor person "likely to be chargeable to the parish" to his or her legal parish, only increased the problems for parishes with large numbers of laborers and not enough work. Thus in the first half of the eighteenth century, both legislative and philanthropic efforts were directed at providing employment for and encouraging industriousness on the part of the poor.[45] Parliamentary acts in 1722 and 1723 made it easier for parishes to establish workhouses and to deny relief to those who refused to enter them. But the workhouses were expensive to maintain, did not turn the profit they were expected to produce, and proved unpopular with the poor who were supposed to be served in them.[46] The carpet and rug manufacture the Millenium Hall ladies established is thus put forward as an alternative to the workhouse. Not only does it provide employment for the poor of all ages within their parish but it has "enrich[ed] the country round about" (201) and, since the fourth year, "has much more than paid its expenses" (205). Because the "ladies have the direction of the whole," including keeping "the distribution of the money in their own hands" (201), its success serves as an argument for the superiority of a philanthropic venture that can, as in this case, be administered entirely by women, over political solutions to the problems of poor relief and vagrancy. *Millenium Hall* implies that domestic women, who are themselves models of industry and cleanliness, are the best guardians and governors of the poor.

By proposing women's philanthropy, instead of marriage, as the solution to social problems, Scott retained women's position as the source of society's stability and security at the same time that she opened a new space within that position for unmarried women who could now define themselves as something other than "old maids" or prostitutes. *Millenium Hall's* home for indigent gentlewomen provides a literal space for such women. This refuge for single women is a larger scale version of an actual eighteenth-century practice that Olwen Hufton has called "spinster clustering," in which a group of single women lived together and pooled their resources so that they could avoid living as dependents.[47]

Based on the practice of voluntary clustering, the home for indigent gentlewomen in *Millenium Hall* also shares characteristics with the philanthropic female asylums.[48] Like the female asylums, the home for indigent gentlewomen is promoted with a sort of prospectus, outlining its plan and rules. The ladies, recounts the narrator, began by drawing up "several regulations, to secure the peace and good order of the society they designed to form, and sending a copy of it to their acquaintance, told them that any gentleman's daughter, whose character was unblemished, might, if she desired it, on those terms be received into that society" (65). The ladies' home, like the female asylums, takes inmates only voluntarily. Each woman is to have a room to herself, but the "eating-parlour and drawing-room [are] in common" (66). Likewise, the philanthropic prospectuses specify that the Magdalens have privacy to facilitate meditation, prayer, and repentance, while working, eating, and spending what leisure they have in common rooms. Like those who supervised Magdalen asylums, the ladies spend most of their time and attention during the first year of the establishment "endeavouring to cultivate in this sisterhood that sort of disposition which is most productive of peace," which they do by "leading" the inhabitants to "industry"—"shew[ing] it to be necessary in all stations, as the basis of almost every virtue" (67). As with the Magdalen asylums, there are provisions for expulsion, and inmates are allowed to leave voluntarily if they find that such a secluded life does not suit them.

The Millenium Hall ladies' asylum, however, is not for prostitutes, nor is it for the refuge of any woman considered to have fallen sexually; the "character" of any woman received must be "unblemished." In other words, these female victims, unlike the Magdalens, are not sexualized; likewise, they are neither too dependent nor too independent. Once the indigent gentlewomen have internalized the rules of the asylum, they, like their benefactors, also engage in philanthropy. Scott's female asylum, unlike similar male-run philanthropic institutions, does not aim to govern its objects' unruly desires by restoring them to the domestic sphere; Scott's victims have no unruly desires. Instead, they are taught cleanliness and industry so they can assume the position of benefactors in a "new world" in which the mutual obligations philanthropy creates substitute for bonds between landowners and dependents that contemporaries feared were being disrupted by the unsettling social changes that had prompted the century's new philanthropic enterprises (24).

Another key charity at Millenium Hall is the education of orphaned daughters of poor gentlemen. This charity, too, resembles a popular type of male-run charitable institution—the asylum for orphaned and deserted females who were thought to be at risk of becoming prostitutes. In the narrative common to philanthropic discourse and the sentimental novel, such young women of decent birth and good education but no fortune were most likely to succumb to the wiles of the wealthy rake or unscrupulous squire. At Millenium Hall, however, the girls' dangerous desires are carefully rooted out and replaced with the skills that would enable them to be self-supporting by qualifying them as governesses or housekeepers. To remind them of this goal they are put "under the immediate care of the housekeeper, with whom they are allowed to walk out for an hour or two every fine day, lest their being always in our company should make them think their situation above a menial state" (112). This precaution is, according to the charitable scheme of the novel, not meant to thwart or demean the young women but rather to keep them from aspiring to use their superior education to catch a rich husband, which would expose such portionless girls to the wiles of men "above them." To further the process of desexualization, the ladies ensure that the girls are "clad coarse and plain . . . as nothing has a stronger influence on vanity than dress" (112). "Vanity," of course, is a code word for sexual awareness; while a major snare for women of any class, it was considered particularly dangerous for girls such as those being educated at Millenium Hall. Only extreme modesty and virtue can ensure their safety in a world where rank and fortune no longer always go together, as the stories of their benefactors attest.

The six Millenium Hall ladies are no strangers to the plight of the orphaned girls they educate. Three of the six were young women of genteel birth but little or no fortune. While their stories use the conventions of sentimental novels, they also reveal the danger of such stories for young women such as those being educated at Millenium Hall. Louisa Mancel's story, for instance, begins as a typical tale of sensibility, reminiscent of Sarah Fielding's *David Simple*[49] and looking forward to Henry Mackenzie's *Man of Feeling*: a man rushes out crying, a woman lies on a bed dying, a beautiful orphan stands at the bedside; a young male character, apparently a man of sensibility, rushes in to hear the story and render aid. In *Millenium Hall* this young man, whose name is Mr. Hintman, adopts the young orphan and provides her with an excellent education befitting her obviously genteel birth, and he earns her gratitude and affection. By the time the beautiful Louisa reaches young womanhood, however, she and her friend Miss Melvyn (later Mrs. Morgan) discover to their horror that Mr. Hintman has lavished all his benevolent care on her in order to make her his mistress: "Among his friends he made no secret of his designs in all he had done for her, and boasted frequently of the extraordinary charms which were ripening for his possession" (50). Although she is saved from seduction by Mr. Hintman's timely death, Miss Mancel's troubles are far from over. Since Mr. Hintman has failed to provide for her in his will, she is still penniless and subject to yet more distress because of her unfortunate combination of beauty and poverty. It is fortuitous for Miss Mancel, however, that Mr. Hintman died just when he did; had his death occurred a few days later, after his intended seduction, she would have been both fallen and penniless. According to the usual story, she would, sooner or later, have become a prostitute.

Mr. Hintman's designs are the reverse of those of the philanthropic institutions, including the one at Millenium Hall; the education he provides for his deserted orphan is aimed *at* seduction instead of against it. Miss Mancel's story therefore discloses the unspoken potential for exploitation built into men's philanthropic institutions for victimized women. Because as an object of charity the woman is expected to repay her benefactor's gift with gratitude and obedience, she is in a position of further risk. The promoters of organized philanthropic institutions had a solution for this problem; most prospectuses propose that both a paid matron and female inspectors, women whose sexuality was properly channeled into marriage, interpose as mediators between the male philanthropist and the object of his charity. Better yet for all women, Scott's novel implies, is to eliminate the male benefactor with his power and dangerous desires and establish in his place a "home" where women help women.

Although Louisa Mancel's next adventure ends more happily, it is also cautionary. The again penniless but still virtuous heroine is prevented by her extraordinary sense of duty from marrying the wealthy and wellborn man who loves her. The charitable Lady Lambton takes Louisa into her home, but she opposes a marriage between her grandson and the penniless and orphaned Louisa, despite Louisa's manifest excellence. Although

Sir Edward, we are told, "might have conceived hopes of obtaining any other woman in her circumstances on easier terms" (89), Louisa's virtue leads him to propose marriage. Maintaining her virtue, however, Louisa not only refuses his offer but also conceals her love for him. Not until her rank and fortune are restored does Miss Mancel admit to her desires and agree to marry the man she loves.

Miss Mancel's reward for "the force . . . put on her affections" (112) is not, as it would be in most sentimental tales, marriage and supposed fulfillment of her desires; instead she loses Sir Edward, who has died for love of her, and retires to Millenium Hall with the widowed Mrs. Morgan. In Miss Mancel's eyes, this is a reward, for "had she married Sir Edward Lambton, her sincere affection for him would have led her to conform implicitly to all his inclinations" (112); she would have lost "all the heart-felt joys she now daily experiences" (113). In *Millenium Hall* heterosexual relationships always involve loss and distress, even when they are legitimate. By teaching the young orphans under their tutelage not to imagine themselves as the heroines of sentimental novels, but instead instructing them in skills that will enable them to support themselves in the only occupations available to women of their class, the Millenium Hall ladies enable their charges to follow their example by refusing the position of sexualized victim.

As Miss Mancel's story demonstrates, however, to refuse the position of sexualized victim was necessarily to reject what was most central to the domestic ideal—love and marriage. Thus the outcome of Scott's use of philanthropy to enlarge upon the possibilities domesticity allowed women was, paradoxically, an exposure of the contradictions of domesticity. According to the domestic ideal, love defined a woman, but it also annihilated her. Marriage was the safe and proper place for a woman, but once married she legally ceased to exist. Sentimental stories taught women how to practice virtue, but they could also seduce. Women were the moral saviors of society, but only if they allowed themselves to be reduced to an image of sexuality. And asylums for female victims were safe, but they were also prisons.

Early in their stay at the place they call Millenium Hall, the narrator and his companion come across an enclosure, painted green and lined on the inside with a thick hedge of seven or eight feet, which they assume is for wild animals. The ladies insist that it is not, and the narrator's companion, Lamont, asks a pertinent question: "But still I am puzzled; what we behold is certainly an inclosure, how can that be without confinement to those that are within it?" (19). The men are soon informed that the enclosure "which makes such an extraordinary impression" on them is the asylum for "those poor creatures who are rendered miserable from some natural deficiency or redundancy" (19). The Millenium Hall ladies have "purchased these worst sort of slaves" (20) from tyrannical "wretches, who seem to think that being two or three feet taller gives them a right to make them a property, and expose their unhappy forms to the contemptuous curiosity of the unthinking multitude" (19). To rescue these people, the ladies have "purchased" them; to "enfranchise" them, they have built an enclosure that is also a confinement (20). Like Millenium Hall, which is situated in a remote location and surrounded by a thick growth of trees, the asylum for the "poor creatures" both frees and imprisons its inmates.[50]

Significantly, the objects of this unique charity, who are both victimized and valued for their appearance, are in many ways similar to victimized women. Like young women who spend the better part of their waking hours dressing in order to catch husbands, the "monsters" are put on display for public viewing. The word "monster," which is used at least twice in Millenium Hall to describe these people, in fact originally meant "to be shown."[51] Like the unmarried women in Millenium Hall, however, these "poor creatures" have retreated from the gazing public eye to the asylum of the sheltered country estate. In one of the inset narratives, for instance, Miss Mancel, who is renowned for her unparalleled beauty, stops attending church because people come from all around the county to stare at her—as if she were a "monster." Accordingly, the Millenium Hall ladies rebuild a special gallery and make arrangements to transport their "monsters" to and from church in covered carriages to prevent the congregation from looking at them (23). Covered galleries also prevented penitent prostitutes from being seen by onlookers at the chapels attached to Magdalen asylums.[52] The use of this detail in Millenium Hall in connection with both the "monsters" and the beautiful woman underlines their connection with the prostitute as sexualized victims.

The identification of the "monsters" and women is further developed in the description of their "vanity." The "monsters," like many of the "shewey" women set against the Millenium Hall ladies in the inset narratives, have their form of vanity, of which their benefactors must cure them. What the "monsters" boast about is how much money their keepers earned by "their being so much farther from the usual standard of the human form" that they became "a more extraordinary spectacle" (22). In their asylum at Millenium Hall, however, the "monsters" realize that vanity and self-display constitute a "malady of the mind" and an "internal source of unhappiness." Lady Mary Jones, another of the Millenium Hall ladies, has also had to learn the consequences of "too great vanity" (146) before she earns her asylum in the female philanthropic community. Both the "monsters" and Lady Mary learn that vanity is the consciousness of one's body that makes one a victim. For women to renounce their sexuality, however, does not really change their victimized position; it merely limits their participation in the world outside the enclosure. An asylum such as Millenium Hall represents an escape from the forced display and legal servitude to which both women and "monsters" could be subjected; but it also represents a withdrawal from the world, which they can never again enter without again taking on the position of victimized object.

Because victimization is built into domestic ideology's prescription for women, the only safe alternative turns out to be same-sex love, emptied of all sexual content. This desexing of women works to strip domesticity of its definitive characteristic. The "family" that resides at *Millenium Hall* is not only all women but it is without any traces of sexualization. Although there is strong affection and attachment at Millenium Hall (Miss Mancel and Mrs. Morgan's relationship is even described as a marriage), the narrator carefully avoids describing such attachments in erotic terms. While such "romantic friendships" might historically have included sexual relations, in the case of *Millenium Hall* there were compelling reasons to exclude sexuality from such female friendships.[53] Heterosexual relations are even more unthinkable.

The only man of comparable rank with the ladies who resides at Millenium Hall is an elderly Italian gentleman, who has himself been an object of charity. Because a proper Englishman, however sensible or philanthropic, who had the power to enforce his will and his desires, would be dangerous to the founding purpose of their female asylum, the ladies

who seek refuge in the "family" at Millenium Hall choose the grandfatherly Mr. d'Avora as their only male associate.[54] Not only is Mr.
d'Avora an object of charity but he is also Italian. In eighteenth-century
England, the word "Italian" was almost synonymous with vice—not
only with sexuality but with deviant or "unauthorized" sexual behavior
as well.[55] Like undomestic women, Italians were represented as sexually
voracious, and unlike Englishmen, their sexuality was seen as unproductive. Mr. d'Avora is represented as anything but sexually deviant; like the
Millenium Hall ladies, he is desexualized.[56] Any unnatural desires that
might be associated with women living together are thus displaced onto
a desexualized elderly Italian object of charity—a man who is as unlike
an Englishman and as unthreatening as it is possible to be. Like the ladies,
Mr. d'Avora can offer asylum but not change the world that makes such
asylums necessary.

Those male philanthropists who, unlike Mr. d'Avora, had the power
to change the world used philanthropy to diagnose social problems as
sexual ones and to treat them by returning sexualized victims to their
"proper" place inside the family. Scott, by contrast, uses philanthropy to
purge domesticity and women of what domestic ideology declared to
be their most essential characteristic, their sexuality. As is the case with
Mr. d'Avora, men who enter Millenium Hall must also be desexualized.
Even Lamont, the rake, is finally neutered by his contact with the Millenium Hall ladies.

However, there is also another way to read Lamont's conversion at
the end of *Millenium Hall*. If Scott's attempt to create a viable alternative
for unmarried women within domestic ideology is in a sense doomed by
the very notion of the asylum as a retreat from a larger world that remains
as inhospitable as ever, it is in another sense retrieved by the male observers who penetrate the pale and observe the asylum—the novel's male
narrator and his companion, Lamont. In making the private asylum public in a philanthropic letter, the narrator invites the world not only to
view the ladies within but also to imitate them. By holding up the ladies'
philanthropic system as a model for imitation, *Millenium Hall* thus explicitly attempts to produce nonsexual, ambitious desires in its women
readers. The "conversion" of the narrator's rakish companion, Lamont,
on the last page of the novel suggests that, despite their exile from tradi-

tional domesticity, female philanthropists might have a chance of motivating changes in the world outside the asylum. If Lamont the rake could be converted not only to religion but to a new respect for the value of women as charitable agents rather than as sexual objects or marriageable fortunes, then the conditions that objectified and victimized women might also be susceptible to change.

"The Care of the Poor Is Her Profession"

Hannah More and Naturalizing Women's
Philanthropic Work

IN AN 1841 LETTER TO William Ellery Channing, the critic and historian Lucy Aikin noted that the practice of visiting the poor had now
become "a fashion and a rage" among Englishwomen, thanks in large
part to a novel published in 1808 by Hannah More, the famous Evangelical writer, philanthropist, and educator.[1] The novel was entitled *Coelebs in Search of a Wife*.[2] Aikin credits More and her fellow Evangelicals
with originating a shift both in the moral tone of nineteenth-century
society and in the role of women: "This philanthropic impulse acted at
first chiefly within the Evangelical party; but that party became, at length,
great enough to give the tone to society at large; and the practice of
superintending the poor has become so general, that I know no one cir-
cumstance by which the manners, studies and occupations of Englishwomen have been so extensively modified, or so strikingly contradistin-
guished from those of a former generation." Writing eight years after
More's death and more than thirty years after the publication of More's
educational works for women, Aikin identifies the kind of women's volunteer philanthropic work that More promoted and practiced as the dis-
tinguishing trait of the women of England.[3]

By the time of Aikin's letter, the charitable labors of Lucilla Stanley
and Lady Belfield, the heroines of More's *Coelebs in Search of a Wife*,

seemed a natural part of the role of middle- and upper-class women. Countless mid-nineteenth-century Englishwomen visited hospitals, prisons, workhouses, and the homes of the poor on a regular basis.[4] While Scott's *Millenium Hall* advocates women's philanthropy as an alternative to marriage, More's novel, conduct books, and tracts portray charitable works as a necessary part of the role of all women of the middle and upper ranks. As Aikin recognized, More's works played a central role in naturalizing philanthropy as an extension of women's domestic duties in nineteenth-century England. Ladies, taught More, could use their influence and their knowledge of domestic economy to superintend the lives, homes, habits, and attitudes of the poor. As both More and Aikin envisioned it, women's philanthropic work was vital to women and to the security and stability of society because it was a way of relieving the distress that could lead to unrest and of instilling "correct" values in the laboring classes.

More's conduct books, novel, and tracts made middle-class women's participation in philanthropic works seem natural by taking the upper-class woman's traditional Lady Bountiful role that had served to reinforce paternalism's hierarchical bonds of deference and refashioning it to suit the new social, political, and economic conditions of her time. Because she rejected the language of the marketplace, More seemed to react against the capitalist economy that was coming to dominate England; her new-styled paternalism, however, used philanthropy's gift economy to replicate capitalism—without seeming to. Preserving and expanding well-to-do women's part in philanthropic activities, More assigned them a crucial role not only in maintaining harmonious class relations but also in fueling a consumer market. Instead of using the language of the marketplace, however, More drew on the rhetoric of Evangelical reform and the conventions of conduct book literature—not only to reinforce "strictures" of female propriety but also to stimulate women's rational desires for increased public usefulness through broadly defined charitable activities.[5] Thus while on the one hand, More's works upheld domestic ideology's prescription for women, on the other, they posed an inherent challenge to that ideology's confinement of women within the private sphere of the home by making their participation in publicly useful activities outside the home seem simply an extension of their domestic role.

Despite the crucial part More played in redefining women's roles in nineteenth-century England, only recently have scholars begun to take account of the cultural import of her writings. Like Lucy Aikin, the historians Leonore Davidoff and Catherine Hall credit More with "setting the terms for the characterization of domesticity and sexual difference," while Mary Poovey notes More's role in placing women on "the Victorian pedestal."[6] Mitzi Myers uses social anthropology to "carefully disinter" the strategies of reformist women such as More during the turbulent 1790s. She explains how More reinterpreted domestic culture to provide active roles for women, defining domesticity in terms of social responsibility and political questions as moral and religious problems that women could solve. Thus, Myers maintains, More's program of "aggressive virtue" made her "a female crusader infinitely more successful than [Mary] Wollstonecraft or any other competitor."[7]

Like Myers, a number of other recent historical critics have focused on the new possibilities More's revision of domesticity opened for women. Arguing that More's program for women was a strategy for displacing anxiety about her own body, Elizabeth Kowaleski-Wallace claims that any gains More achieved for herself and other women were secured through her complicity with patriarchy and were hence "tragically inadequate" to the task of freeing women from the dictates of patriarchy.[8] Kathryn Sutherland and Christine L. Krueger, by contrast, place More in a tradition of women writers whose works extend the possibilities for women through their domestic role. The feminized familial domain that More's writings promote, Sutherland argues, "cut[s] through a bankrupt patriarchal model of social relations."[9] Emphasizing More's connection with a tradition of women preachers, Krueger maintains that More "intends to teach women how to gain access to social discourse and demands that men repent of their efforts to exclude them."[10] While Myers, Sutherland, and Krueger recognize that philanthropic work was a key component of the "aggressive virtue" More believed would reform society, however, none of these critics explains how naturalizing female philanthropy as part of domesticity rewrote the terms of paternalism and also helped to generate ambitious desires that posed a challenge to the domestic ideology that "good works" were supposed to support and extend.

Even more recently, the critic Beth Fowkes Tobin has focused specifically on More's version of philanthropy in *Superintending the Poor*. Tobin casts More as a spokesperson for the rising middle class against the landholding gentry and aristocracy who had "abdicated their paternal responsibilities" to the rural poor (3). Middle-class women, writes Tobin, filled the void left by the abdication of the masters with their charitable labors. More was "confident that women of the middling classes, who had mastered the microtechnologies of self-regulation, could change the hearts of the poor, teaching them to accept with humility and gratitude their place in the paternal order" (123). While it is true that More criticized the landowning classes for their moral laxity and neglect of responsibilities, I maintain that her goal was to reform, not replace, the aristocracy; in fact, as I argue, *Coelebs in Search of a Wife* represents reformed aristocratic women as the most influential exemplars of domesticity and the most important practitioners of philanthropy. And, although she did portray a societal model based on paternalistic ties, More's version of paternalism was not merely a return to an idealized past but was rather a new paternalism that could accommodate and serve a consumer-driven market economy and could be administered by both middle- and upper-class women.

Lady Bountiful and Refashioned Paternalism

More's refashioning of paternalism depended on the traditional association of women of the landed classes and charitable activity. While well-born landlords exercised power over their social inferiors through their control of property and the legal system, the Lady Bountiful figure also had an acknowledged and socially important role in maintaining the hierarchically organized relations among different classes of people that characterized traditional rural paternalism.[11] Women of the landed classes had typically visited and aided the poor on their estates and in the surrounding villages, overseen and taught in charity schools, and donated money for hospitals and almshouses. Their expenditure of time, money, gifts, and advice had been crucial in sustaining the bonds of deference that tied laborers to the land and its owners.[12]

The eighteenth century, however, had seen significant changes in the organization of society that challenged these traditional bonds. An evolving capitalism, both industrial and agricultural, steadily pushed (or attracted) laborers away from the small villages and into larger towns and cities. The historian Harold Perkin points out, for instance, that by 1801 only about one-third of English families were engaged in agriculture, while a far higher number worked in trade, manufactures, and commerce.[13] With neither physical proximity to nor traditional ties with urban laboring people, women of the landed classes had little contact or influence with them. Further, along with these shifts in the distribution of the population had come new methods for dealing with the poor, the sick, and the unfortunate that implicitly devalued the informal social contributions of wealthy women. Among the changes were the charitable subscription societies modeled on joint-stock companies as well as emerging new attitudes toward poor relief that eventually resulted in the New Poor Law of 1834.[14] By reclaiming a Lady Bountiful–like role for upper- and middle-class women, More's writings worked to restore women to active leadership in charitable endeavors, both institutional and noninstitutional. Thus More's oft-disparaged commitment to paternalistic social relations was more than simply patriarchal complicity or a political blind spot; it was a fundamental and necessary condition of the "profession" she claimed for middle- and upper-class women—the profession that was to give them access to the public sphere outside their homes.[15]

More, whose Evangelical agenda included a new and more central role for women, held to what seems like a traditional paternalistic social order based on the mutual responsibilities of rich and poor. Women, through their superintendence of the poor, were both vital to the functioning of this imagined social order and dependent on it for their sense of usefulness and authority. More's belief in a paternalistic system is particularly evident in one of her most explicitly political pieces in the *Cheap Repository Tracts,* "The Riot: Or, Half a Loaf Is Better Than No Bread, In a Dialogue between Jack Anvil and Tom Hod" (1793) (which is credited with having stopped a riot near Bath).[16] In this ballad one of the arguments steady Jack uses to counter Tom's democratic sentiments is that "the gentlefolks" will help out during bad times. As in traditional paternalism, More's rich have as strong a moral obligation to help the poor as the poor have to work for the rich. The solution Jack offers to the problems attendant on bad times is not, however, that landlords will take care of tenants and tenants of laborers in a hierarchical system of interlocking responsibility; instead, he imagines that the rich will fulfill their obligations to the poor by subscribing to organized philanthropic causes: "the gentlefolks" will help by giving up "their puddings and pies" in order to subscribe to charities.[17]

The modification of traditional notions of paternal responsibility that Jack expresses in More's ballad was necessitated by the breadth of the current distress—not only were too many of the poor displaced, or not attached to any particular estate or village, but also (presumably) there were too many in need during such times of crisis for individual land-owners to supply. While a Lady Bountiful might have succored the poor on the family estate in times past, More now calls on subscription soci-eties to meet a more widespread need. But, as More implies throughout her published works and the example of her own philanthropic career, she expects women to maintain what had been their casual and unofficial role as dispensers of charity even in new and more public forms of phi-lanthropy. Thus More relies on a traditional version of paternalistic values but adjusts them to current problems in such a way that she can retain and even enhance the role women play in handling the problems of the poorer classes. Unlike the traditional system, however, women need not be rich to act the role of charitable lady, because their contribution in-volves managing more than dispensing charity.

That women's philanthropy means much more in More's view than dispensing food and blankets to distressed individuals is especially clear in several of her tracts addressed to "persons of the middle ranks" (*Works*, vol. 4). In these pamphlets, More gives specific instructions and practical advice aimed at teaching women with little money how to reform their communities. In "A Cure for Melancholy," the newly impoverished widow Mrs. Jones manages to work a reformation in people of all ranks in the parish in which she lives, even though she has no money to con-tribute (4:325−57).[18] Mrs. Jones's story, some of it based on Hannah More's firsthand experiences in charitable work, is a model of the kind of charity More advocated for her new Lady Bountiful.

On the advice of the vicar Mr. Simpson, Mrs. Jones sets out not to give monetary assistance but to educate the poor of the parish and moti-vate them to reform what she sees as their bad habits. For instance, she convinces the local women to avoid tea and white bread and butter (which are expensive and thought to be inappropriate to their station in life) by teaching them to cook more appetizing meals; bake their own (coarser and cheaper) bread; and brew their own beer, which keeps their husbands away from the public houses and contributes to temperance—which yields better laborers. In her visit to inspect the local charity school, Mrs. Jones teaches the girls to cut and sew, mend, wash, and iron, thus making them better potential servants. Through her skill at explaining their duties to others, she effects other reforms as well—she manages to prevent a dishonest baker from selling substandard loaves of bread (by instructing a local butcher in the merits of becoming an "informer"); to arrange for fresh milk and dairy products for the poor without jeopardizing the profits of large-scale dairymen; and to get villagers to boycott a shop that does business on Sunday. She convinces the gentry to buy only the more expensive cuts of meat so the poor can make soup from the poorer cuts, instigates the closing of all but two public houses, and institutes a Sunday school. Thus almost single-handedly Mrs. Jones manages to solve the most pressing problems of the parish through her philanthropic educational efforts.

While Mrs. Jones is busy educating the poor of her parish and solving problems on their behalf, Hannah More is also educating her reader. Through her description of the process Mrs. Jones goes through to set up her Sunday school, for instance, More gives the reader advice on finding a teacher, regulating the school, and setting the curriculum, and she also teaches her how to overcome the kind of resistance from local farmers that More faced in setting up her Sunday schools in Cheddar ("The Sunday School" 4:358–86). Using Mrs. Jones as a model, More is able to point out to her middle- and upper-class female readers that their inspection and supervision is vital to the success of philanthropic projects, whether or not they have money to contribute.

Through Mrs. Jones, More also outlines her vision of reformed paternalist relations. As Mrs. Jones explains to the vicar (and the reader, whether poor or rich):

> Providence, in sending these extraordinary seasons of scarcity and distress, which we have lately twice experienced, has not only excited the rich to an increased liberality, as to actual contribution, but it has led them to get more acquainted with the local wants of their poorer brethren, and to interest themselves

in their comfort; it has led to improved modes of oeconomy, and to a more feeling kind of beneficence. Above all, without abating any thing of a just subordination, it has brought the affluent to a nearer knowledge of the persons and characters of their indigent neighbours: it has literally brought the rich and poor to meet together. (4:356)

The lesson that the rich need to relearn, in More's view, is the value of the face-to-face contacts with the poor that paternalism formerly was supposed to ensure. The "extraordinary seasons of scarcity and distress" of the 1790s were, as More's readers were well aware, also periods of profound fear of working-class unrest and even revolution. Her antidote is to maintain "a just subordination" through active, local charity that mimics old-styled paternalism in a new situation in which the affluent no longer have "a near knowledge of the persons and characters of their indigent neighbours." This is to be accomplished, of course, through women such as Mrs. Jones, whose influence in the community eases conflicts among the classes and teaches all—characters and readers—to do their Christian duty for one another.

This technique of educating her more affluent readers through texts ostensibly addressed to those socially beneath them is used frequently in the stories and ballads More wrote for the *Cheap Repository Tracts*. The tracts, which were initially printed below cost to compete with (or, rather, it was hoped, to supplant) vulgar ballads and chapbooks and seditious pamphlets by Thomas Paine and others, were marketed directly to the poor through hawkers as well as to persons of the upper ranks (at a higher price than hawkers paid) for free distribution to the poor.[19] They were read by people in every class, including the king (who "expressed his delight openly," says one biographer).[20] By 1796 the tracts were being published on cheap paper for sale by hawkers and on better quality paper and in bound editions for the gentry, many of whom bought them for their children or their own libraries.[21] Thus the tracts had a dual audience: the poor to whom they were explicitly addressed and those who in a sense read over their shoulders. This enabled More to provide lessons not only to the poor in how to do their duty and to live happily within their means and station but also to instruct their "betters" in their responsibilities to the poor. By representing the concerns, customs, dialect, and attitudes of the poor, the tracts helped to accomplish More's aim of teaching her middle- and upper-class readers to understand "the persons and characters of their indigent neighbours."[22]

When More addresses the landed classes explicitly, she invokes a traditional paternalistic vision of a society held together by interlocking bonds of duty and interest. *Coelebs in Search of a Wife,* for instance, is a conduct book written in the form of a novel to reach readers who were affluent enough and likely to buy novels or frequent circulating libraries.[23] The main characters, like those of most sentimental novels, are either aristocrats or gentry and, like the poorer characters in the tracts, are meant to serve as either negative or positive models of the behavior More would like to inculcate. For persons at this level of society, who do have landed estates, More's aim is partly to reawaken their sense of their paternalistic responsibilities. Mrs. Stanley, for instance, explains how "subordination" can be "just": "The largest bounty to the necessitous on our estates, is rather justice than charity. 'Tis but a kind of pepper-corn acknowlegement to the great Lord and proprietor of all, from whom we hold them. And to assist their own labouring poor is a kind of natural debt, which persons who possess great landed property owe to those from the sweat of whose brow they derive their comforts, and even their riches" (2:22). Fashioning justice and charity as synonymous makes it possible for the rich to feel morally upright and equitable without redistribution of wealth or destruction of social hierarchies, while it benefits the poor by giving them a claim on the bounty of the rich. As long as the rural laboring classes can be made to adhere to "a just subordination," even during periods of distress such as that of the 1790s, the rich will owe them the "natural debt" that theoretically holds the classes together.

Economies of Charity

Even in her works for the landowning classes that seem to uphold a traditional version of paternalism, however, More invokes a slightly different vocabulary that works to redefine, or modernize, paternalism. This redefinition constitutes More's most significant contribution to early-nineteenth-century discussions of social and economic relations. In *Coelebs,* for instance, Charles, the hero of the novel, speaks to the Stanleys' lame gardener, who details all the kind things Lucilla and her family have done for him. The gardener ends his recital with, "At Christmas they give me a new suit from top to toe, so that I want for nothing but a more thankful heart, for I never can be grateful enough to God and my benefactors" (2:53). While some of the kindnesses of the Stanleys work to fulfill their "natural debt" to their dependent, this final instance, the Christmas suit, is a gift in excess of debt because it creates an unrepayable debt: "I never can be grateful enough." This language labels the favors of the rich as charitable gifts rather than as "natural" debts. The charitable gift to the poor inspires a sense both of obligation and insufficiency in the recipient. Defining the bounty of the rich as charity confirms a set of relations based on a gift economy, as described by the anthropologist Marcel Mauss, rather than as an employer-employee relation characteristic of an emerging market economy.

Mauss identifies the gift exchange system of primitive societies with almsgiving, or charitable giving. What distinguishes the gift economy from a market economy, says Mauss, is that in the gift exchange system the objects exchanged take on moral and spiritual value. The most important of these "spiritual mechanisms," he writes, "is clearly the one which obliges us to make a return gift for a gift received."[24] There is in addition in a gift exchange system an equally meaningful obligation to accept a gift that is proffered. Thus those who are unable to repay a gift in kind must still accept it, but they must repay it in other ways, such as in service and gratitude.[25] If, like the lame gardener, one can never be grateful enough to repay the gift, then one must not only work for the giver but also behave with deference toward the benefactor and allow the benefactor to superintend one's life, as well as one's work.[26] While this relationship between benefactor and the object of charity resembles traditional paternal relations, in More's program it applies not only among landlords, their Lady Bountiful wives and daughters, and their dependents but also between middle-class women such as Mrs. Jones and the poor with whom she has no obvious connection besides the fact that she pays them charitable visits.

According to Peter M. Blau, who applies Mauss's observations to a capitalist society in his *Exchange and Power in Social Life,* the dual obligation to receive and to repay a gift "makes it possible for largess to become a source of superordination over others, that is, for the distribution of gifts and services to others to be a means of establishing superiority over them" (108). Lucilla's charity, then, is a gift that marks her generosity, but it is also a way of establishing superiority and power over those socially beneath her, as well as changing the meaning of the exchange of goods and services between them. The gardener, as an employee on the Stanley estate, receives pay for work done, and, under the terms of a market economy, he could be seen as a "free" agent exchanging his labor for a wage. By extending charity toward him, the Stanleys displace the market system with a gift economy that obligates the gardener and makes his labor insufficient as a repayment for goods received.[27] Thus the "economy of charity," based on the type of gift exchange in which there is a "unilateral supply of benefits," makes the poor or laboring-class recipients of philanthropy "obligated to and dependent on those who furnish [these benefits] and thus subject to their power," whether the poor are dependents on a rural estate or urban laborers.[28] Of course, if women are the primary agents in charitable giving, this way of defining their activity puts them in a position of considerable power and authority over those they "serve"—a position they would not normally hold in customary market exchanges.

To fill and maintain this position of power and authority, women thus need for the poor to remain poor. This may explain at the most basic level why women (and also, to some extent, men) committed to helping the poor through philanthropy were also committed to maintaining a paternalistic, gift-based social system.[29] Commenting on what had happened in women's philanthropy during the nineteenth century, Lucy Aikin wrote that "a positive demand for misery was created by the incessant eagerness manifested to relieve it."[30] While More was genuinely committed to improving the lot, both spiritual and temporal, of the lower classes, she was equally convinced of the need to keep the poor in their place (both literally and figuratively); to teach them to be content with their situation (and not to work to raise their social status); and to urge their gratitude toward their benefactors. As long as there were poor to be educated and relieved, there would be work—and authority—for charitable women.

Thus, while the philanthropic act could fulfill the poor person's need, it was necessary also to generate a new need, which would require another philanthropic act. Accordingly, once children were taught to read in the Sunday schools, they needed appropriate reading materials—such as, *Cheap Repository Tracts.* Or, once a child learned to read, as does Hester in the companion tract to "A Cure for Melancholy" and "The Sunday School," the parent develops a desire to read, which requires an evening school for adults in addition to the Sunday school or charity school. Hence, while in More's system charitable acts displace market exchanges between employers and laborers, at the same time philanthropy expands according to the same logic as capitalism.

Ultimately, of course, many of the working-class people who took advantage of philanthropic programs, especially schools, did eventually develop desires that could not be filled by philanthropic ladies but instead led to the very things More was trying to prevent—labor unions, universal suffrage, and so on.[31] That the possibility was built into the idea of educating the poor is evident in More's often noted unwillingness to teach writing in her schools. Says Mrs. Jones, echoing statements made elsewhere in More's voice,[32] "I do not in general approve of teaching charity children to write. . . . I confine within very strict limits my plan of educating the poor. A thorough knowledge of religion, and of some of those coarser arts of life by which the community may be benefited, include the whole stock of instruction, which, unless in very extraordinary cases, I would wish to bestow" (*Works* 4:352). Mrs. Jones treats the poor with respect and rails against those who "think that any thing is good enough for the poor" (4:353), but that the poor remain poor is necessary to her endeavor—which, in her case, as a single, widowed gentlewoman, is the only endeavor available to her. In a way, Mrs. Jones needs the poor far more than they need her—hence her (and her author's) reliance on a system such as the gift economy that obliges (or hopes to oblige) the poor to receive her charity because every gift (or philanthropic act) generates an insufficiency, a need for another gift (or philanthropic act).

Along with the implied power that philanthropy gives to the benefactor in More's vision of an ideally functioning society comes the right and responsibility of the philanthropic woman to superintend those she relieves. Philanthropy creates an unrepayable obligation; it also affords the upper-class woman the right to supervise the household of the poor. One of Lucilla's philanthropic projects, for example, involves her orchard and garden. When one of the servants or a girl from the charity school marries—"provided they have conducted themselves well, and make a prudent choice" (*Coelebs*, 2:48)—Lucilla "presents their little empty garden with a dozen young apple trees, and a few trees of other sorts, never forgetting to embellish their little court with roses and honeysuckles" (2:50). This, recollects Charles, explains the "many young orchards and flourishing cottage gardens" in the village that "embellish poverty itself" (2:52), rendering it pleasing to the eye of the tasteful rich. Besides nourishing their aesthetic sense, these flowers, although transplanted to the gardens of the poor, still evidently belong to the rich—another characteristic of a gift exchange economy.[33] Charles cuts a bouquet of roses for Lucilla from the bush outside the cottage of one of "her poor" without even mentioning it to the inhabitants of the cottage present in the room (2:278). And Lucilla, Charles learns, makes "periodical visits of inspection [to '*her* poor'] to see that neatness and order do not degenerate" (2:52).

Such gentle coercion, which not only teaches but forces the poor to "do their duty," is "well-becoming the tenderness" of the female sex, says More (*Strictures* 7:135). Ladies should "consider the superintendence of the poor as their immediate office," she explains, because "They are peculiarly fitted for it; for from their own habits of life they are more intimately acquainted with domestic wants than the other sex; and in certain instances of sickness and suffering peculiar to themselves, they should be expected to have more sympathy; and they have obviously more leisure" (7:135). This sympathetic superintendence, then, extends not only to the charity school and the home but even to the most intimate details in the lives of the poor. Despite (or perhaps partly because of) the fact that the sexual functions of their own bodies are unmentionable ("certain instances . . . peculiar to themselves"), philanthropy gives upper-class women the opportunity to oversee even the sexuality of the lower classes, thus maintaining the existing social and political structure at its most basic levels.[34]

More's revised paternalism, based on the exchange of gifts and obligations and requiring the services of women as the agents of charity and supervision for the lower classes, also participated in and reacted against a boom in the consumer economy. According to the historian Neil McKendrick, consumerism reached "revolutionary proportions" in the third quarter of the eighteenth century: "men, and in particular women, bought as never before."[35] This new ability to spend, while uneven, spread to a certain extent across all classes, rather than being confined to the affluent as it had been in previous ages. Even those in the lower ranks wanted and were occasionally able to purchase clothing, furniture, and food that had traditionally been available only to the well-to-do, even if such articles were cheaper imitations. During this period, many in England began to realize that the social emulation that spurred consumerism was productive of economic growth because it impelled trade. But, explains McKendrick, "the unleashing of the acquisitive instincts of all classes still posed too great a threat" to many observers because "self-improvement through spending implied genuine social mobility." [36]

More's writings show that she shared this anxiety about the breakdown of social distinctions through the poor emulating the rich by eating the same foods, wearing the same clothes, and so forth. As we have seen, much of Mrs. Jones's effort in "A Cure for Melancholy" was devoted to convincing those she was attempting to "help" that it was more economical for them to eat foods appropriate to their station: home-baked dark bread rather than white; home-brewed beer instead of purchased spirits; fresh meat (of poorer cuts) rather than butter; and, most of all, milk or water instead of tea. Tea was for many, including the famous eighteenth-century philanthropist Jonas Hanway, "the apotheosis" of "needless extravagance by the poor." [37] As More phrased it, for the poor to give up these luxurious practices and eat home-prepared food suitable to their station would be one step toward restoring the "good old management" (*Works*, 4:342). Yet Mrs. Jones's advice to the poor on these subjects should not be read as a rejection of the growing consumer economy but rather as a redirection: if the poor practice domestic frugality by spending less on (healthier) food, they will be capable of supplying more and better labor and they may have more to save toward less perishable goods (such as *Cheap Repository Tracts*). Mrs. Jones also contributes to the smoother functioning of trade by teaching local storekeepers to respond to customer demand for milk by keeping their own cows—which facilitates the large-scale sale to urban markets of dairy products produced on local farms (4:348). Thus the charitable activities More proposes for women through the example of Mrs. Jones do, in a sense, work both with and against the growing consumer economy. Although More opposed widespread social mobility, social emulation was in some ways the mainspring of her theory of reform because this identification registered the influence of the upper classes. Such emulation on the part of the poor, however, when it involved tea and white bread—and the idleness that supposedly went along with "taking tea"—was also a source of anxiety.

More's ideal woman philanthropist also participates in a consumer economy through her role as consumer. In More's family-based philanthropic scenario, the husband/male-philanthropist accumulates money through investments and/or rents; the wife/female-philanthropist puts the money back into the economy by spending it[38]—and by enabling the poor to spend. In More's scheme, women's philanthropy facilitates this gendered circulation of money both indirectly and directly. Lucilla, for instance, rather than denying her pleasures "imposes on herself" an act of charity with each "personal indulgence" (*Coelebs,* 2:51). "From this association she has acquired another virtue," she smilingly tells Dr. Barlow, the clergyman: "she is sometimes obliged to content herself with practicing frugality instead of charity. When she finds she cannot afford both her own gratification, and the charitable act which she wanted to associate with it, and is therefore compelled to give up the charity, she compels herself to give up the indulgence also. By this self-denial she gets a little money in hand, for the next demand, and thus is enabled to afford both next time" (2:51). In this situation Lucilla practices frugality, the hallmark of domestic economy, and philanthropy at the same time, while also disciplining her desires. She is the perfect female consumer: her father's (and soon her husband's) money, dispersed both frugally and wisely, goes directly into the larger economy when she spends on "personal indulgences" and indirectly when she gives it out to the poor in acts of charity. Following Lucilla's virtuous example, Lady Belfield performs the role of ideal female consumer on a greater scale. When she builds an expensive conservatory on her country estate, she also establishes a charity school "associated" with the conservatory, to balance her expenditure—or rather, to double it (2:343).

The charitable economic activities of Lucilla and Lady Belfield are contrasted in *Coelebs in Search of a Wife* with the example of Lady Melbury. Rich and beautiful, Lady Melbury squanders her substantial allowance at the gaming table, behavior that forces her to leave her cre-

ditors unpaid. By chance, Lady Belfield brings Lady Melbury to the
home of one of the victims of her vice, a young woman named Fanny.
Fanny, whose tradesman father died in debtor's prison for a debt of the
same amount Lady Melbury owed him, lives on crusts of bread while
tending her dying mother, who is paralyzed from a stroke brought
on by her husband's arrest (1 : 147–48). Horrified at the consequences
of her own profligacy, Lady Melbury repents of her vices and, like
Lady Belfield, is converted to domestic economy and the proper administration of philanthropy. Illustrating the process of her conversion,
Lady Melbury describes a visit taken with her exemplary aunt, Lady
Jane:

> In the neighborhood of the Castle, Lady Jane carried me to visit
> the abodes of poverty and sickness. I envied her large but dis-
> criminating liberality, and the means she possessed of gratifying
> it, while I shed tears at the remembrance of my own squandered
> thousands. I had never been hard-hearted, but I had always given
> to importunity, rather than to want, or merit. I blushed, that
> while I had been absurdly profuse to cases of which I knew noth-
> ing, my own village had been perishing with a contagious sick-
> ness. (2 : 399)

Coelebs, the novel that is continually searching for examples of perfect wives, ends with this conversion of Lady Melbury (there is only one
chapter, summarizing Charles's later activities, following the description
of her turnaround). Lady Melbury's case, one among many in the two-
volume novel, is given so much weight because she represents the woman
at the top of the social scale. Addicted to gambling, fashion, and other
forms of dissipation, Lady Melbury has committed almost all the female
sins identified throughout the book (except adultery—that would prevent her final reclamation).[39] She has defrauded her creditors, ignored the
plight of the poor on her estates, and dispensed charity to affecting cases
according to feeling and sensibility rather than the "pure motive" of glo-
rifying God. Further, her charity has done little good because it was applied indiscriminately, without the supervision or "management" that
should be directed toward the lower classes. Lady Melbury's philanthropy
has been a vice of self-indulgence rather than a virtue with proper reli-

gious and political force; although it has had some economic effect, its impact has been limited because she has not taught the poor to spend their money to best effect. Charles observes, however, "as Lady Melbury had been the 'glass of fashion,' while her conduct was wrong, I hoped she would not lose her influence by its becoming right" (2:412).

One major aim of More's conduct writing is to promote Charles's hope—to convince highborn ladies such as Lady Melbury to follow in her footsteps. The example and active philanthropic efforts of women of the higher classes would serve to disseminate the principles of domestic economy and proper philanthropy throughout all classes of women, thereby creating a reformed social order based on, but not identical to, traditional paternalism.[40] Although such principles have been associated with the rising middle class, More attempted to inculcate them in women of the landed classes as well, because her vision of a reformed society involved marrying the paternalistic bonds of the landed order with the values of the middle classes, particularly the Christian values of the Evangelical reform movement. Central to the accomplishment of this vision are exemplary women of all classes, teaching one another and men. But, as Lady Melbury's story indicates, More hoped that aristocratic women who have reformed themselves and learned to administer charity properly will lead the way.

Proper Philanthropy

In *Strictures on the Modern System of Female Education,* More condemns the kind of charity Lady Melbury initially practiced. In More's system, virtues that rise out of Rousseauian sensibility are "almost more dangerous than the vices" (1:36).[41] In language that perfectly describes Lady Melbury, More complains that "The chief materials out of which these delusive systems are framed are characters who practice superfluous acts of generosity while they are trampling on obvious and commanded duties"; "it is considered as a noble exemplification of sentiment that creditors should be defrauded, while the money due to them is lavished in dazzling acts of charity to some object that affects the senses; which paroxysms of charity are made the sponge of every sin, and the substitute of every virtue: the whole indirectly tending to intimate how very *benevolent people are who are not Christians*" (1:36, 38). Even the ideal Lucilla is tempted to perform charitable acts out of sentiment instead of as part of her devotion to God and the mission of reforming those she aids:

> As to my very virtues, if I dare apply such a word to myself, they sometimes lose their character by not keeping their proper place. They become sins by infringing on higher duties. If I mean to preform [sic] an act of devotion, some *crude plan of charity forces itself on my mind,* and what with trying to drive out one, and to establish the other, I rise dissatisfied and unimproved, and resting my sole hope, not on the duty which I have been performing, but on the mercy which I have been offending. (2:105, emphasis added).

Charity done (or even thought about) for its own sake, or, rather, charity that is performed in response to a feeling of pity in order to generate a feeling of self-satisfaction, is both "crude" and selfish. While charitable and benevolent feelings, including pity, are godlike and necessary to philanthropic endeavors, for More such emotions seemed uncomfortably close to the indiscriminate and sentimental philanthropy that counterfeits Christian charity but leads neither to God nor to reform.

Besides its use as "the substitute of every virtue" and "the sponge of every sin," sentimental charity is directly linked to at least three sins: theft, by defrauding creditors; vanity, through the display of "dazzling acts"; and sensuality, since its "paroxysms" are motivated by "object[s] that affect the senses." It was important to More to distinguish between what she saw as proper philanthropy and the kind of charity that resulted from such sensual and vain benevolence, particularly because the two might be mistaken for each other. As I have mentioned, it was to counteract the novels of sensibility that promoted such unchristian acts of charity that More undertook to write her novel. *Coelebs in Search of a Wife,* although short on plot and incident, provides not one but many positive and negative models of Christian charity—but without the heart-rending stories of distressed victims or the exquisite feelings of pity and its relief in pleasure from the act of charity that characterize so many sentimental novels.[42] The charitable acts of the characters in *Coelebs* are meant to instruct women in pursuits that will extend their opportunities for usefulness, not to elicit their emotions. More's unsentimental novel substitutes disciplined, rational desires for the self-indulgent, sensual desires that had long been attributed to women.

Unlike one who sentimentally indulges in showy philanthropic acts, the woman who exercises charity properly does not compliment herself on her benevolence or sensibility, but rather she sees herself only as the "underagent of Providence" (1:3). Fulfilling such a role is not only her duty but also the reward of duty. For instance, in *Coelebs* the Stanleys have taught even their youngest daughters that the coveted reward for good behavior is the opportunity to perform acts of charity for their poor neighbors and tenants: "Almost the only competition among them is, whose [drawer] shall be soonest filled with caps, aprons, and handkerchiefs" worked for their indigent neighbors (1:183). Most important, however, Charles reports that "It is all done so quietly, and when they meet at their meals they are more cheerful and gay than if they had been ever so idle" (1:183). Yet Mrs. Stanley cautions Charles against praising her daughters for their extraordinary attitude toward charity: "should the little ones find that their charity procures them praise, they might perhaps be charitable for the sake of praise" (2:23). Praise, of course, is likely to produce vanity, and vanity is a sin against God as well as a characteristic of the kind of aristocratic womanhood More is trying to supplant with her new domestic heroines. To fill the role More has in mind for her, a woman must not be vain about her sensibility or even her Christian good works.

More's new woman must also be on guard against taking too much pleasure in charity.[43] Lucilla Stanley enjoys charitable activity so much that she worries it may be sinful—that she is doing it from her natural desires rather than for the glory of God. For More this kind of sentimental charity indulges the sensual. Her view resembles that of Thomas R. Malthus when he compares the benevolent impulse to sexual excitation: both, he observes, are "natural passions excited by their appropriate objects."[44] According to More's program, women are to subdue any natural desires by directing them toward God. However, *Coelebs in Search of a Wife* and More's conduct books work to generate another kind of desire in women and men. While More denies women sensual pleasures, she offers them authority and a power that reinforces the behaviors necessary to a Christian version of the emergent capitalist economy. Thus as long as desires for such power are kept in line with promoting God's glory,

More encourages them. Page after page is devoted to representing the advantages women can gain from repressing their sensual desires and acting on their more ambitious (if selfless) ones. At the same time, by making the central character of her novel a young man searching for a wife, More attempts to create male desire for her new ideal woman by demonstrating to male readers the benefits of having such a wife—instead of a wife who indulges in sensual pleasures or exhibits showy accomplishments. Lucilla, the wife Charles finally chooses, exemplifies More's ideal so thoroughly that even her charity is rational and godlike, rather than impulsive and emotional.

While More distrusts the sensual attractions of sentimental charity, however, she also uses the implicit connection between sexual excitation and benevolent urges to make women essential to charitable projects, be they informal or, by implication, institutional.[45] Throughout *Coelebs,* men, like women, participate in philanthropy—but only by giving money, usually for the women to distribute. Seeing the touching distress of the young woman ruined by the careless economy of Lady Melbury, Charles puts his purse into Lady Belfield's hands, "declining to make any present [him]self" (1 : 149). Charles does not make his gift personally for fear the onlookers will suspect his motives. By characterizing upper- or middle-class men's charity as sexually threatening to such victimized women, More makes direct philanthropic efforts by men dangerous, leaving the field open for middle- and upper class–women, whose sexuality presumably has been concealed under the label of modesty.[46] It is Lady Belfield who uses the money Charles contributes to rescue Fanny and restore her to a respectable situation. By representing even the charity of the exemplary Charles as a potential sexual threat, More guarantees middle- and upper-class women's place at the center of philanthropic activity, but only at the cost of suppressing their desires for pleasure, even pleasure in performing benevolent deeds. Instead, More counsels, their desires should be directed toward pleasing God and reforming society according to His plan, a design that accords women a more major role in managing society than do earthly political systems.

Charity performed for the sake of pleasure, like charity performed for praise, also smacks of vanity, that "ubiquitous" vice that "is on the watch to intrude every where, and weakens all the virtues which it cannot destroy" (2 : 106), because taking pleasure in charity is a kind of display to oneself. Display, whether of the body, modish accomplishments, or sentimental acts of charity, is for More the chief obstacle to women's fulfilling the expanded role she offers them.[47] In *Coelebs* More uses the voices of Charles and Sir John Belfield to condemn ostentatious female philanthropy. Sir John describes philanthropic women in London who have so many arguments to prove their forms of charity are the best that they appear less like "benevolent lad[ies] than chicaning attorney[s]" (1:326). Nothing, observes Charles, corrects this "bustling bounty" so completely "as when it is mixed up with religion, I should rather say, as when it flows from religion." That "is the only sort of charity which 'blesses twice.' All charity, indeed, blesses the receiver; but the blessing promised to the giver, I have sometimes trembled to think, may be forfeited even by a generous mind, from ostentation and parade in the manner, and want of purity in the motive" (1:326–27). By using these male voices to condemn ostentatious charity and recommend religion as a corrective, More strives to convince young female readers and their prospective husbands that display of any sort, even of good works, will not increase women's value. Benevolence "set at work by vanity," says Mrs. Stanley, is "the iniquity of holy things," which "requires much Christian vigilance" (2:23) because it is so insidious.

In keeping with More's general insistence on religion as the only proper basis for charity, Mrs. Stanley, the model wife and mother in *Coelebs,* comments that the noblest charity is that which "cures, or lessens, or prevents sin": "And are not they the truest benefactors even to the bodies of men, who by their religious exertions to prevent the corruption of vice, prevent also, in some measure, that poverty and disease which are the natural concomitants of vice?" (2:26–27). While Lucilla insists on religious motivation as a necessary condition for proper charity, in Mrs. Stanley's formulation, overt religious instruction is also an essential component of proper charity, not only because it will save the souls of its recipients but also because it will lead to improvements in their physical conditions. Although they are to provide pecuniary assistance where necessary, converting the poor from lives of vice and indigence is the more valuable form of service for More's exemplary women. Providing relief from distress, of course, is what sentimental charity usually does—in response to the sensation of pity, the giver acts to remedy the situation. But true charity, responding not merely to feelings of pity but to a call from God, seeks not only to remedy the current distress but to work a change in the individual, the family, and in society at large—a change of heart that convinces the object of pity to accept uncomplainingly his or her God-given place in the social order.

More's emphasis on religion as key to her vision of a reformed society was not solely a function of her Evangelical beliefs. Christianity in England had long offered roles to women that extended beyond or offered alternatives to their domestic duties. Various dissenting groups, notably the Quakers, granted women a key role in administering charitable works, and Catholicism had left a legacy of Sisters of Charity, whose primary occupation was practical philanthropy. While there were no sanctioned religious sisterhoods in England in the eighteenth century, there were informal groups of women who lived together and devoted their lives to good works. Scott's *Millenium Hall,* for instance, represents what could be called an unofficial Protestant sisterhood. The religious association of women and charitable works was thus another important historical precedent for More's project of reclaiming the Lady Bountiful role in a time when capitalist individualism was replacing traditional paternalistic bonds.

In claiming philanthropy as a natural and necessary part of women's domestic role, More built on women's traditional roles as Lady Bountiful and Sisters of Charity. Her promotion of women's philanthropy for women of the middle as well as the upper classes worked to extend what seems to be a narrow domestic prescription and to assign it an importance that was both parallel to and part of the political and economic realms associated with men. Through her representations of women performing systematic, rational philanthropy attended with authority over and gratitude from the poor, More hoped to motivate women of both the upper and middle classes to repress their "natural" sensuous desires and replace them with desires to become publicly, as well as privately, useful and powerful. To represent the kind of world she imagined, in which women's philanthropy would play such a crucial role, her conduct book writings call into play two conflicting vocabularies that enabled her to rewrite not only traditional paternalism but also the public market.

The Domestic Model of Philanthropy

While it supported the behaviors essential to the emergent capitalist economy, More's rewriting of charity gave these behaviors a different emphasis, one that appears in the vocabulary by which she described philanthropy. While male writers often used the vocabulary of politics or the marketplace to portray philanthropic ventures, domestic writers, including More, more typically characterized women's charitable activity in terms of domestic values. For instance, in a preface to her political pamphlet *Remarks on the Speech of Mr. Dupont,* addressed to the "Ladies, &c. of Great Britain," More links charity with two other virtues of her ideal woman, modesty and domestic frugality:

> Even your young daughters, whom maternal prudence has not yet furnished with the means of bestowing, may be cheaply taught the first rudiments of charity, together with an important lesson of oeconomy: they may be taught to sacrifice a feather, a set of ribbons, an expensive ornament, an idle diversion. And if they are on this occasion instructed, that there is no true charity without self-denial, they will *gain* more than they are called upon to *give:* for the suppression of one luxury for a charitable purpose, is the exercise of two virtues, and without any pecuniary expense. (2:268)

If mothers teach their daughters to avoid vanity and display, and to practice domestic economy, the daughters will save enough money to contribute to charity. However, by attaching to a political pamphlet a preface that urges women to "relieve distress," More connects women's domestic values—charity, modesty, frugality—directly to politics and national security and, indirectly, to the economic exchanges of the marketplace. By frequently urging the example and charitable activity of domestic women as a cure for urgent social and political problems, More implicitly makes the home the controlling metaphor for all human activity, including the state.[48]

If, in More's view, domestic values are appropriate to the world outside the home, domestic organization also has a wider application. The ideal home that More represents in *Coelebs in Search of a Wife* is an ex-

ample of the kind of domestic arrangements the literary-historical critic
Nancy Armstrong describes, in which the man provides the income but
the woman is responsible for transforming "a given quantity of income
into a desirable quality of life."[49] By the early nineteenth century, this
domestic organization was beginning to be mirrored in philanthropic
practice, where women turned men's pounds not only into food, medicine, and advice for the poor on their estates but also into schools, hospitals, asylums, properly run prisons, and tracts.[50] Because men tended to
use the vocabulary of business and politics to characterize these philanthropic projects, women such as More could also call on this vocabulary
to describe their "domestic" part in the undertaking. Hence More calls
charity a woman's "profession" or her "trade." Says Mrs. Stanley, the
model mother in *Coelebs:* "I have often heard it regretted that ladies have
no stated employment, no profession. It is a mistake. Charity is the calling
of a lady; *the care of the poor is her profession*" (2 : 20).[51] By using the language
of male occupations for women's philanthropic work, More gives such
work a status equal to men's work. The conjunction of the vocabularies
of business, politics, and domesticity at the site of philanthropic discourse
allowed women such as More—women who did not confine their activity to the domestic sphere—to define themselves as "proper" and
"feminine," even while they took an active role in political and economic
activities usually associated with men.

The two major projects on which More's fame as a philanthropist
rested were the Sunday schools in Cheddar and the *Cheap Repository
Tracts.* Following the domestic model, both ventures were suggested and
financed by men but carried out by women. In 1789, while visiting More
at her home in Cowslip Green, More's friend and fellow Evangelical William Wilberforce returned from a picnic in the Mendip Hills appalled at
the poverty and degradation of the inhabitants of that area. More's sister,
Martha "Patty" More, records his reaction:

> The servant, at his request, was dismissed, when immediately he
> began, "Miss Hannah More, something must be done for Ched-
> dar." He then proceeded to a particular account of his day—
> of the inquiries he had made respecting the poor. There was
> no resident minister, no manufactory, nor did there appear any

dawn of comfort, either temporal or spiritual. The method or possibility of assisting them was discussed until a late hour. It was at length decided in a few words by Mr. W's exclaiming, "If *you* will be at the trouble, *I* will be at the expense."[52]

More responded by establishing her first Sunday Bible school, along with a school of industry (which taught spinning and housework to girls) and a women's friendly society.[53] By 1791 More and her sisters had nearly one thousand children attending their schools in ten parishes.[54] More did not teach or work in the schools, but she served as chief administrator over all of them. Seeing to the distribution of Wilberforce's financial contribution, like a wife disbursing a husband's income, More acted as a "professional" female philanthropist.[55]

Similarly, the *Cheap Repository Tracts* were also suggested by a man but carried out by More. This time the project was suggested by Beilby Porteus, bishop of London. Beginning with "Village Politics, by Will Chip," More began writing the series of tracts, which enjoyed phenomenal sales—"No such sale has ever been heard of in the annals of England," said one of her three publishers.[56] The tracts were financed at first by members of the Clapham Sect and later by a philanthropic society that solicited subscriptions to finance the printing, although the tracts were so popular they eventually generated a profit for their publishers.[57] Even though the records of the financial dealings involved with the *Cheap Repository Tracts* are somewhat sketchy, it is clear that while the project was financed by others, More took an active role in the marketing as well as the editing, which she did almost single-handedly. More's tracts were an important and trend-setting experiment in the mass production of reading materials, similar to what manufacturers such as Josiah Wedgwood were doing with other consumer goods.[58]

Some feminist critics have argued that because many of the projects More managed and supervised were proposed and paid for by men, she was merely serving patriarchal interests to gain approval from those men.[59] While there is no doubt that More's projects furthered patriarchal interests by promoting the doctrine of separate spheres and reinforcing the primacy of women's domestic roles, it is also true that including the "profession" of philanthropy in her vision of women's sphere posed an inherent challenge to the ideology that restricted women's activities to their homes and families. Because she defined the male-oriented world of business and politics as a larger version of the domestic, where both men and women had critical roles, More was able to occupy a position from which she could participate prominently in that public world and still be considered an appropriately "feminine" woman. Her professional activities—administering school systems; writing, editing, and market-ing books and tracts; and taking a public role in political and religious discussions and controversies—could still be considered part of a wom-an's proper profession: a philanthropy that both mirrors and is an exten-sion of the home. While this gained More personal fame and fortune, it also served as a model of what other women could do.[60] Women's philan-thropy was so important to More's vision of "woman's mission" that she refers to it approximately sixty times in *Coelebs in Search of a Wife.*

One of Hannah More's biographers, M. G. Jones, asserts that More was "a woman of far richer personality and of greater significance in the history of her time than has been commonly acknowledged."[61] Just as her personality was sanitized by early biographers, her importance as a writer and public figure to the history of women has been obscured by her apparently conservative attitudes toward women and the working classes. Yet More's claims for expanded opportunities for women of her class depended on those apparently conservative views. A religious pater-nalistic society in which the poor maintained "a just subordination" was a necessary condition for affluent women to act with authority in settings outside the home as the "underagent[s] of Providence" (*Coelebs,* 1:3). Advocating the same kinds of rational desires and behaviors for women philanthropists that later political economists would recommend for men in the business world, More helped to ensure that middle- and upper-class women would play a central role in social and economic relations. Although she insisted on the difference between men and women, and assigned women to the domestic sphere, More used women's traditional association with charity to recast the political, economic, and social world associated with men as simply a wider version of the domestic that not only allowed but required women's participation. While earlier propo-nents of women's philanthropy, such as Mary Astell and Sarah Scott, had proposed all-female utopian societies as alternatives to the domestic sphere for upper-class women, More's conception of women's philan-thropy enabled her to expand that sphere so that it could encompass alternatives. By representing women's philanthropy as not simply an alternative to women's domestic role but rather as a key part of that role, More appealed to—and helped to generate—middle- and upper-class women's desires to participate in the world outside their homes and to define themselves as something other than objects of men's desires. If More's domestic prescription for women had a lasting impact on the lives of nineteenth-century "angels in the house," her strategy of domesticating the public sphere was used by later feminists to bring the angels out of the house and into social work, higher education, paid professions, elected offices, and other visible and significant arenas for women.

3   Hannah More's Heirs

Women Philanthropists and the
Challenge of Political Economy

IN ONE OF HARRIET MARTINEAU'S tales in her *Illustrations of Political Economy* (1832), a reform-minded surgeon remarks on "the failure of British benevolence." What Mr. Burke characterizes as a "failure" of benevolence does not come from a lack of sympathy, devoted service, or substantial financial contributions; rather, the "failure" comes from too much of these things: despite "funds raised for the relief of pauperism in this country [that] exceed threefold the total revenues of Sweden and Denmark" and "exceed the whole revenue of Spain," "distress is more prevalent than ever and goes on to increase every year."[1]

While Hannah More had argued that charity, properly administered by educated and religious women, would perform an important political function by contributing to social harmony and stability, laissez-faire political economists such as Martineau worried that philanthropy, combined with poor relief the state dispensed, would have the reverse effect; by attempting to subvert the so-called natural laws of political economy, relief to the poor, whether private or public, would convert ever-increasing numbers of independent laborers into paupers who would demand support as a right and refuse to work.[2] Thus while thousands of English-women followed the advice of Hannah More in the early decades of the nineteenth century and took up the practice of visiting the poor or joined societies that sponsored charitable works, these philanthropic practices were being hotly debated. Although few would have denied the need for any philanthropy at all, many urged that philanthropic practice must be reconciled with the laws of political economy; others, such as More, saw it as a way to generalize paternalism so it could serve as a model for social relations in urban and industrialized, as well as traditional agricultural, settings. Adherents of both political economy and a revitalized paternalism, however, shared a growing concern about the effects of charity on its working-class recipients in what seemed a time of serious economic and social upheaval. With philanthropy under attack, of course, the role of women within it was also jeopardized; what direction philanthropic practice would take was thus of crucial import to women anxious to preserve—and extend—the usefulness and authority More's writings had seemed to guarantee them. It is ironic that, despite a documented increase in the number of women performing charitable work, most of the women writers whose works were published in the decades immediately following the publication of More's works were less confident about representing women doing philanthropic work.

Although few literary or nonliterary works written between 1809 and the late 1830s portray women performing philanthropic works on the scale represented in Sarah Scott's *Millenium Hall* or Hannah More's *Coelebs in Search of a Wife,* many novels aimed at a female readership do assume charitable activity as a natural feature of a wealthy woman's life—especially if the woman belongs to the landed classes or is the wife or daughter of a clergyman. A brief but important scene in Jane Austen's *Emma* (1816), for instance, shows the heroine visiting the poor and exercising a benevolent understanding and influence that her less genteel friend Harriet cannot match (56). Emma's aptitude for charity is one of the redeeming qualities that qualifies her to marry Mr. Knightley, the most notable paternal figure in the community; as his wife, she will exercise the traditional authority of a Lady Bountiful, a role that many saw as even more crucial in the nineteenth century than it had been in the eighteenth.[3] Even the silver-fork novels popular in the 1820s presume that their aristocratic heroines will demonstrate their worthiness by the appropriate administration of charity.[4] Although philanthropic work is assumed as part of a woman's role in these works, however, none focus more than passing attention on it.

By the 1830s, however, three key women writers took up More's strategy of using the discourse of philanthropy as a way to enter public debates about important economic and political issues. Although her opinions differed from More's in many ways, Harriet Martineau's popular tales in *Illustrations of Political Economy* are modeled on More's work in *Cheap Repository Tracts,* and the heroine of her novel *Deerbrook* shares many characteristics with More's rational philanthropic heroine in *Coelebs in Search of a Wife.*[5] Only a few years later, Frances Trollope used her novel *The Life and Adventures of Michael Armstrong, the Factory Boy* to expose child labor conditions and campaign for factory reform legislation, while almost simultaneously Charlotte Elizabeth Tonna, an avowed disciple of More, also entered the factory reform debate with her novel *Helen Fleetwood.* Yet, while all three of these writers, like More, use philanthropic discourse and try to imagine a role for middle-class women in urbanized, industrial social relations, actually representing women in such a role proves imaginatively impossible, given the constraints of the historical moments in which they were writing.

Harriet Martineau and the Principles of Political Economy

The writer of an 1832 review of Martineau's *Cousin Marshall* in *Fraser's Magazine* described the tale as "a long tirade against all charity."[6] This reviewer was only one of many, both at the time and since, to identify Martineau with a utilitarian view that condemns charity and advocates leaving all social relations in the hands of the "natural" laws of political economy. Such a view, in the reviewer's eyes, is particularly wrongheaded and reprehensible because, as a woman, Martineau should be promoting charity. The terms of the reviewer's attack show how entrenched the connection between women and charity had become: "What a frightful delusion is this, called, by its admirers, Political Economy, which can lead a young lady to put forth a book like this!—a book written by a *woman* against the *poor*—a book written by a *young woman* against *marriage!*"[7] Charity, in this passage, is as much identified with a woman as marriage, both considered part of her natural role. The reviewer is partly right when he claims Martineau's tale is against marriage; the principle illustrated in *Cousin Marshall,* Thomas R. Malthus's law of population, preaches against the poor marrying too early and having more children than they can support.[8] Neither this tale nor any of the others, however, argues against charity for the poor; what it does do is redefine charity, in much the same way that More and other serious thinkers about philanthropy had done, as education rather than alms. In so doing, Martineau implicitly gives middle-class women as important a role in managing social relations as More had done; although Martineau's rationalized charity is consistent with the principles of political economy, it is also compatible with the revised paternalism that More imagined to extend and enhance the influence of women.

The passage from *Cousin Marshall* that leads the *Fraser's* reviewer to accuse Martineau of condemning charity is a dialogue between the surgeon Mr. Burke and his sister, a workhouse visitor.[9] In this dialogue, Mr. Burke explains his conscientious objections to several charities for which he serves as medical advisor, particularly the Lying-In Hospital and the Foundling Hospital, as well as almshouses for the elderly. These charities, as he sees it, encourage the poor to have more children than they—or the economy at large—can support. The dialogue, set as a familial conversation over tea, is the tale's principal scene of instruction. As Mr. Burke elucidates the principles of political economy to his sister, she asks appropriate questions and supplies additional examples from her experience. The scene ends with Miss Burke endorsing her brother's decision to resign, on principle, as medical advisor to the charities of which he disapproves.

Although she is cast as the listener in the exchange, Miss Burke's role is crucial, not only in this scene but also in Martineau's vision of a society reorganized according to the principles of political economy, because the surgeon's sister is a philanthropic worker. When she listens, learns, and contributes her examples to her brother's explanation of economic principles, Miss Burke stands in for the reader, and the inclusion of her character in this role implies that Martineau expected that many of her readers would also be middle-class women. Speaking to them through Miss Burke, the surgeon explains how crucial the right kind of charity is: "There are some [charities] which I would extend as vigorously and perseveringly as possible; via., all which have the enlightenment of the people for their object. Schools should be multiplied and improved without any other limit than the number and capabilities of the people" (3 : 40). The surgeon, a professional medical man, is not directly involved with the schools he advocates so strenuously, but his sister is. The one scene in the tale in which she takes center stage is her visit to the work-house school, where she inspects the activities of the paid teacher and tactfully corrects the teacher's handling of a classroom conflict through her superior example. Although most of the scenes in *Cousin Marshall* focus on the working-class characters, these two scenes featuring Miss Burke learning and practicing an enlightened charity that is consistent with, even indispensable to, the smooth functioning of the economy demonstrate that Martineau envisioned a pivotal role for middle-class women in the ideal society she imagined.

It is significant that while in the workhouse Miss Burke encounters a male visitor, who is portrayed as too stupid to comprehend either polit-ical economy or his proper role as a visitor. While it would be unrea-sonable to conclude from this encounter that Martineau disapproved of all male visitors, the incident does reinforce the effectiveness of well-educated women such as Miss Burke, who understand the skills of do-mestic, as well as political, economy. In fact, Martineau's introduction to the series, *Illustrations of Political Economy,* stresses the analogy of political and domestic economy; like More, she casts the nation as a larger family, with political economy doing for the nation what domestic economy does for the individual family: as domestic economy, in Martineau's for-mulation, has already civilized families, the nation needs political econ-omy to become truly civilized (i:vi–vii, viii). Martineau's linking of women's domestic skills with political economy distinguishes her from the other most famous apologist for political economy, Thomas Chal-mers. Although their views are alike in many ways and Martineau's name was often linked with the charismatic Scottish clergyman's (the *Fraser's* review does it repeatedly), the key difference between them is that Mar-tineau managed to preserve a central role for women philanthropists even in a world envisioned as running strictly according to the rules of political economy.

Chalmers published his *Christian and Civil Economy of Large Towns* from 1821 to 1826, about ten years before Martineau's *Illustrations of Po-litical Economy.* In *Christian and Civil Economy* Chalmers describes the sys-tem of parochial visitation he had developed and supervised in Scotland, a system that uses individual religious instruction of the poor to ensure the steady functioning of a laissez-faire economy.[10] Chalmers had main-tained that because religion was not an essential need such as food or shelter, the desire for it had to be generated; in the case of the poor, this was to be accomplished by personal contact with social superiors who understood its value and usefulness. The underlying aim of generating a desire for religion and moral education was, according to the literary-historical critic Mary Poovey, to develop the "disciplinary individualism" essential to the functioning of a capitalist economy and a bureaucratic state.[11] Martineau's tracts share this aim; if all members of society, especially those of the laboring classes, were educated in political economy, then (she assumed) they would discipline themselves and their desires according to its principles. Although Martineau advocated the principles of political economy alone, without the religious instruction Chalmers insisted on, Martineau believed as strongly as Chalmers in the need to stimulate a desire among the working classes for this kind of disciplinary education. Mr. Burke, for instance, explains to his sister that the function of the charity schools he advocates is not only to educate the poor but also to convince them that they need education—enough that eventually they will be willing to pay for it themselves.[12]

In Chalmers's experiments and in his published writings, however, the home visitors are always male—clergymen such as Chalmers or lay visitors, presumably businessmen; professionals such as Mr. Burke; or leisured gentlemen.[13] While many of Martineau's tales also feature men in tutelary roles—in *A Manchester Strike,* for instance, it is a fair-minded (male) factory owner who teaches the principles of political economy to the striking workers—the important role of Miss Burke in *Cousin Marshall* mirrors Martineau's position as a woman teacher, ideally suited to instructing the poor because of her domestic skills, including the management of servants, and the traditional role women had played in both visiting the poor and teaching in or managing charity schools.[14] While Mr. Nugent, the male workhouse visitor in *Cousin Marshall,* has good intentions, he lacks the qualifications Miss Burke seems to possess naturally. Martineau's project of using *Illustrations* to educate the public in the "natural" laws of political economy to create an informed and compliant workforce resembles Chalmers's enterprise for reconciling religion and political economy, with the crucial difference that, like Hannah More, Martineau claims a key role for women, including women writers.

Although Martineau's social vision followed Hannah More's in preserving and extending the role of middle-class women, her religious and political views do seem to diverge radically from her predecessor's. As an avowed exponent of the laissez-faire principles of political economy, Martineau appears to eschew the benevolent paternalism that More advocated in *Coelebs in Search of a Wife*. When More has Mrs. Stanley, her wise Lady Bountiful figure, say that "to assist their own labouring poor is a kind of natural debt, which persons who possess great landed property owe to those from the sweat of whose brow they derive their comforts," she endorses the view that the working classes have a "right" to assistance and to a basic subsistence (2:22). Martineau, of course, vehemently disagrees. Mr. Burke explains to his sister how dangerous it is for the poor to assume such "rights": "There is harm enough done by the poor taking for granted that they are to be supplied with medicine and advice gratis all their lives: the evil is increasing every day by their looking on assistance in child-birth as their due; and if they learn to expect food and warmth in like manner, their misery will be complete" (3:38). *Cousin Marshall* illustrates this principle in the character of Mrs. Bell, a working-class woman whose skillful manipulation of both "the gentry" and the administrators of the old poor laws has made her selfish, spiteful, and, most important, unable to support herself and her family. Arguing explicitly against government poor relief and implicitly against any kind of intervention in regulating the economy, Martineau has Mr. Burke denounce the metaphor of paternalism as "a fallacy" and a "false analogy" (3:45).

Despite Martineau's apparent rejection of paternalism as a model for social relations, whether the traditional paternalism of the gentry for the poor on their estates or the newer notion of state paternalism, her vision, like that of Chalmers, does have significant similarities to the revised paternalism More recommended. Although paternalism as traditionally defined included taking care of the material needs of the poor, in More's version, as we have seen, the educative function of one-to-one contacts with the poor was more important than the material assistance offered. In the case of Mrs. Jones, the protagonist of several of More's tracts for "persons of the middle ranks," little if any monetary charity was given—or needed. The major contribution of the middle-class philanthropist was her influence—her moral teachings and domestic skills as well as her personal concern and tact. Likewise, in Chalmers's *Christian and Civil Economy* the visitors are to create bonds of gratitude and respect among the poor through the power of their personal interest in both individuals and families, not primarily through material gifts. It is key that while many political economists and bureaucrats had begun to view the poor in the abstract, as statistics,[15] Chalmers and Martineau insisted that even the laws of political economy would be more likely to work toward society's good if they were taught and reinforced by the personal acquaintance between upper- and lower-class people that characterized paternalism. While political economists such as Chalmers and Martineau denied the responsibility of the paternal classes to provide for the poor's material needs, they by no means abandoned the duty to educate or the authority that paternalism granted to those in a superior social position.[16]

Deerbrook, the novel Martineau published in 1839, for instance, explicitly attempts to teach the gentry their real paternal responsibility to the poor of their neighborhood. Virtually all the characters from the lower classes, including shopkeepers, laborers, and the indigent, are easily swayed—even manipulated—by their social superiors, whether the wife of the local manufacturer or the family of Sir William Hunter, the local squire. When the town and surrounding area are struck by an epidemic, Sir William and his family are roundly condemned by the novel's protagonists and the narrator for neglecting their paternal duty to the distressed:

> Sir William Hunter and his lady are enough to paralyse the morals of the whole parish at a time like this. Do not you know the plan they go upon? They keep their outer gates locked, lest any one from the village should set foot within their grounds; every article left at the lodge for the use of the family is fumigated before it is admitted into the house: and it is generally understood that neither the gentleman nor the lady will leave the estate, in any emergency whatever, till the disease has entirely passed away. Our poor are not to have the solace of their presence even in church, during this time of peril, when the face of the prosperous is like light in a dark place.[17]

The Hunters do provide money; Dr. Levitt, the clergyman, reports that he spends Sir William's money "as freely as my own at a time like this" (477). Their real duty, in the scheme of the novel, however, is not to provide money but instead personal contact: "I tell him that one hour of his presence among us would do more good than all the gold he can send," says Dr. Levitt (477).

The failure of the gentry to fulfill their (rightly defined) paternal duty in *Deerbrook* is eventually overcome by an alliance reminiscent of More's relationship with her male sponsors, Wilberforce and Bishop Porteus—a partnership between professional men and philanthropic women. Dr. Levitt asks Margaret Ibbotsen, the novel's heroine, to give "her time and talents for such services as we gentlemen cannot perform," inviting her to become a "fellow-labourer of your sex, no less valuable in her way than my friend Hope [the doctor] in his" (477). Unlike Lady Hunter, who not only fails in her Lady Bountiful role but also frightens the shopkeepers she patronizes out of doing their duty, Margaret becomes a necessary and equal partner with the clergyman and the doctor. Martineau does not reject the idea of the paternal responsibility of the gentry, male or female; rather, she condemns those individuals, such as Sir William and Lady Hunter, who abrogate their duty. Ideally, Martineau implies, rightly conceived paternalism on the part of the gentry would work hand in hand with the efforts of educated professionals united with informed women philanthropists to ensure the smooth working of "natural" laws that promote society's general welfare.

In representing education of and personal contacts with the poor as essential to the functioning of the laws of political economy, Martineau not only preserves a role for women philanthropists but makes their intervention in social relations necessary. This, of course, provides the rationale for her venture into a field that many—like the reviewer for *Fraser's*—saw as inappropriate for women. Building on the precedent of rationally educated women writers such as More, Martineau assembled a successful career as a professional writer, not of silver-fork or domestic romances but of serious works on topical political, social, and economic issues.[18] There are, however, no characters quite like Martineau herself in her writings; Miss Burke appears only briefly in *Cousin Marshall* and Margaret Ibbotsen is soon absorbed into *Deerbrook*'s romance plot. The contrast between Martineau's career and her writings suggests that while individual women might achieve success, prominence, and even political influence by taking on the role of the philanthropic woman, representing that role for women in general was still fraught with difficulty.

Frances Trollope and Factory Reform

Another woman writer who used the discourse of philanthropy to write and publish fiction on controversial social and political issues during the 1830s was Frances Trollope. The mother of the now more famous Anthony Trollope, Frances wrote thirty-five novels, many of them dealing with social issues such as slavery, the poor laws, and factory reform.[19] Although Trollope did not explicitly address political economy, as Martineau did, her popular novels represent—and critique—a world dominated by its principles. One of these, *The Life and Adventures of Michael Armstrong, the Factory Boy,* was the earliest major example of the genre variously labeled condition-of-England novels, social-problem novels, factory novels, and proletarian novels.[20] Published in shilling numbers from March 1839 to February 1840, Trollope's novel was the first by a woman to take advantage of this new and lucrative method of publication;[21] it sold well enough that it appeared shortly after in both one- and three-volume forms.

An early reviewer of *Michael Armstrong* suggested that "the author . . . deserves as richly to have eighteen months in Chester Gaol as any that are there now for using violent language against the 'monster cotton mills.'"[22] Those already in the Chester Gaol were trade union leaders and labor agitators, several of whom Trollope had consulted and entertained on a fact-finding mission to Manchester earlier in 1839.[23] By linking Trollope with these political reformers, the reviewer included her novel in the political debate in which working-class spokespersons such as Richard Oastler, J. Doherty, and Joseph Raynor Stephens and reform-minded writers and professionals such as Michael Sadler, Lord Ashley (later, Earl of Shaftesbury), and Edwin Chadwick participated. This response to the novel indicates that Trollope's book was taken seriously as a commentary on contemporary social and political issues.

Trollope wrote *Michael Armstrong,* which features a nine-year-old factory worker and a wealthy middle-class factory owner's daughter as protagonists, to generate support for protective factory legislation. Castigated by both contemporary reviewers and some modern scholars as propaganda for the Ten-Hours Bill, the novel advocates the state paternalism that Martineau eschewed in her *Illustrations of Political Economy.*[24] Although Trollope's view of political economy was the reverse of Martineau's, however, Trollope assumed many of the "natural" principles Martineau espoused; Trollope's project is not to reject political economy but to temper it with laws that will allow the revised paternalism More envisioned to function side by side with a strong capitalist economy.[25] By focusing on a victimized child laborer and a sympathetic middle-class philanthropist, Trollope's novel attempts to create a space where workers, and especially middle-class women, can participate as agents—not just as passive objects—within the economy.[26]

Like More and Martineau before her, Trollope implicitly justified her intervention into political and economic issues by taking up the position of the middle-class woman as philanthropist-educator, while at the same time drawing on the conventions of sentimental fiction. One of the primary intended functions of *Michael Armstrong* is to teach readers unfamiliar with factories and factory workers the effects of the factory system, particularly on child laborers. Trollope's description of Sir Matthew Dowling's mill, for instance, takes the inexperienced reader on a tour of the factory, beginning with the exterior and moving inside to view the operatives firsthand.[27] Her vivid portrayal enables readers to experience the sensations Trollope wants them to feel at the sight of the factory: "The ceaseless whirring of a million hissing wheels, seizes on the tortured ear; and while threatening to destroy the delicate sense, seems bent on proving first, with a sort of mocking mercy, of how much suffering it can be the cause. The scents that reek around, from oil, tainted water, and human filth, with that last worst nausea, arising from the hot refuse of atmospheric air, left by some hundred pairs of labouring lungs, render the act of breathing a process of difficulty, disgust, and pain" (80). In describing the child workers, Trollope carefully chooses her language: the children are "helpless," "suffering" "infants," their "premature old age" is "hideous," and, most inflammatory of all, the "dirty, ragged, miserable crew" are characterized as "little slaves," prodded by "over-lookers, strap in hand."[28] Trollope's emphasis in this description is on the tortured bodies of children, a tactic intended to garner maximum sympathy from the reader, especially the female reader accustomed to melodramatic and sentimental fiction. Using words such as "slaves," of course, not only elicits an emotional reaction but also draws on the rhetoric of the abolition debates in which many middle-class women took part.[29]

Finally, Trollope focuses her description on an individual child worker:

> The miserable creature to whom the facetious doctor pointed, was a little girl about seven years old, whose office as *"scavenger,"* was to collect incessantly from the machinery and from the floor, the flying fragments of cotton that might impede the work. In the performance of this duty, the child was obliged, from time to time, to stretch itself with sudden quickness on the ground, while the hissing machinery passed over her; and when this is skillfully done, and the head, body, and outstretched limbs carefully glued to the floor, the steady-moving, but threatening mass, may pass and repass over the dizzy head and trembling body without touching it. But accidents frequently occur; and many are the flaxen locks, rudely torn from infant heads, in the process. (80–81)

Fulfilling her role as educator, Trollope introduces the uninitiated reader to the vocabulary of factory life—here the "scavenger" and later the notorious "billy-roller," for instance, are both defined and pictured for the reader. Mingling matter-of-fact tour guide description—"but accidents frequently occur"—with the horrifying details of the little girl continuously forced to undergo a dangerous and terror-inducing experience, Trollope uses the conventions of both sentimental fiction and educational explanation to evoke a visceral response from her readers (79–81). These readers include, the author makes clear, most of those who live in luxury from the profits of such labor; such readers are represented in the characters of Mary Brotherton, the heroine, and Martha Dowling, Sir Matthew's ugly but sympathetic daughter.[30]

Thus, while other nineteenth-century factory novels, as the literary-historical critic Constance D. Harsh points out, tend to represent the evils of the industrial system by showing their effects on the domestic sphere,[31] Trollope also takes her readers into the factory workrooms and forces them to experience the pain of suffering children's bodies.[32] Although Trollope was not an advocate of the utilitarian and laissez-faire principles of political economy, as Martineau was, this focus on victimized children enabled her to avoid a contradiction of those seemingly natural laws. By drawing attention to the suffering bodies of the children the factory system exploited rather than the adult laborers who were supposedly free agents, Trollope could campaign for protective legislation and hope to gain support even from those engaged in or profiting from the mills and factories.

The legislation that *Michael Armstrong* (both the novel and the character) advocates is, as I have mentioned, the Ten-Hours Bill that would restrict the hours of factory labor to ten hours without a diminution in pay.[33] While it is the heroine Mary Brotherton through whom the reader experiences and learns about the effects of factories, the political explanation of the need for and ramifications of the bill are put into the mouth of the Reverend George Bell of Fairly. The character of the Reverend Mr. Bell is closely based on the Reverend Mr. Bull of Brierly (popularly known as the "Ten-Hours Parson"), whom Trollope met and conversed with on her fact-finding trip to the manufacturing district in Lancashire.[34] Thus, although the daring investigation into and observation of appalling factory conditions is carried out by the ingenious efforts of Mary Brotherton, she does not herself become involved in political agitation or reform. Instead, as several feminist critics have observed, the figure of a male professional, the clergyman Mr. Bell, is made the spokesperson and activist for the political views expressed in the novel. The only role Mary is allowed to play in solving the problems she investigates, despite her potentially powerful position as daughter of a factory owner, is to rescue, educate, and provide for individual factory workers. Convinced by Mr. Bell that neither her fortune nor her philanthropic efforts to aid and educate factory workers will have any effect on the real problems in the factories, Mary takes the child workers she has rescued—Edward Armstrong, Fanny Fletcher, and, finally, Michael—and leaves England, using her fortune to form a small utopian community in Germany. Thus Trollope seems to suggest that women have no voice in political discourse, but they only contribute to a reformed society through individual acts of service and compassion, thus reinforcing the doctrine of separate spheres that consigned women to the supposedly apolitical private sphere of home and family—and posing no threat to a laissez-faire economy.

However, the sentimental ending of *Michael Armstrong,* which many critics have labeled apolitical or escapist, can be read in a different way. Harsh, for instance, argues that Mary's voluntary exile to Europe is a solution to the version of industrialism represented in the book because it rejects the industrial values controlling England in favor of the non-patriarchal domestic utopia she builds in Germany with Edward, Fanny, and Michael.[35] Compelling as Harsh's reading is, however, it ignores Trollope's role in promoting industrial legislation as a resolution to the problems Mary observes. While the time is not yet ripe for Mary to intervene in industrial affairs on a large scale, Trollope does intervene; in effect, she takes over the male voice of the historical activist Rev. Bull and re-creates it, on a grander and more effective scale, as the fictional Rev. Bell, putting her words into his mouth. Thus Trollope the novelist is allowed a role that her character is not.

In another sense, however, even in the context of the novel Trollope uses the character of Mary Brotherton in two ways. By having Mary leave England and set up an alternative society, Trollope can represent the destructive effects of the laissez-faire doctrines of Sir Matthew Dowling and his obsequious theorist, Dr. Crockley, as unredeemable and therefore reject them; but by representing in detail the process of Mary's political and moral awakening through her investigations and the explanations of Mr. Bell, Trollope also holds out a solution to the industrial problem that goes beyond the specific legislation Mr. Bell is promoting—a remedy that necessarily involves domestic women as well as enlightened male reformers.

Even though Mary is in a sense forced to leave England to refashion society, the novel's championing of the Ten-Hours Bill cannot be overlooked as a proposed solution to industrial ills in which even she could participate. What I suggest is that this piece of legislation is represented as only the first enabling step in a larger process of factory reform that necessarily involves women in their by now accepted role as philanthropists. I argue that it is philanthropic discourse that permits Trollope to represent Mary as involved even in the observing and investigating role she is allowed in the novel and that, despite her inability to act on the Ten-Hours Bill, Mary's role as a female philanthropist is a political statement of the claims of middle-class women to authority in a newly expanding social sphere.[36]

The Trollope critic and biographer Helen Heineman, like Harsh and a number of other readers, makes a point of claiming that in *Michael Armstrong* Trollope rejects not only the severe laissez-faire values of industrialism but also any type of philanthropic reform. Heineman contends that

"*Michael Armstrong* was an early criticism of the effectiveness of private philanthropy and presented powerful arguments that only public legislation . . . could bring relief to the sufferings of the industrial poor," citing statements such as this one from Mr. Bell: "That you may save your own heart from the palsy of hopeless and helpless pity, by the indulgence of your benevolence in individual cases of distress, I need not point out to you; but that any of the ordinary modes of being useful on a larger scale, such as organising schools, founding benefit societies, or the like, could be of any use to beings so crushed, so toil-worn, and so degraded, it would be idle to hope."[37] Obviously, such statements critique the effectiveness of private charitable schemes. The novel also gives a parody of philanthropic efforts on behalf of factory workers, namely Sir Matthew Dowling's "adoption" of Michael that puts the plot into motion. This deed is represented as a sham act of charity designed to calm the complaints of and impress the workers, while ironically puffing Sir Matthew as a kind and benevolent master. In addressing Mary Brotherton, Sir Matthew caricatures his surveillance of his employees as "charitable visits of inquiry" (130). The narrator describes Michael as suffering the "horrible bondage of Sir Michael's charity" (113). In addition to this parodic inversion of philanthropy, Trollope also shows the ineffectiveness of traditional charitable projects by having Mary visit a Sunday school attached to a factory, where the children are berated in the name of the Bible on Sunday by their weekday master—but they fail to heed the lecture because they are asleep from the long hours of overtime they have spent in the factory (240–41).

Despite these examples, however, *Michael Armstrong* should not be read as whole-scale rejection of philanthropy as a cure for the problems of the industrial poor. Mr. Bell's statement, for instance, that any philanthropic project will only do good to Mary's feelings and not to the workers is prefaced by another statement: "if any proof were wanted of the depth and hopelessness of the wretchedness which the present system produces, it might be found in the fact, that despite the inclination I feel both for your sake, and that of the poor operatives, to encourage your generous benevolence, I cannot in conscience tell you that is in your power effectually to assist them" (208). Mr. Bell here implies that the fact of philanthropy's ineffectiveness is the worst indictment of "the present system"—a system he wants the passage of the Ten-Hours Bill to rectify. In other words, Mr. Bell claims that once this piece of legislation is enacted, benevolence and philanthropic projects will again assume their rightful role in helping the poor. The Sunday schools, for instance, are not criticized per se but only because the children are too sleepy to benefit from them (and have the wrong teachers); limit the children's hours of labor, however, and they will be ready and willing to take advantage of the benefit offered, as Edward Armstrong immediately takes advantage of the charity school Mary Brotherton has instituted on her estate for the children of the servants—once he is released from the need of working long hours in the factory. Similarly, the motherless Drake girls, another family Mary Brotherton visits, are unable to take advantage of Mary's gift of fabric for new clothes because they work such long hours that they have not had time to learn to sew. Again, however, limiting their hours of labor would put such girls in a position to benefit from individual gifts such as Mary's, or from clothing societies, because they would not only have time after work to sew and mend their own and their families' clothing but they would be able to attend charity schools, where they would be taught domestic skills—thus becoming "like all other decent young women" (156).

The "other decent young women" to whom Mary Brotherton refers are not factory girls but women from two other significant groups of working-class people—servants and the agricultural poor. As Trollope envisions it in *Michael Armstrong,* the solution to both the physical suffering and the perhaps even more serious problem of moral degradation, marked in this instance by the Drake girls' lack of domestic skills, is not to get rid of machines or factories (Mr. Bell goes on at length about the "magnificent power" of machinery rightly used), or even of children working in them, but rather to regulate their hours of employment in order that they may become like other English working people. By means of this legislation, Trollope suggests, factory relations can be re-formed on the model of traditional social paternalism.

It is obvious that the traditional social paternalism Mary Brotherton (and Trollope) espouses is idealized. The state of things that allows some to be richer than others is "natural," Mary reasons, "but that among those whom fate or fortune had doomed to labour, some should be cherished, valued, honoured by masters who received and paid their industry, while 'other some' were doomed, under the same compact of labour and payment, to the scorn, avoidance, and contempt of the beings whose wealth and greatness proceeded from their toil, was an enigma she could in no wise comprehend" (98). Mary's reasoning, of course, is based on a naive conception of the working of paternalism, not only in her assumptions about appreciative, respectful masters but also in her simple equation of the employer–employee relation in a paternalistic agrarian economy with the labor relations of capitalism. Even though it is both anachronistic and simplistic, however, there is an important reason that Trollope has her independent heroine believe so fervently in the efficacy of the interlocking bonds between the landed gentry and their servants and laborers. For, while this model of social relations has been repeatedly characterized by twentieth-century feminists as oppressively patriarchal, it nonetheless offered a definite and significant role to women as managers of class relations in the capacity of Lady Bountiful. By holding on to her idealized vision of agricultural class relations, Mary also preserves her role as a key player in the field of social regulation. Following the explanation that Poovey gives of the formation of new domains, preserving the Lady Bountiful role from feudal relations would seem in some ways contradictory and irrational because it is the "trace" of an older domain in the newer domain of the "social."[38] Such apparently contradictory or irrational traces, however, could sometimes be usefully exploited. In this case, then, preserving the landed woman's role in founding and teaching in charity or Sunday schools; providing employment, advice, and gifts to the poor; and, most important, knowing them individually and claiming their loyalty and deference is a way of transporting these useful mechanisms for social management into the industrial world of the factory and city as well as a system of ensuring women a vital role in a field of knowledge and activity increasingly being claimed by professional men — political economists, social investigators, journalists, doctors, clergy, as well as politicians. In *Michael Armstrong,* for instance, Dr. Crockley maintains his claim to advise (and profit from) Sir Matthew Dowling on the basis of his "scientific" interest in and knowledge of the factories and factory workers. His knowledge, however, is shown to be both superficial and self-serving, while Mary Brotherton's, based as it is on systematic investigation, clear reasoning, and sound moral principles as well as genuine sympathy, is presented as more accurate, reliable, and helpful.

Mary's knowledge, however, is not only based on her investigation of factory conditions; she also has her experience in managing numerous employees—her servants. For in *Michael Armstrong,* the ideal servant economy is likewise organized according to paternal principles whereby behavior is regulated by loyalty and deference, in response to fair and sympathetic treatment.[39] Mary's servant nurse Tremlett, for instance, will do anything for her, as will virtually everyone else who has ever worked for Mary, while Sir Matthew's servants mock him when in his service and immediately decamp when he fails because neither he nor his wife and daughters understand the interlocking bonds that go further than wages in securing good "service."

Thus Mary Brotherton's central role in a novel about factory relations, even though she is represented as being politically ineffectual, is made possible by her position as the mistress of a domestic establishment and by the discourse of philanthropy that rewrote factory relations as paternal. That Mary can even undertake her fact-finding and rescue mission to the mills is justified by recourse to this philanthropic discourse. Her mission is first of all motivated by her desire to aid the destitute but deserving widow Mrs. Armstrong. Although Mary, "the richest young lady in Lancashire rolled off, very literally in search of adventures" (235), this unusual and conventionally unfeminine activity is deemed appropriate with an explanation commonly used to defend single women's participation in all sorts of projects and activities that could be labeled philanthropic: "Do not either of you judge me harshly," replied the heiress with great earnestness; "do not set me down in your judgments as a hot-headed girl, indifferent to the opinions of society, and anxious only to follow the whim of a moment. Did I belong to anyone, I think I should willingly yield to their guidance. But I am alone in the world; I have no responsibilities but to God and my own conscience" (232). Because Mary has no husband or father or ailing relatives to look after—no family responsibilities—then her admirable domestic skills and sympathies can be put to use to serve others in a philanthropic endeavor, even if this endeavor involves subterfuge, bribery, and investigation of spaces that conventional wisdom (and many of the novel's reviewers) believes to be unsuited to women.

Thus, while *Michael Armstrong* as a novel does critique philanthropy as a method of solving industrial problems, it employs the discourse of philanthropy to do it. By another apparent paradox, the novel seems to deny women a role in political discourse while its woman author conspicuously engages in it. Like Martineau, Trollope cannot represent her heroine functioning in a literal political or economic role, but by putting Mary Brotherton's investigations and opinions center stage, she does take Martineau's portrayal of female philanthropists a step further. While Trollope's heroine must in the end be exiled to Europe, her novel at least imagines a way for a woman to participate in an industrial England dominated by the principles of political economy but tempered by protective legislation—through her role as a philanthropist.

Charlotte Elizabeth Tonna's Revised Paternalism

Like Trollope's *Michael Armstrong,* Charlotte Elizabeth Tonna's industrial novel *Helen Fleetwood* portrays the evils of a factory system based on the principles of political economy rather than benevolent paternalism and calls on middle-class women to rectify it. Published serially from 1839 to 1840 in *The Christian Lady's Magazine,* only a few months after *Michael Armstrong* began publication, *Helen Fleetwood* is aimed at a female readership, although it was widely read by a more various audience when it appeared in a one-volume edition priced at seven shillings the following year.[40] Like *Michael Armstrong,* Tonna's novel is designed to introduce its readers to the suffering and oppression—both physical and moral—that the factories inflicted on workers, particularly children. Both *Michael Armstrong* and *Helen Fleetwood* feature sympathetic working-class protagonists; both take the reader inside factories, describing the horrible conditions but also explaining technical terms and procedures; and both advocate protective legislation as a (partial) solution to factory problems, thus taking part in contemporary factory debates. While both novels also call for the intervention of middle-class women in a reformed factory system through their role as philanthropists, *Helen Fleetwood* is even more explicit in outlining this role than is *Michael Armstrong,* giving women significant responsibility both in getting needed legislation passed and in superintending the reformed factory system the author imagines. Even though Tonna goes further in outlining women's participation in the world of the factory, however, she, like Trollope, cannot actually represent this intervention under existing conditions. Tonna makes it clear that the factories must be reorganized on the principles of a revised paternalism, instead of the harsh "laws" of political economy, before women can fully take on the role she envisions.

Helen Fleetwood begins in a setting similar to that portrayed by Hannah More and imagined by Trollope's Mary Brotherton. Tonna's protagonists are rural cottage laborers who embody all the qualities of an idealized English working class. This model working-class family is composed of Widow Green, her four orphaned grandchildren, and Helen Fleetwood, another orphan she has adopted. All members of the family, from the aged Widow Green to the eight-year-old Willy, are industrious, independent, religious, respectful, and gratefully loyal to their "betters." The family, however, loses its lease on the idyllic rural cottage where they have lived so happily and industriously, and they are tricked into going into the factories of M—— by an unscrupulous parish overseer who, following the dictates of political economy, wants to prevent them from falling on the parish for support.

The rest of the novel traces the steadily declining fortunes of this model family as they experience factory life in the city of M——. On their arrival in M——, the Greens meet and are contrasted with the other branch of their family, the widow's daughter Mrs. Wright and her sickly and corrupt factory-bred children. Despite the Green family's proper values and Widow Green's best efforts to maintain their physical and spiritual welfare in the face of the factory system, their fortunes go from bad to worse: the girls, who go into the factory of Mr. Z., are persecuted by their peers and beaten by the overlookers; young James dies of consumption, while eight-year-old Willy, employed by an ostensibly Christian master in a silk mill, experiences such bodily fatigue and spiritual corruption that he turns to the gin shop. While the widow unsuccessfully seeks redress from every source of authority in M——, Helen becomes a model of submissive suffering, finally dying just as they are about to be rescued and returned to their initial rural setting. The remaining family members are eventually allowed to return to the country but not to their former happily independent state; instead, Widow Green goes into the workhouse and the rest of the family is separated when they each take jobs as waged agricultural laborers, demonstrating the spreading negative effects of laissez-faire economics even in the rural agricultural economy.

Portraying both the admirable qualities of the model Green family and the misfortunes they experience when plunged into an antipaternalistic factory economy allows Tonna to mount a devastating critique of a society run solely in accordance with the supply and demand principles of political economy. Not only do the factories cause enormous physical suffering but the factory world turns the poor from industrious citizens into statistical abstractions.[41] Widow Green, for instance, behaves with exemplary deference, humility, and politeness in all her encounters with those "above her" in M——, from the factory agent to the owner Mr. Z., but she is not in turn treated with the respect to which she has been accustomed in the country. Both agent and owner refuse to address her by name, even when they remember it, but rather they stress her interchangeability with all other "old women": "Widow Green, Brown, Black, or White, do you think I have a memory for all the colours that pass before me every day?" says the agent Mr. M., while even Mr. Z. addresses her as "Mrs. Thingimy."[42] Helen, a model of modesty and femininity, is subjected to coarse taunting and insinuations by her employers and the town magistrates because they see her only as a "mill girl."[43] That it can rob even these two exemplary feminine women of their individuality and turn them into interchangeable units is one of the novel's harshest indictments of a world driven by political economy.

Seeing working people only as abstractions—units of labor—is troubling to Tonna because it denies or ignores that they have souls. An avowed admirer of Hannah More and her writings, Tonna used her novel as a platform to teach her readers about factory conditions as well as to instill principles of Christian forbearance and acceptance of God's will, whatever that may entail in terms of temptation and suffering. Like the exemplary working-class characters in More's *Cheap Repository Tracts*, Widow Green, her grandson James, and Helen Fleetwood meet grinding poverty, physical suffering, and contemptuous treatment with Christlike submission and forgiveness. When she is unjustly beaten by an overlooker, for instance, Helen responds: "Dearest granny, don't be distressed: it was a trifle, and I hardly feel it now at all. Such things cannot sometimes be helped in a place like the mills. Be satisfied that I did not intentionally deserve a blow; and that by the grace of God I was enabled to take it patiently, and to forgive. So now, granny, let us forget it too; for you know the command is, 'Forgive *as* ye would be forgiven'" (111). In Tonna's view, Helen's admirable response to both violence and injustice makes her superior to her capitalist employers, despite her low economic status. In addition, her goodness gives her the power of influence. In this scene, Helen's superlative behavior and forgiving words affect not only Widow Green but also the Irish papist Mr. Malony. Even though Tonna's working-class characters often initially react to injustice or indignity with outrage, anger, and a desire to fight back or even seek revenge, throughout the novel Christian forbearance is represented as the better way to meet tyranny, oppression, and maltreatment. It is significant that these exemplary working-class characters are not promised or given earthly rewards for their suffering or forbearance, but they are assured of their reward in heaven—and they also win converts such as the Catholic Malonys and the crippled Sarah Wright, a girl in the other branch of Widow Green's family. While this is a common tactic for keeping the poor in their place, for Tonna this Christian response to the evils of the factories is set up as an alternative to the radical social activism embodied in Chartism and socialism, and it is a necessary part of the solution she envisions for the depravity of the factory system.

Tonna, again following Hannah More, made paternalism central to both the novel's Christian message and its reforming social and political mission. For her, the system of agrarian paternalism, where masters and laborers are linked in mutual bonds of loyalty, deference, and respect, is divinely instituted. That even the social and economic relations of rural England are being threatened by the incursion of political economy is a secondary, but crucial, warning to Tonna's readers. "There are districts in the land," Tonna's narrator assures her presumably skeptical readers, "still retaining much of the primitive character of English rusticity—places where *the blight* has not come" (117). She goes on to describe the harvest celebration in L——, the Greens' country home:

> The 'Squire was pleased at the diligence with which [the workers] had availed themselves of the favourable season; the men were gratified by his praises, and no less by his liberality; while the women and elder children, who had found plentiful employment too upon his extensive lands, had similar causes for gladness. As for the little ones, they were delighted to gambol and exhibit their activity in the presence of the 'Squire's family, whose daughters took no small pains in disciplining the urchins

at their infant school, and marshalling them for an orderly march
to the church door. Each, both old and young, enjoyed that peculiar feeling, the value of which the poor are seldom aware of
until they experience its absence, "My employer knows me; I am
not in his sight a mere piece of machinery, regarded only while
it works in his service. There's a tie between us that he, though
a rich man, would not disown. If he is everything to me, I and
mine are something to him." (118)

While this description seems on the surface merely an idealized and nostalgic vision of a past golden age, a closer look at its language suggests it
is instead a carefully articulated call for a kind of social relations that could
be transferred to the urban environment of the factories—as well as
needing to be preserved in the country. Tonna emphasizes that the interests of the squire and the laborers are bound up with each other—the
bountiful harvest has contributed to their mutual happiness. And she insists on the value of face-to-face contacts between employer and employee, interactions in which workers and masters treat each other with
respect. But Tonna contrasts these nostalgic social bonds with impersonal
factory relations where masters regard their anonymous hands as "mere
piece[s] of machinery." Although enclosed in quotation marks as if taken
from the thoughts of the country laborer, this analogy is the narrator's,
since these workers have not experienced factory life and are not aware
of what they have not lost. The passage, including an earlier section in
which even the landscape is described in paternalistic terms, is meant primarily as a lesson on how factories should be run: mill owners should
appreciate and praise the labors of their workpeople; their families, especially their daughters, should be known to and involved with the workers; adults and older children should all be productively employed while
small children are allowed to frolic and go to school; and the property
owners should acknowledge and not disown a tie between themselves
and the workers that goes beyond the cash nexus and that involves the
whole family—on both sides. Thus, the idyllic rural scenes in *Helen Fleetwood* should not be read merely as nostalgia for an idealized past but as
a specific—and God-ordained—program for the industrial present and
future.[44]

Along with her pastoral descriptions of social relations, Tonna's novel also provides examples of the destructive effects of the loss of such rela-tions in the urban factory environment. Accustomed to viewing the squire and his family as protectors and benefactors, Widow Green visits Mr. Z., the factory owner, at his country home to seek his assistance in preventing the physical and moral abuse her family has been facing in his factory. The widow trusts the owner because "I know he is a father, and he must feel; I know he is a gentleman, and he will not mock a poor old woman for appealing to his heart and conscience, on behalf of two help-less orphans" (96). She finds, however, that her trust is misplaced; both fatherhood and gentlemanliness are dissevered from their paternal roots even in the elegant homes of the owners, imitating, as they do, the landed gentry in situation and style (96). Mr. Z. treats Widow Green dismissively and, as the "laws" of political economy prescribe, takes no responsibility for the welfare of those who work in his factories, however faithful or exemplary they may be.

Besides the failures of the managers and owners to behave in a pater-nal role, Tonna also points out the exclusion of their daughters from all contact with the working people who supply their fortunes as an equally egregious lapse of social responsibility. Mr. Z.'s daughter listens to the widow's story with interest and compassion, but her father immediately expels her from the room and reprimands the widow "for introducing such improper subjects in the presence of a young lady, whose ears ought not to have been assailed by discourse so unfit for a delicate mind" (100). His statement, of course, is meant to be ironic since Helen Fleetwood, the orphan on whose behalf Widow Green is pleading, has been shown to have as "delicate" a mind as any middle-class young woman could have.[45] Mr. Z.'s daughter, however, is more responsive to Widow Green's story than is her father, and she follows and offers money to the aged widow:

> "Dear young lady!" replied the widow, "it is not money that I want: but if I could win your father's protection for my poor girls, how thankful I should be!"
>
> "Oh," exclaimed Amelia, looking frightened, "Papa never al-lows any of us to interfere in the least about the mills—I must not say one word to him on that, because"—here a side door opened, and an elder domestic appeared, who, darting a look of

anger at the poor woman, said in a very testy voice, "Miss Amelia, your Mamma wants you directly. Directly, Miss." (100)

Even the servants combine to protect the daughters of mill owners from exercising what Tonna represents as their natural sympathy with and desire to aid the less fortunate and from exercising her feminine influence on either her father or the poor. Widow Green, accustomed to rural paternalism, can still hardly grasp how differently social relations are organized in M——: "Yet there lingered in her mind a sort of incredulity as to the possibility of such a state of things existing in England, simply because it was England" (101).

That the factory town and its inhabitants, of both upper and lower classes, are un-English is Tonna's severest condemnation of them. She frequently applauds England's superiority to other nations because of its independent and industrious working classes, its law that apply to all, and, especially, its abolition of the slave trade. Yet in M——, all these have been overturned. The working classes are repeatedly characterized as slaves, a court scene proves that the laws are unequally applied, and the recruitment of factory workers is linked with the slave trade. Worst of all, however, is the moral depravity of the workers, represented most forcibly by the Wright family. The Wright children, except the crippled Sarah, are not only physically stunted but are ignorant, profane, and violent; the two youngest boys are drunkards and the eldest, it is implied, is a thief, while Phoebe, the eldest daughter, is sexually promiscuous. Their mother, Mrs. Wright, has become so hardened that she has little feeling for her children or her mother, Widow Green; and the father, although less hardened, is portrayed as weak and ineffectual. The family, despite being such close relations, torments the Greens. Phoebe is primarily responsible for the humiliation, beating, and eventual death of Helen— merely because Helen insists on being good and not succumbing to the vices of the other factory girls, something the hardened (but apparently conflicted) Phoebe cannot stand.

The Wrights are an especially poignant example of the depravity the factories caused because, like the Greens, the parents were reared in the country and Mrs. Wright, Widow Green's daughter, has had the same pious upbringing as do the orphaned grandchildren the widow is raising. Yet neither the Greens nor the novel blame the Wrights or the other factory laborers for their fall from grace. As the factory worker Mr. South explains to Richard Green: "just ask yourself what you would most likely now be if you had been taken out of your bed every day at early morn, and shut up in a close, hot, dirty, unwholesome building, where you'd never have heard a syllable of good advice, but cursing and swearing, and filthy talk from morning to night; then to go home, so tired you had no thought for any thing but to get to sleep as fast as could be, and up again for the same purpose. This to go on from Monday morning to Saturday night" (136). Interrupted by an anguished exclamation from Green, South explains, "I wanted to prove to you that the wickedness of the factories is not to be charged on the poor labourers, so much as on the vile system that makes slaves, not servants, of them" (137).

Because the resolution of *Helen Fleetwood* can only send the Greens to heaven or back to the country to escape the depravity of the factory system, some readers have criticized the novel—along with most other factory and social-problem novels—for failing to advance a solution to the problems it so graphically represents. In response to the un-Englishing of the factory towns, however, Tonna did propose a comprehensive plan, one that involved re-envisioning the "unnatural" relations the factory system spawned, along with specific legislative action and significant educational efforts. And, like her predecessor Hannah More, Tonna saw women as essential to the accomplishment of the social and political reform she envisioned:

> Compelled by a legal enactment to allow their poor little labour-
> ers a scanty portion of the day for the purposes of education,
> what a noble field was opened to the mill-owners for supplying
> an antidote to the worse evils of their system! [Widow Green]
> thought of Amelia Z. and imagined her, with others like her,
> devoting two hours of their vacant morning to the sweet and
> sacred task of superintending the instruction of their young ser-
> vants in religious and useful knowledge; shaming vice, overawing
> insolence, encouraging modesty, industry, and cleanliness, by the
> mere force of their frequent presence and occasional admoni-
> tions. A clean, airy room, regular arrangements, a few minutes
> allowed for thoroughly cleansing their soiled skin and brushing
> their clothes, with easy, but distinct tasks assigned, and suitable

rewards for such as excelled—all under the personal direction of the employer's family: oh, what a refreshment to body and mind would this have secured to the poor little toil-worn creatures! by what a tie of respectful affection, and consequent diligence and integrity in his service, would it have bound them to their master! (116)

Tonna here outlines her plan: an enforced "legal enactment" would first compel the mill owners to allow the time; then the daughters would initiate and superintend appropriate education, thus binding the children to their masters by ties of deference and gratitude; by implication, then, these children would grow up to be responsible workers and parents, hence preventing not only rampant vice but also potential rebellion.

Tonna, as we have already seen, was by no means alone in advocating a revised version of paternalism as a model for factory relations. Her novel is in effect a visualization or embodiment of the principles advocated by the Christian political economists and reformers who promoted interventionist legal measures. Thomas Chalmers, along with Harriet Martineau, for instance, strongly recommended a moral paternalism even though they believed in economic individualism.[46] Many reformers and Evangelicals went even further and promoted paternalistic measures that were both economic and moral. The difference in Tonna's novel, however, is the explicit inclusion of women as the key figures in the process of generating paternalist relations out of protective legal enactments. By the time in which her novel is set, a number of protective laws had already been passed, including some that restricted hours and ages of employment for children and the one that required factory owners to release children for a set time each day to go to school. What *Helen Fleetwood* demonstrates so graphically, however, is that even protective laws are useless unless they are legally enforceable—and unless there are able and willing volunteers to make use of the opportunities the law provides. It is significant that Tonna called on women to act in order to remedy both of these impediments to reform.

Late in the novel, Tonna has Richard Green attend "a select meeting of the labourers, about to assemble for the consideration and adoption of future plans" (147). Far from being a socialist or Chartist meeting, however, this turns out to be a meeting of Christian reformers from the arti-

san and working classes, followers of Lord Ashley, the great reforming
legislator. The problem they face, remarks the president of the group,
is that "we cannot rouse a manly feeling in the legislature" (149). The
solution, therefore, says Green's new friend Mr. Hudson, is to enlist
women:

> Now suppose a lady, the mother of a young family, looking upon
> her own children and thinking what she would feel if they were
> situated like the wretched little ones in the factories,—or sup-
> pose another, employed in teaching or overseeing a nice school
> of girls, and comparing their comforts and advantages with what
> our little labourers want, and what they suffer,—don't you think
> these ladies would use their influence over their own husbands,
> fathers, brothers and friends, to make it a point with the candi-
> date they vote for, that he should support our cause in the Parlia-
> ment? (150)

Women will exercise their influence over the voting male members of
their families, claims Hudson, and, if sufficiently informed of the nature
of the problem, they will organize, establish societies, take up collections,
and spread information—as they have done in the case of slavery and
educating the "heathens." "Oh that we had a few of those Christian
ladies to take the hard case of our factory little ones into their kind and
zealous hands!" cries Green enthusiastically (151). Thus, in Tonna's novel
not only working-class women such as Widow Green but also responsible
and reform-minded working-class men call on middle-class women to
aid and further their cause, while the middle-class men who hold authority—both the mill owners and Parliament members—are accused of
a failure of "manliness." If women actively and aggressively assert their
femininity in the realm of social relations and politics, however, Tonna
hopes that the men in power will reassert their own "manly," that is fatherly and paternal, role in social and political relations; in other words,
they will enact, enforce, and observe just and protective laws, which will
free women to do their part in educating and superintending the laboring
poor. In effect, like More, Tonna thereby advocated a "marriage" between male reformers—capitalists, professionals, and legislators—and
female philanthropists as the foundation of her ideal paternalist factory
world.

Thus, although only one middle-class woman appears in *Helen Fleet-wood,* and only for the briefest moment, the novel nonetheless represents a central role for them in the newly developing social sphere through their acknowledged aptitude for philanthropy. Although the plot focuses on working-class women, its primary intention is to convince middle-class women that factory workers are not frightening and depraved but good—or potentially good—people who need their help and assistance. While Trollope's *Michael Armstrong* shows its heroine dashing off to dangerous and unfeminine adventures, *Helen Fleetwood* generalizes the potential role of middle-class women by merely asking its readers to do the same sort of charitable activities that many of them are already doing—to organize societies, push their husbands and sons to pass protective legislation, and form one-on-one paternal relationships with working-class people by teaching in charity schools and visiting in their homes.

One might ask, then, where does that leave Helen Fleetwood, the working-class heroine on whom most criticism of the novel has naturally focused? As Constance Harsh concludes, "Helen is the great active and positive force in the novel, easily outstripping South and his shady schemes and even those well-intentioned Christians who look to Lord Ashley for help." Not only does her exemplary death move her "from prominence in the home to eminence in the outside world" but she also succeeds in quashing socialism in her mill by mobilizing some of the workers.[47] And Helen is also a teacher, informally, among her family and fellow workers, but also formally, in the Sunday school in the country and in the city. Thus, if the active femininity of middle-class women is recruited by Tonna as a necessary part of her solution to factory problems, it is also required of educated working-class women such as Helen and Widow Green. In Hudson's appeal to middle-class mothers and teachers, he stresses their essential likeness with working-class women. So, even though Tonna might be seen as casting the working-classes as children in order to assure a role for middle-class women, she is also holding out the possibility of working-class women profiting from and participating in the role she claims for women by representing the public world outside the home as merely a larger version of that home—a home where manly men and feminine women act in their separate, but equally important, spheres to preserve the Englishness of their nation in the face of radical economic and social change.

By bringing the domestic into the commercial and public world of the factory through women's traditional association with philanthropy, Martineau, Trollope, and Tonna all attempted to put Hannah More's revised paternalism into practice in a new and modern space organized according to the economic principles of political economy. Without rejecting political economy entirely, they tried to temper its "laws" in such a way that women, and the more "humane" values with which they were associated, could also inhabit that space. Redefining Lady Bountiful–like charity as education, they were able to imagine a sphere outside the home where women would still play a crucial role. Women philanthropists and writers of succeeding generations would go on to theorize and represent middle-class women acting in this sphere, although, as might be predicted, their access to it would not go unchallenged.

4 "The Communion of Labor" and *Lectures to Ladies*

A Midcentury Contest between Male Professionals and Female Philanthropists

"WOULD YOU MAKE CHARITY a profession?" asks an imaginary antagonist of Anna Jameson in her second lecture on women's philanthropy, "The Communion of Labor," in 1856. "Why not?" answers the author. "Why should not charity be a profession in our sex, just in so far (*and no farther*) as religion is a profession in yours!" [1] When Hannah More, writing in the first decade of the nineteenth century, claimed philanthropy as a lady's "profession," she had in mind that charitable works would become a natural and necessary part of domestic women's calling as wives, mothers, and daughters. [2] While More used the word "profession" metaphorically to elevate middle- and upper-class women's domestic and charitable activities to the same level of importance and value as men's occupations, Jameson applied the term in a more literal sense. By the middle of the century, and partly because of the influence of More's metaphoric formulation of woman's sphere as a profession equivalent to men's, Jameson conceived of philanthropic work as a profession in nearly the same sense as educated men's paid professional endeavors: philanthropy could be a profession for women like "religion is a profession" for clergymen.

Calling women's philanthropy a profession in 1856 put Jameson in the middle of contemporary debates about women, philanthropy, and professionalism. Philanthropy was by then accepted as the natural extension of the domestic sphere, and thousands of women visited the poor regularly, in their homes as well as in workhouses, hospitals, and even prisons.[3] Philanthropy was often proposed as a solution to the "redundant woman problem" triggered by the widely publicized 1851 census figures; women who could not marry could make charitable work their occupation.[4] However, although it seemed a natural pursuit for all middle- and upper-class women and was touted as especially suitable for unmarried women, women's philanthropy also raised anxieties for some contemporaries, especially those who belonged to the emerging class of male professionals. Charles Dickens's biting satires of women "philanthropists by trade" in *Bleak House,* for instance, may indicate in part his anxiety about his status as a professional writer.[5] Even the writings of ardent supporters of serious women's philanthropy, such as the Christian Socialists F. D. Maurice and Charles Kingsley, reveal concerns about women philanthropists competing with male professionals for authority in a newly defined social sphere.[6]

Like Sarah Scott, Hannah More, and other women philanthropic writers before her, Jameson addresses these anxieties about women's philanthropy by employing the metaphor of the home as model for society, reassuring her listeners and readers that women, however well-trained and professional, will play the same subordinate role in philanthropy that they have in the home. Further, women philanthropists will be distinguished from the male professionals they assist because they will not be paid for their services. Despite these self-conscious restrictions, Jameson's vision of women's role in philanthropy pushes against the boundaries of the dominant domestic ideology of separate spheres. As hard as she works to make women's philanthropy a middle ground between domestic work and paid professional occupations, Jameson's writings—and male professional responses to them—bring out the tensions inherent in using philanthropy to extend the domestic sphere for women. They also make evident the need for more opportunities for education and paid employment, particularly for middle-class women.

Women and the Social Sphere

In their lectures about women's philanthropy, both Jameson and the group of male professionals F. D. Maurice gathered to deliver the *Lectures to Ladies on Practical Subjects* envisioned women performing a crucial function in a "larger social sphere" that was at once an extension and a mirror of their role in the home (*Sisters,* 166). This social sphere, as it was constructed in the nineteenth century, was both an ideological and a material space. Ideologically and practically, the social fell between what were defined as public and private spheres, and it blurred the boundaries between them. Thus, although the domestic ideology that promoted the privatized and feminized home as a separate sphere and a refuge from the hostile public world of men was accepted as natural and true in nineteenth-century England, neither the public nor the private sphere was as unified or discrete as it was proclaimed to be.[7] Moreover, both public and private spheres were also internally divided. What is usually called the public sphere, for instance, was actually an aggregate of diverse activities and interests, encompassing government, education, business, manufacturing, science, the arts, and so on. While all these activities might have been characterized as public, and therefore part of the man's appropriate sphere, not all men had equal access or authority in any or all of these areas. The various sub-realms vied with one another for primacy and power within the larger sphere of the public; all, however, were defined as public by their difference from activities marked as private by being associated with women. While the political and public had almost always been synonymous, and the commercial or economic realm had long been recognized as a public domain, the social realm was a relative newcomer to the public sphere.[8]

Denise Riley describes some of the activities that characterized the "newly conceived space" of "the social":

> The nineteenth-century "social" is the reiterated sum of progressive philanthropies, theories of class, of poverty, of degeneration; studies of the domestic lives of workers, their housing, hygiene, morality, mortality; of their exploitation, or their need for protection, as this bore on their family lives, too. It is a

blurred ground between the old public and private, voiced as a field for intervention, love, and reform by socialists, conservatives, radicals, liberals, and feminists in their different and conjoined ways.[9]

While Riley uses spatial terms such as "ground" and "field" metaphorically to specify the ideological work "the social" was supposed to accomplish, the nineteenth-century social sphere also had its material spaces—the tenements and cottages of the poor, the streets and sewers of the cities, the lanes and bogs of the country, and the comfortable rooms of the middle-class home, as well as the hospitals, prisons, penitentiaries, and workhouses that housed those who seemed most threatening to social health and harmony.

The social sphere, with its theories and studies, could be classified as a public realm because it was associated with the middle-class male professional and his expertise. However, because the object of social observation and intervention was most often the family, women, too, could be represented as experts. The private home was defined by the newly constituted social science as a public space that was both political and apolitical, commercial and antimarket.[10] All women's work, even that strictly isolated within the home, could now be defined as social, or as at least partly public. And when a middle-class woman left her home to visit in the homes of the poor, she used her domestic expertise to authorize herself as an expert, masculinized observer of the social. Since all sorts of concerns identified as public—industrial relations, political unrest, regulative legislation, sociological investigation, and scientific experimentation—fell under the rubric of the social, it was thus possible to imagine these realms as appropriate work for women. Although the social sphere may have been in one sense inherently feminized, however, it was by no means automatically ceded to women.[11] Rather, as Jameson's lectures and the response of Maurice and his professional colleagues demonstrate, professional men and middle-class women competed for access to and authority over the social sphere. While both sets of lectures helped to construct this social sphere and to make a place in it for women philanthropists, the subtle differences between them give evidence of this struggle between male professionals and female philanthropists.

Jameson, a well-known writer of art and travel books who had also become interested in women's issues, gave the first of her two lectures on the subject of women's philanthropy, "On Sisters of Charity Abroad and at Home," in February 1855, shortly after the first reports of Florence Nightingale's success with volunteer nurses in Crimean War hospitals in the winter of 1854–55.[12] In her frequent travels abroad, Jameson had visited several European hospitals and was impressed with the work of both Catholic and Protestant Sisters of Charity. By her own account, Jameson had long contemplated the possibility of women's increased involvement in social work in England as well, and the heavily publicized achievements of Nightingale and her nurses made the time seem right for Jameson to expound her ideas (149).[13] The lecture was enthusiastically received by a large private audience and was published "by desire" in March.[14] The book sold so well that a second edition was published within three months, with a third a year later, another in 1859, and an American edition in 1857.

In the eyes of Jameson and many others, Nightingale's efficient and humane management of the war hospital in the Crimea proved that women were not only capable of reforming and operating public institutions without losing their femininity but also that they deserved the kind of training that Nightingale had obtained for herself in the preceding years.[15] Jameson used Nightingale's notoriety to argue for the necessity of preparing large numbers of women for action in the social sphere:

> people were heard congratulating each other on "the lucky chance" that a Miss Nightingale should have been forth-coming just at the moment she was wanted. Suppose there had been no Miss Nightingale at once able and willing to do the work,—no woman in a position which gave her social influence to overcome the obstacles of custom and prejudice,—suppose that the example of noble courage and devotion which led the way for others had been wanting,—is every crisis of danger, distress, and difficulty involving human life, human suffering, human interests of the deepest consequence, to find us at the mercy of "a lucky chance?"—at the mercy of people who have never thought seriously on any great question, or taken the trouble to

make up their minds one way or another? I trust that England has many daughters not unworthy of being named with Florence Nightingale. (115)

Stressing that Nightingale's "noble courage and devotion" can be cultivated in "many daughters" so that their skillful intervention will be available at every "crisis"—as Nightingale's was for the Crimean mission—Jameson insists that Nightingale was not an "exceptional" woman. Many women, she urges, those "people who have never thought seriously on any great question," could be trained to be "at once able and willing to do the work" of making England's social institutions run as smoothly and efficiently as the ideal English home.

Although Hannah More's earlier use of a familial metaphor to describe the public world of politics, economics, and institutional philanthropy implicitly justified her personal success as a public figure, even in her own terms she was largely an "exceptional" woman. Sometimes classed as one of the "great men" of the Clapham Sect, More advised most women to keep their charities local so as to promote the face-to-face encounters so vital to her revised paternalism.[16] Jameson, however, in what seems a direct response to "strictures" such as More's, calls for all educated women to take their place in public, as well as private, philanthropy: "but why should not charity assume functions publicly recognized,—openly, yet quietly and modestly exercised? why is female influence always supposed to be secret, underhand, exercised in some way which is not to appear?" (269). Jameson asks that women such as More or Nightingale, who assume a womanly but public role in the social sphere, become the norm rather than the exception. Accordingly, she calls for both more serious training and more opportunities for middle- and upper-class women to perform meaningful work as volunteers in social institutions.

Jameson's Challenge to Male Professionals

Jameson's call was both heeded and contested by the Reverend F. D. Maurice, Christian Socialist and principal of the Working Men's College. Maurice had already had a great deal of experience in women's education. He had been one of the founders of Queen's College in 1848, where he is said to have influenced several women who were later to become active in promoting basic and higher education for women.[17] After being fired from a prominent position at King's College in 1854 for unorthodox views, Maurice and a group of his fellow Christian Socialists founded the Working Men's College. According to J. F. C. Harrison's *A History of the Working Men's College,* "the first Circular advertising the College in 1854 said that it was hoped ultimately to provide teaching for both the wives and children of the working-men students" (106). Maurice explained his commitment to educating working-class women as well as men: "We were told in various quarters, that we should do nothing with our scholars unless we could improve the character and the knowledge of their wives and daughters; that they were already less instructed than the males of their own class; that if we succeeded at all, we should make the distance between them wider and more hopeless. It was impossible not to listen to these remonstrances, especially when they proceeded, as some of them did, from ladies who were using great exertions to raise their own sex, which they accused us of neglecting."[18]

Although Maurice had already planned to introduce classes for working women, Jameson's "Sisters of Charity" lecture prompted the idea that "the proper foundation of a College for Working Women would be a college in which ladies should learn to teach" (*Lectures,* 7). Thus, in a direct response to Jameson's proposal, Maurice initiated plans for a college for working women that would be staffed by middle-class ladies in training as teachers and philanthropists.[19] To launch the project, Maurice organized a series of lectures that not only explained the plan of the college but also instructed interested ladies in a number of branches of social work. Maurice's lecture, for instance, based on his experience as a hospital chaplain, was entitled "The College and the Hospital." Charles Kingsley gave instruction on women visiting the poor in "The Country Parish." Other lectures, given by clergymen, physicians, lawyers, and the secretary to the General Board of Health, covered topics such as mental stress among the poor, dispensaries, district visiting, poor laws, sanitary law, and workhouse visiting, as well as teaching. Thus the lectures, which were published soon after as *Lectures to Ladies on Practical Subjects* (1855), went far beyond the specific aim of educating women at the Working Men's College toward the larger goal of utilizing women's skills and qualities to further the positive effects of all social institutions—as Jameson had advocated. Hailed as the implementation of a "radical idea," the published *Lectures* were seen by both men and women as an important step for and "respectful tribute" to women.[20]

Although the proposed college and the *Lectures* seemed to open new avenues for women's philanthropic activity and to accord them more responsibility in the developing social sphere, even this apparently progressive proposal to include women amateurs in social work may be read as an attempt to reinforce the monopoly of these professionals. The sociologist Magali Sarfatti Larson explains nineteenth-century professionalization as "the process by which producers of special services sought to constitute and *control* a market for their expertise," and a "successful project of professionalization" was one that came "close to attaining the goals of market monopoly, social status, and work autonomy." Successful professionalization, writes Larson, became visible when professionals "collectively outrank[ed] (or eliminate[d]) competitors" and obtained "supervisory or controlling authority over related occupations."[21] Since monopolized training is so central to professionalization, Jameson's plans for training middle-class women could have threatened the position of male professionals. Implementing Jameson's proposals for trained women's social work under the umbrella of established male professional authority, however, was a way of neutralizing this potential threat. On the one hand, the "progressive" nature of Maurice's college demonstrated the "service ideal" of professionalism;[22] on the other hand, the project of sharing (a limited portion of) their professional expertise was a way of emphasizing its value. Thus Maurice and his fellow lecturers simultaneously mobilized female helpers to perform some of the least skilled parts of their work and taught these potential rivals that their "natural" or commonsensical methods were wrong or insufficient.

Although philanthropic work by the middle of the nineteenth century was perceived to be a natural and necessary part of women's role, its very naturalness served as a target for male professionals who needed to define women's work in the social sphere as amateurish rather than professional in order to consolidate their own social and economic positions. Maurice's offer to teach middle-class women how to "help" in the social sphere, for instance, characterizes male professionals as "experienced," "efficient," "practical," as well as open and scientific: "Nothing is more reasonable than that men who have had experience in different occupations should say, 'We are convinced that women might help us very much in what we are doing. Some of them have tried to help. We think they would be more efficient if they had more instruction, and certain practical hints which we could give them. If they, or any of them, are of the same opinion, we shall be willing for our parts to make the experiment'" (286). Conversely, Maurice implies that women who participate in social work on their own authority without male "instruction" are inefficient and ineffectual; their attempts to "help" may in fact be obstacles to social progress and men's professional goals.

While Jameson welcomed Maurice and his colleagues' offer of sharing their professional expertise with women philanthropists, her lectures use women's supposedly natural aptitude for charity to argue for their expanded participation and authority in the social sphere, which implicitly contests the male monopoly of professional skill. Jameson requests access to male professional knowledge not only to help male professionals but also to provide something similar to professional opportunities for middle-class women. Although Jameson claims she is opposed to women becoming doctors or interfering at all with the male sphere, for instance, she expends a great deal of energy defending women medical workers against the charges male physicians leveled at them. For one such defense, Jameson uses the voice of a male physician, a Dr. Gooch, rather than risking these statements in her own voice:

> Many will think that it is impossible to impart a useful knowledge of medicine to women who are ignorant of anatomy, physiology, and pathology. A profound knowledge, of course, would not, but a very useful degree of it might: a degree which, combined with kindness and assiduity, would be far superior to that which the country poor receive at present. I have known matrons and sisters of hospitals with more practical tact in the detection and treatment of disease than half the young surgeons by whom the country poor are commonly attended. (98)

Supposedly in defense of nursing, and in the voice of this male doctor, Jameson comes close to suggesting that women could become doctors and perhaps better ones than many men. Despite an avowed allegiance to the doctrine of separate roles and occupations for men and women, at times like this Jameson nearly crosses the fragile but critical boundary between them.

Maurice and his professional colleagues, of course, have a stronger investment in keeping the boundaries between men's professional and women's amateur occupations intact. To be certain that his proposal to train women philanthropists is not misconstrued, Maurice emphasizes the difference between lady volunteers and male professionals:

> I hope . . . I have guarded myself against the suspicion that I would educate ladies for the kind of tasks which belong to *our* professions. In America some are maintaining that they should take degrees and practise as physicians. I not only do not see my way to such a result; I not only should not wish that any college I was concerned in should be leading to it; but I should think there could be no better reason for founding a college than to remove the slightest craving for such a state of things, by giving a more healthful direction to the minds which might entertain it. (13)

Maurice defends himself against the probable suspicions of other male professionals by portraying his women's college as a project to reinforce rather than undermine the embattled position of male professionals. He projects suspect desires to relax the boundaries between men's and women's separate spheres onto Americans; his goal, as he represents it, is to turn ambitious women's minds in a more "healthful" direction. By defining women's "craving" for public activity as unhealthful, Maurice casts not only physicians but himself and other male professionals as "doctors," thereby shifting the category of persons at risk from male professionals to ambitious women. Maurice's formulation characterizes women and their aspirations as "unhealthy," thereby solidifying his (and other professional men's) right to diagnose (that is, define) and prescribe for (that is, exercise control over) them.

Virtually all the other lecturers in Maurice's book echo in some form his anxieties about women competing with male professionals, and, like him, they move to reinforce their right to control women. One of the most interesting of these moves is Kingsley's. Lauded as the "most popular" of the series, a "good specimen of this author's fearless and striking manner" (a tribute that itself fortifies the noted author's masculinity), Kingsley's lecture "The Country Parish" addresses the issue of appropriate women's work.[23] What is perhaps most "fearless and striking" about the lecture is its forceful, even dictatorial, tone. This tone is achieved partly through the recurrent use of the imperative mode: "Be not deceived," "Fancy not," "believe me," "Be sure," "Do but say," "Let him see," "Let him slip," "Consider to whom you go," "In God's name, encourage," and on and on. The style of the lecture is also characterized by the use of short declarative sentences and clauses that seem almost to hammer on one's ears:

> I must begin by telling you frankly,
> that we must all be just
> before we are generous.
> I must, indeed, speak plainly on this point.
> A woman's first duties are to her own family, her own servants.
> Be not deceived:
> if any one cannot rule her own household,
> she cannot rule the Church of God.
> If any one cannot sympathise with the servants
> with whom she is in contact all day long,
> she will not really sympathize with the poor
> whom she sees once a week. (53)

These balanced and repetitive phrases, peppered with imperative words such as "must," "ought," "should," "cannot," "never," and "has to," leave no openings for hesitation or disagreement. As Kingsley repeatedly makes clear, he "knows" what is right, best, and appropriate for women working under the rule of his authority.

It is ironic that most of Kingsley's lecture is devoted to teaching middle-class women philanthropists how to reach working-class women without dictating to them. He gives his female audience instructions on how to create bonds of sympathy with working-class women, thereby opening opportunities to teach and direct them, without erasing the boundaries that keep them in a subordinate position. Kingsley's instructions are enlightening with regard to his position as a self-styled teacher of middle-class women:

> They [poor women] scramble through life's rocks, bogs, and thornbrakes clumsily enough, and have many a fall, poor things! But why, in the name of a God of love and justice, is the lady,

rolling along the smooth turnpike-road in her comfortable carriage, to be calling out all day long to the poor soul who drags on beside her over hedge and ditch, moss and moor, bare-footed and weary-hearted, with half-a-dozen children at her back—"You ought not to have fallen here; and it was very cowardly to lie down there; and it was your duty, as a mother, to have helped that child through the puddle; while, as for sleeping under that bush, it is most inadmissible?" Why not encourage her, praise her, cheer her on her weary way by loving words, and keep your reproofs for yourself—even your advice; for she does get on her way, after all, where *you* could not travel a step forward; and she knows what she is about perhaps better than you do, and what she has to endure. . . . But do not be a stranger to her. Be a sister to her. I do not ask you to take her up in your carriage. You cannot; perhaps it is good for her that you cannot. . . . All I ask is, do to the poor soul as you would have her do to you in her place. (61–62)

Kingsley here does to his women listeners just what he advises them not to do to their "poor sisters." His lecture is an example of the kind of direction he abjures for them. His encouragement and praise for the work of the women he supposedly admires and respects as equal is minimal. And while he might invite a middle-class woman to ride in his carriage, he certainly has no intention of letting her drive.[24]

The Home as Metaphor for the Social Sphere

While Jameson and Maurice and his fellow lecturers demonstrate an awareness of the tensions generated when philanthropic women and professional men share the work of the social sphere, they also have a way of imagining the sphere that helps to allay such anxieties. Both Jameson and Maurice's group use the metaphor of the middle-class home to represent men's and women's roles in the social sphere; not surprising, however, the way they deploy the metaphor differs. Maurice's lecturers, for instance, exhibit strong loyalties to the Victorian domestic ideal, particularly the notion of the superior English family as the backbone of society. "An English household of the educated classes," says J. S. Brewer in his lecture

"Workhouse Visiting," is not "the growth of a year, or a life, or a century; it is the very marrow of our national life—the essence of our national experience. To it not only have our great worthies in literature and science contributed, but every art and almost every invention has added its quota" (277).

Jameson, too, links the state of the family to the state of civilization:

> As civilization advances, as the social interests and occupations become more and more complicated, the family duties and influences diverge from the central home,—in a manner, radiate from it,—though it is always there in reality. The man becomes *on a larger scale,* father and brother, sustainer and defender; the woman becomes *on a larger scale,* mother and sister, nurse and help.
>
> Of course, the relations thus multiplied and diffused are less sacred, less intense, but also less egotistical, less individual, than in the primitive tent of the Arab, the lodge of the red-man, or within the precincts of the civilized hearth; but *in proportion as we can carry out socially the family duties and charities, and perform socially the household-work,* just in such proportion is society safely and harmoniously constituted. (27, emphasis added)

While Brewer and Jameson would agree that God made "*domestic* life the basis of all social life" and "all *social* life the basis of all national life" (*Sisters,* 166), Jameson's interpretation of the way in which the analogy between home and society operates is slightly different from Brewer's. For Brewer, all of man's highest accomplishments center on—and are traceable to—the home. And yet, although the home is the center of society, the reason for its existence, it is still something separate from the (male) world of science, business, literature, art, and (presumably) government. The two spheres are interdependent but essentially different. For Jameson, however, the home is not only the center from which civilization radiates into society; home is reproduced at the level of society. The domestic sphere usually associated with women and, subtly or not, considered the subordinate or inferior one, for Jameson becomes the sole sphere. The organization and relations of the home are for her rewritten at the level of the professions, social institutions, and the state.

Jameson as well as Maurice's lecturers take the analogy of home and society literally. Large segments of Jameson's essays and many of the lectures in Maurice's books are taken up with examples of social institutions that were significantly improved by modeling them on the home. According to Brewer's experience, for instance, the explanation of social deviance is that those who deviate were deprived of a happy home; the solution is to provide them with one:

> Turn to the police reports in our newspapers, or only watch for yourselves the boys and girls who join in the disorders of this metropolis, and fill our prisons—no longer prisons to them—and you will see how imperative it is that something should be done to rescue them. They are mainly the produce of the workhouse and the workhouse-schools. Over them society has no hold, because society has cast them out from all that is humane. They have been taught to feel that they have nothing in common with their fellow-men. Their experience is not of a home or of parents, but of a workhouse and a governor—of a prison and a gaoler as hard and rigid as either.
>
> *Yet even these women and boys do become steady sometimes, when they are married.* (279, emphasis added)

The purpose of Brewer's lecture to the ladies is to encourage them to use their influence to ensure that such newly created homes are modeled on middle-class ones. Those women who have been trained as domestic servants in these homes "have advanced as their mistresses have advanced," while those unable or unwilling to achieve the proper domestic model are "utterly deficient": "they remain to this day unmoved and unshaken as they were centuries ago. Everything else has improved about them— knowledge of the laws of health, food, dress, means of life and comfort; but in their households there is little or no change for the better, and there has not been for ages; if possible, there is more waste, more dirt, more want of order, of comfort, and of economy" (276). Like Brewer, several of Maurice's other lecturers believe in the model of the middle-class wife's home management as one of the chief remedies for social ills; and several suggest ways in which it may be promulgated—most effectively, as both Brewer and Kingsley note, through the middle-class wife's influence on her domestic servants and through effective home or workhouse visiting and charity school work. Women's homelike touch would also be appreciated, say these professional men, in institutional settings such as the hospital, prison, and penitentiary.

Jameson would not disagree with these men who stress the importance of the middle-class woman's example in the homes of the poor or her softening touch in the institution. Jameson's examples of the practical application of the principles of the happy middle-class home to philanthropic and social work, however, go even further. On her travels in Europe, Jameson had made "exhaustive studies" of European social institutions, "visiting every hospital and charitable institution to which she could get admission."[25] Her two lectures are filled with dozens of descriptions of hospitals, reformatories for prostitutes, homes for the disabled, prisons, and refuges for the poor, virtually all of them run by women. While the details vary from one institution to the next, the refrain is the same: institutions managed and staffed by women are reminiscent of model middle-class homes; they are clean, light, airy, and cheerful; every inmate, hired nurse, or paid orderly is in his or her assigned place doing his or her job, with a serene mother overseeing all and a fatherly doctor or chaplain checking in from time to time. Guards are unnecessary, even for the most hardened social victims, and many inmates choose to stay on after their terms have expired. These are not, like the ones Maurice's lecturers envision, male-run institutions softened by the woman's touch. They are institutions served by "women acting *with,* as well as *under,* authority" (69).

Notably, the one European hospital Jameson cites that is not described in approving terms is one that, despite being "the most richly endowed hospital in all Europe," is mismanaged by a secular board of six male governors—a business rather than a family model of administration (184). Even worse, Jameson implies, was the state of the hospitals in Turin before Sisters of Charity were invited into the hospital to lend their influence to its management. Medical students complained about the new system of management—what Jameson calls "the strict order and surveillance exercised and enforced by [the Sisters] wherever they ruled"— because it prevented their sexual exploitation of "poor young female patients" (185). The Sisters, in other words, transformed the "morally lax" ("I might give it a harder name," Jameson adds) male-run hospital into a model Victorian home, where not only dirt, disorder, and despair are proscribed but illicit sexuality is policed. In this home, a father (doctor, government official) is a necessary and important person, but, since it is a home, the mother is the primary force (in Catholic hospitals, of course, she is even called Mother).

Jameson takes yet a further step in her claims for the home as the foundation of society. While Maurice's lecturers sometimes make conventional statements about the English home being the basis of the healthy nation, Jameson implies that the state, like social institutions, should operate on the family model. Jameson begins "The Communion of Labor" with a consideration of property law as it relates to women. Although she starts this discussion with a tribute to "the manly intellect" and "the sympathy of the manly heart," and claims that the unjust laws "are under the consideration of wise and able men, and may be safely left in their hands" (153–54), she devotes the next fifteen pages and some of her strongest rhetoric to doing just the opposite—considering those laws and all their implications in detail. Without going so far as to advocate that women vote or hold office—she denies that she is concerned with the "rights and wrongs of women"—Jameson insists on women's equality before the law and their right to participate in "national life." She makes this argument plausible by extending the domestic model to the functioning of the nation:

> How, then, shall our social *and national* life be pure and holy, and well ordered before God and man, if the domestic affections and duties be not carried out *and expanded, and perfected in the larger social sphere,* and in the same spirit of mutual reverence, trust, and kindness which we demand in the primitive relation? It appears to me that when the Creator endowed the two halves of the human race with ever-aspiring hopes, with ever-widening sympathies, with ever-progressing capacities,—when He made them equal in the responsibilities which bind the conscience and in the temptations which mislead the will,—He linked them inseparably in an ever-extending sphere of duties, and an ever-expanding communion of affections; thus, in one simple, holy, and beautiful ordinance, binding up at once the continuation of

the species and its moral, social, and physical progress, through all time. (166–67, emphasis added)

While Jameson does not quarrel with the doctrine of different roles for men and women, her overdetermined "ever-" expressions—"ever-aspiring," "ever-widening," "ever-progressing," "ever-extending," and "ever-expanding"—explode all limits to her ideal domestic model. Jameson does not advocate that women compete with men, but she does insist that women be allowed to work side by side with men as equals in a "communion of labor" that extends to all facets of human experience.

"Redundant" Women and the Issue of Paid Work

Although both male professionals such as Maurice's lecturers and women philanthropists such as Jameson believed they could share the social space without competing with each other, as men and women did in the home, that belief was challenged by the 1851 census. The results of the census, which counted more women than men in the population, forced the recognition that many Englishwomen could not marry and would need to earn their own livelihood. Because of the "problem" of "redundant" women, the issue of women competing with men for the same jobs became a pressing concern. A decade earlier, in the "hungry forties," working-class men had already focused on working women their anxiety about competition for scarce jobs.[26] The results of the census, however, were threatening not only to working-class men but to male professionals as well, since not all middle-class women who needed to work could or would be accommodated by governessing or seamstressing.[27]

Florence Nightingale had opened the possibility of nursing as another potential occupation for single women, but initially not many middle-class women were attracted to it because nursing had traditionally been done by servants and hence seemed to entail a lowering of their class status. Nursing gradually became more acceptable to middle-class women as it became more professionalized; as it became more professionalized, however, it moved closer to competing with male medical professions. Even philanthropy, as we have seen, raised anxieties about competition with male professionals. The crucial difference between women's philanthropy and male professions, though, was that philanthropy was unpaid labor. When some, including Jameson, wondered why, if philanthropy was an appropriate occupation for unmarried women, it could not also provide them a livelihood, the critical distinction between professional and amateur was jeopardized.

Although Maurice and the other lecturers were aware of the "redundant woman problem"—several of them had been involved in founding Queen's College for the purpose of better educating governesses [28]—their major tactic for dealing with the issue of social work as a potential paid employment for middle-class women was silence. This silence is an indication of how important it was to male professionals that women, however much their domestic skills might be a help in the social sphere, not cross the line that kept them from direct competition with men of their own class. Maurice, for instance, stresses that the separation between the provinces of men and women is God-ordained. He laments the confusion that arises when "a notion gains currency that there is no specific work in which women may engage; that what they undertake for the good of their fellow-creatures is a sentimental recreation, not a serious business, to be pursued with just as much settled purpose, just as much in a regular and distinct method, as any business to which we devote ourselves" (13). Maurice grants women "just as much settled purpose" and "just as much in a regular and distinct method" as men's business or professional pursuits—but he is silent when it comes to the point of just as much pay. What is conspicuously absent from Maurice's analogy between women's and men's work is the most important difference between the two. A few pages later, Maurice suggests that the reason women need the kind of education he is so committed to is "not only to show them what they can do, but what they cannot do and should not attempt"—that is, to compete with professional men for employment. The "profound consolation"—and to professional men it is a consolation—"which one derives from the remembrance of Miss Nightingale's services in the war," claims Maurice, "is that they entirely confound the notion that only paid jobs are done effectually." "The tasks that have been done most thoroughly," he continues, "have been done from a divine inspiration"—but not for pay (17).

Jameson often echoes Maurice's sentiments about the value of unpaid female labor situated above the values of the marketplace. Like Maurice,

Jameson applies to the social sphere the notion that women's work is valuable precisely because it has no market value. But Jameson's commitment to keeping middle-class women as volunteer rather than paid workers is not as strong as that of Maurice and his professional colleagues. By asking the question with which I began this chapter—"Why should not charity be a profession in our sex, just in so far (*and no farther*) as religion is a profession in yours!"—Jameson provides a rationale for women to be paid for their Christian "vocation" as professional clergymen are.

It is with the notion of vocation that Jameson covers over the ideological contradiction that troubles her text far more than it does Maurice's. While by the 1850s "profession" implied payment for skilled services, the synonym "vocation" still carried the sense of a religious calling.[29] Hence, by defining philanthropy as a "holy, heartfelt vocation" (268), Jameson equates a woman's "profession" with that of a clergyman, a man with both a vocation and a profession; yet she still avoids suggesting outright that women be paid. What she describes instead is the European system of Sisters of Charity that she hopes to institute in England. According to her plan, women will not be paid individually for their services, as male professionals are, but instead women will band together like continental Catholics to live—and be paid—communally.

Jameson, of course, was not the only one in England to propose Protestant sisterhoods as a solution to the "redundant woman problem." Contemporary journals were full of articles debating the feasibility and advisability of such communities. Because these sisterhoods were so tied up in the English mind with Catholicism, however, the idea often created more fears than it quieted. Several sisterhoods were established, but few lasted more than a short time.[30] The primary thing about the idea for Jameson, though, was that it was the only solution she could imagine to the problem of women supporting themselves through social work without putting them into direct competition with male professionals and crossing the all-important boundary between male and female spheres.

Jameson's uneasiness with her solution to the problem of paid women social workers is evident, especially when she makes the argument that there should be two classes of professional women social workers: "those who receive direct pay, and those who do not" (274). She continues to insist that the women working for hire (that is, working-class women) will be subordinate to unpaid women—that "order of women quite beyond the reach of any remuneration that could be afforded" (275). Jameson realized, however, that some middle-class women needed respectable paid employment, and she sensed the difficulty of maintaining the hierarchy of volunteer over paid services once women received the professional training she advocated. Thus she clearly admits at least the possibility of paid female professionals. If such women, who are both trained and paid, seem to compete with professional men, Jameson has a judicious answer. Using female doctors as an example, she diplomatically shifts the grounds of competition from gentlemanly physicians to "the ordinary run of country apothecaries": "Be it remembered . . . that the choice is not between such women and a profound and perfect physician or surgeon (if there is such a person), but between such women and the ordinary run of country apothecaries; the latter laboring under the additional disadvantage of wanting time for the application of what skill they have" (95). Despite all Jameson's ploys to deflect male professionals' anxieties about competition from paid female professionals, the potential for such competition—which is denied or passed over in silence by Maurice's group—is built into her arguments and proposals. In addition, her parenthetical remark—"if there is such a person"—implicitly casts doubt on the "profound and perfect" male professional.

Critical Differences

Jameson and Maurice and his lecturers, then, used the figure of the trained but unpaid woman philanthropist to sanction women's participation in the developing social sphere. Positioned on the cusp between volunteers and professionals, and between men's and women's "natural" spheres, the figure of the trained woman philanthropist could be used to bridge such gaps—or "chasms," as they are frequently called in these texts—while still maintaining subtle but crucial lines of distinction. For Jameson, the task was to come as close as possible to crossing the line of difference between the sexes without arousing anxiety and provoking reaction from male professionals and others concerned about what they considered the defeminization of women. For Maurice and his fellow lecturers, the ideal relation between male professionals and female philanthropists was to smile and hold hands across the chasm without bringing the two precipices too close together. For Jameson, the model for all relations between men and women is the home where, although the man provides the seed and the support, the woman creates an environment after her own image; for the male lecturers, the model is rather a college, where women teach, to be sure, but only as they are in the process of being taught by men. Perhaps the difference between the two models is best illustrated by the two most striking images in these texts.

Most of Jameson's book *Sisters of Charity* consists of arguments, quotations, statements of feeling, analogies, and descriptions of institutions—the kinds of rhetoric usually associated with the lecture setting. There is virtually no narrative and even illustrative anecdotes are used sparingly. People are described in groups, for the most part, rather than as individuals. In her descriptions of the institutions, Jameson generally focuses on their history and method of operation and on her overall impression—almost invariably, they are clean, light, airy, and cheerful, or they are characterized by filth, sloth, immorality, disease, and insubordination. Instances that deviate from this pattern thus call attention to themselves. Probably the most memorable—and telling—of these occurs in a description of the Hospital of Saint John in Turin, which is "clean, and neat, and cheerful" (192). Jameson is particularly impressed at "the neatness with which the food was served" in this institution (193). Her next sentence, however, uses an image unlike any other in either of Jameson's lectures: "I remember being touched by the sight of a little dog which, with its fore-paws resting on the bed and a pathetic wistful expression in its drooping face, kept its eyes steadfastly fixed on the sick man; a girl was kneeling beside him, to whom one of the Sisters was speaking words of comfort" (193). There it all is: the man (sick and helpless), the daughter (caring and concerned), and the motherly Sister with all the physical arrangements so under control that she can stand by to offer comfort and sympathy (administering, in both its senses). The final touch, however, is the dog. Not only the family, the institution, the nation, but all creation is included in the well-run home, presided over by a competent woman. The dog looks at the man, "wistful" at his weakness; but the little animal is there, the final stroke in the touching familial picture, by the grace of the woman, without whose influence man's seed is the source of "change, discord, and decay" (140).

Jameson's grateful family with its equally grateful dog makes an effective contrast to another striking image that Kingsley uses in his lecture. In directing his women auditors on how to use their womanly sympathies with working-class women, Kingsley wields the image of a pistol to describe the goal of philanthropic social action. Without "humanity"— "the smile of the lip, the light of the eye, the tenderness of the voice" that women are to supply—the pistol, which is the social institution, is an "iron tube without the powder, unable to send the bullet forth one single inch" (55). Women are vital in their role as providers of the powder, but it is the man who aims and fires, and the phallic and violent image of the pistol suggests something far different from Jameson's gentle tableau.

Jameson is not a "sentimental" lady novelist; neither are Kingsley, Maurice, and their colleagues notable for aggression or the depiction of violence, which is why these two images are so arresting. Although Jameson and Maurice's group of Christian Socialists seem in many ways to share identical beliefs and ideals for men, women, and their society, and to be working to achieve the same goal of making women's philanthropic work more meaningful, their agendas were quite different. Maurice and the other male professionals who worked with him believed they saw the justice of Jameson's proposals and thought they were implementing them; their plan and lectures, however, indicate that what they had in mind was training middle-class women to utilize their admitted feminine strengths while keeping these helpmeets firmly under professional male direction. Jameson, by contrast, although she praised the efforts of these professional men, envisioned social institutions organized and directed by sympathetic but capable women who sought professional male help only on occasion when needed.

The practical results following from the delivery and publication of these two series of lectures apparently devoted to the same project also give evidence that Jameson and Maurice's group had different investments in the project. Although the Working Men's College did carry a course of classes for working-class women for a time, this endeavor was fraught with difficulties and controversy, and, according to the available evidence, it did not involve middle-class women as teachers except for a brief period in the beginning. A separate Working Women's College was instituted in 1864, but conflicts, from both within and without and not unrelated to the ones discussed here, led to a further split into two colleges for working women in 1874. By the time of the publication of the history of the Working Men's College in 1954, women had still not been admitted to the Working Men's College, nor were women employed—with or without pay—as teachers. The chronicler of the college's history cites a telling anecdote, which, although it occurred almost a hundred years later, echoes the implicitly ambivalent feelings of the college's founders about training women to participate in their "own" sphere as well as it does those of their successors: "Council, having become unintentionally engaged in a fierce controversy on the general principle of the admission of women to the College, was rescued by a brief speech from the back of the room: 'Mr. Chairman, I think we ought to have women, but I move that we don't.'—which was adopted by a large majority." [31]

Jameson's lectures, by contrast, had a far-reaching impact on her "adopted nieces," Barbara Leigh Smith Bodichon, Bessie Rayner Parkes, and the other young feminists involved in the Langham Place Group. [32] Although these younger women sensed the ideological contradictions inherent in Jameson's work that I have discussed, particularly in her position on women receiving pay for their social work, they also recognized the potentially radical implications of much of what Jameson had to say. Jameson is quoted frequently in the pages of *The English Woman's Journal* and in lectures that Parkes, Bodichon, Emily Davies, and others delivered at the meetings of the National Association for the Promotion of Social Science; and Parkes paid Jameson a moving tribute in 1864. [33] These younger feminists were influential in the eventual passing of the Married Women's Property Bill (for which Jameson argued in "The Communion of Labor") and in promoting higher education (which Jameson also advocated) and increased job opportunities for women (which Jameson recognized as a serious need), thus realizing at least in part most of Jameson's dreams for women's legal and social advancement.

While Maurice and his associates are similarly lauded by their admirers and followers, it is rarely for their involvement with the project that the *Lectures to Ladies* was supposed to inaugurate. [34] The contradictions built into their conception of the project—their basic ambivalence about the role women should play in social institutions and their anxieties about educated middle-class women threatening their professional status—

were no doubt a large part of the reason that the "Female College for the Help of the Rich and Poor" never got off the ground. Their dialogue with Jameson on the merits of training women philanthropists, however, reveals what was at stake in the claims many Victorian women were beginning to make on the basis of what had come to seem their natural role in philanthropic social work.

The Female Visitor and the Marriage
of Classes in Elizabeth Gaskell's
North and South

A JANUARY 1856 REVIEW OF F. D. Maurice's *Lectures to Ladies on Practical Subjects* addressed a topic that was by now familiar to its audience:

> It is plain that this whole matter of visiting among the poor,
> whether isolated or organized visiting be in question, is the sub-
> ject of much anxiety to many of the lecturers. . . . It is no wonder
> it should be so. All see how dangerous a thing it would be to
> check these intercourses; often the sole means by which the rich
> obtain an insight into the struggles of the poor. Yet we are con-
> stantly made aware of other dangers arising out of visiting; and
> especially out of District Visiting.[1]

The reviewer's language calls attention to the uneasiness that many
people in mid-nineteenth-century England felt on the subject of female
visitors to the poor. The position of the female visitor, as the reviewer
presents it, is one of double danger: it would be "dangerous" to "check"
their dealings with the poor, but these dealings are fraught with "other
dangers." However well-intentioned, visitors may antagonize the poor
who will "come to regard themselves as the inspected" (150) and who
may pretend to be worse off than they are in order to receive charitable

donations. Proper visitors, by contrast, can foster much goodwill among classes:

> Once in a while a visitor may mediate between the master and the man. So the circle widens and spreads, and who can tell the misery which that one kind woman's call may have averted? And here it is impossible not to allude to a work most fruitful in suggestion on this subject. We mean that part of Mrs. Gaskell's "North and South," which portrays the gradually acquired ascendancy of Margaret [Hale] over the radical and infidel weaver, Nicholas Higgins. The more nearly it is examined, the more genuine and free from blemish does this picture appear. Humility and deep sympathy, on one side, meet in time with the due abatement of pride on the other: the whole coming quite within the range of ordinary possibilities. (151)

As an antidote to the anxieties the figure of the female visitor posed, the reviewer proposes a novel: Elizabeth Gaskell's *North and South,* published serially in Charles Dickens's *Household Words* in 1854–55 and issued in two volumes in 1855. According to the reviewer, Gaskell's novel resolves the disturbing paradox—the double danger—of the woman visitor by portraying a model lady visitor who performs the vital function of mediating among classes with feminine "humility and deep sympathy." Her visits to the poor are not dangerous because they do not jeopardize the relations they are supposed to be mediating. Just as significant, the model lady visitor, as the reviewer describes, does not threaten the position of the paid male professional; while the effects of the "kind woman's call" are important, their value is incalculable and therefore outside the professional market where such services are bought and sold: "*who can tell* the misery which . . . may have [been] averted?" (emphasis added).

This critic's brief notice of *North and South* identifies a crucial aspect of the novel that later critics have almost entirely passed over. Although twentieth-century critics have increasingly recognized the importance of *North and South* as a social-problem novel, an industrial novel, and a protofeminist novel, no one has considered it in the context of the mid-nineteenth-century debate about female visitors to the poor—an issue it raised for contemporary readers. Critics who read *North and South* for its social commentary, from Louis Cazamian's 1904 *The Social Novel in En-*

gland to Sally Minogue's 1990 essay "Gender and Class in *Villette* and *North and South,*" commonly fault Gaskell for failing to follow through with the potentially radical implications—Marxist or feminist—of the social issues she raises in the novel.[2] Specifically, such critics object to the novel's happy ending, which is almost universally read as a retreat from the troubling problems of the public sphere into a romanticized private and personal reconciliation. John Lucas, for instance, accuses Gaskell of "laps[ing] into cosy liberalism," while Minogue, a feminist trying to rehabilitate Gaskell, maintains that "the ending belies the emotional, social and moral complexity of the novel."[3]

Catherine Gallagher, Rosemarie Bodenheimer, and Hilary M. Schor complicate these narratives of failure by focusing on the dynamics of the relation between the public and private spheres throughout the novel. For Gallagher, the "metonymic method of connecting the public and private spheres . . . paradoxically depends on their separation. The novel's solution hides but does not resolve this basic dilemma."[4] While Gallagher's reading is convincing, even her account misrepresents Gaskell's novel because it oversimplifies notions of the public and private in the mid-nineteenth-century England Gaskell portrays in *North and South*. What Gallagher fails to recognize is that many of Margaret Hale's private or personal actions are already coded with a public meaning, a meaning that comes out of the controversy about female visiting. Schor's astute analysis of Margaret Hale's social function recognizes her mediating role between public and private spheres, but she concludes that Margaret's "woman's plot is in danger of getting subsumed into the larger plots (the social conversations, the industrial debate, the ideological imperatives of marriage)."[5] I argue, however, that Gaskell's novel works to construct a social sphere that casts a "woman's plot" as one of these "larger plots." Bodenheimer contends that Gaskell's "refusal to keep [the heroine] 'pure' and separate from the activities generally associated with the male, the public, and the system" allows her to find "an enabling structure within the model of capitalist enterprise itself."[6] Bodenheimer's reading is essentially right, but she does not take into account the crucial role of the female visitor in constructing this "enabling structure."

As the 1856 review indicates, *North and South*'s representation of a lady visiting in a working-class home was embedded in a controversy of considerable moment in midcentury England, a debate on one level over whether and how the poor were to be reached, supervised, and taught proper values. On another level, as we have seen, the question of ladies' visiting was a contest over who had access to and who would control a range of social spaces and practices. While Anna Jameson's published dialogue with the authors of *Lectures to Ladies* illustrates some of the tensions that arose when both professional men and philanthropic women attempted to share responsibility in the social sphere, Gaskell's novel stages this conflict in an industrial setting. Thus her representation of a model female visitor also participates in the construction of the social sphere and the definition of women's role in it. Reading *North and South* as Gaskell's attempt to resolve imaginatively some of the issues involved in the controversy over female visiting allows us not only to make sense of some of the more troubling aspects of the novel, including its happy ending, but also to shed light on the cultural work that Gaskell's novel performed in mid-nineteenth-century England.

North and South does represent, as Gaskell's contemporary maintained in the 1856 review, an exemplary woman visitor and it makes some important claims about her fitness for the role of mediator among classes; it also presses these claims against those of male professionals. Gaskell's novel, however, goes beyond claiming the publicly useful role of class mediator for women. Like Hannah More, Gaskell rewrote the upper-class woman's traditional mediating role as Lady Bountiful. By moving her midcentury Lady Bountiful to an urban setting, however, in her novel Gaskell offers a new model of social relations that is based neither on rural paternalism nor the industrial cash nexus. Rather, women play a vital role in the modernly defined social sphere, a space that is both private and public. The concept of the social sphere, as both Gaskell and Jameson before her portray it, allows the novelist to represent women intervening in the hostile world of the factory, something Martineau, Trollope, and Tonna could only imagine. Gaskell's social model also enables her to extend her claims for women visitors to include women novelists. Her novel is not only about philanthropic visiting; using its narrative structure as a model of the mediating role it projects for women visitors, *North and South* represents the writing of a novel as a philanthropic act akin to visiting. In claiming an independent, autonomous role for women in the social sphere, however, *North and South* does not challenge the private arrangements of the domestic sphere where men rule over women legally, sexually, and emotionally; instead, the novel bases its case for women's mediation among classes on an analogy between marriage and class co-operation.

The Social Sphere and Class Mediation

In the mid-nineteenth century, one major project of what I am calling the social sphere was to heal the "separation between class and class which is the great curse of British society," as Justice Talfourd expressed it in his last speech, in 1854.[7] Although the immediate fears of political and social upheaval that many in the middle classes had harbored during the 1840s had declined with the demise of Chartism and the touted prosperity of the 1850s, a wave of strikes beginning in 1852 provided an occasion for some middle-class writers and thinkers to reopen debates about class relations. This was especially true in industrial areas, particularly those surrounding Manchester, although strikes occurred around the country, including at least one by agricultural workers in a rural area.[8]

Gaskell lived in Manchester, the heart of the manufacturing district where the majority of strikes were taking place, and *North and South* was her contribution to the discussion of strikes and labor disputes. Perhaps the most famous strike was the Preston Strike, or lockout, which began in the summer of 1853 and lasted until the spring of 1854, while Gaskell was writing *North and South*.[9] According to Henry Ashworth, one of the commentators on the much-discussed Preston Strike (writing on the side of the masters), the working classes were dangerous because they began striking not when times were bad, as in the 1840s, but in a period of economic prosperity. In Ashworth's view, the more the workers got, the more they wanted; the strike was not about wages but about power and property. What the working classes—and their middle-class sympathizers—wanted, claims Ashworth, was "to reconstruct society on a new basis": "The right of the master . . . rests upon the principle that he may do as he likes with his own money; it is, in fact, a necessary consequence of the rights of property. If any body of workpeople may justly dictate the limits within which this right shall be exercised, property at once virtually ceases to be private, all private rights are overthrown, and we are in the high road to communism." [10] While there were other views about what was at stake in labor disputes such as the Preston Strike, there was widespread disapproval of strikes. Many were concerned that hostile relations among the classes would jeopardize trade and, hence, the nation's prosperity. Some accused union leaders of creating class hostility to further their self-interest. Others, such as Dickens and Gaskell, declared their sympathy with the working classes and felt a moral responsibility to alleviate the negative side effects of industrial capitalism and to promote class harmony. While social legislation, philanthropic schemes, utopian experiments, and educational institutions for teaching political economy to the poor were promoted as possible solutions to the problem of uniting the classes, many people, including several of the lecturers from *Lectures to Ladies,* favored personal contact between potentially hostile factions as the best way of reconciling what they saw as conflicting class interests. Some, such as F. D. Maurice and his colleagues at the Working Men's College, attempted to form collegial friendships with working men.[11] But the most frequent and common interpersonal exchanges involving members of different classes were those between every middle-class woman and her servants and between female visitors and the poor families they visited.[12] Thus such contacts took on a crucial ideological significance for those concerned about class relations and working-class unrest.

A writer quoted in *The District Visitor's Manual,* a handbook designed to instruct women visitors on proper relations with the poor, stresses the important social—and political—role of these personal contacts:

> It is, in truth, only by means of a more frequent and friendly interchange of feeling than has hitherto prevailed among the different orders of the community, that the bond of social union can be permanently strengthened. Thus alone may the more advanced civilization of the educated ranks be brought to bear upon the tone of morals and manners which pervade the nation at large; and thus alone can the higher classes acquire that intimate knowledge of the wants and habits of their inferiors, which will qualify them wisely to adapt their various plans of beneficence [a footnote adds, "May it not be added—or of legislation?"] to the real necessities of those whom they desire to serve.
>
> Few among the rich are aware how easily they might thus surround themselves with an impregnable barrier of attachment,—a barrier which no political convulsion would be able to destroy.[13]

Women visitors were to shed their moralizing influence on the lower classes, and they were also to serve as the chief investigators of the working-class condition—"thus alone can the higher classes acquire that intimate knowledge of the wants and habits of their inferiors." Despite the notoriety of male professional investigators such as Henry Mayhew or Peter Gaskell, there were many more women in a position to observe the poor firsthand than there were men. Even organizations such as the Charity Organization Society (COS), formed in 1869, which prided itself on its scientific and theoretically sound principles, relied on women visitors to do its fieldwork. In *North and South,* Mr. Colthurst, the noted member of Parliament, is anxious to hear Margaret Hale's "experiences" in working with factory laborers; even the "wisdom" of the innovative industrialist Thornton is based on the insight Margaret has given him into the workings of the lower-class mind.

Women's presumed insight into what was perceived as the real—the individual case rather than the abstract or the theoretical—was the basis of claims about the importance of their participation in the newly constituted field of social science.[14] The reformer Octavia Hill, for instance, wrote a pamphlet titled *District Visiting* in 1877 that argues for the importance to "theorists" of the practical experience of district visitors:

> Statesmen, philanthropists, political economists, try their hands at [solving the problem of poverty], or rather their heads. Do they succeed better than the clergy and the visitors? Do they not often succeed worse? For the clergy and the visitors at least bear witness to the poor of sympathy with them, and deal with the wants around them practically; while the theorists, let their theories be ever so excellent, somehow stand so far off that they bring little practically into operation.
>
> Now these two classes, the studious, more leisurely, generalizing thinkers, and the loving individualizing doers, need to be brought into communication. . . . Each has knowledge the other requires: separated, they are powerless; combined, they may do much.[15]

Hill's list of theorists who need the practical experience of the visitors—"statesmen, philanthropists, political economists"—is a roster of the alternative contenders for authority over the social space. Although Hill links the clergy with the visitors as "loving individualizing doers" rather than "generalizing thinkers," she also (tactfully) accuses them, like the theorists, of failing to solve the critical problems that social experts were supposed to address:

> However earnestly our clergy have desired to solve this problem of how to deal wisely with the temporal condition of their flocks, it remains a problem still. . . . Busy, overworked clergymen, with services and sermons, and churches and schools, and thousands of souls to see to, have inherited systems of relief in their parishes which they hardly have time to reform, and the gigantic pressure of daily duty perpetuates many unwise plans. . . . I believe most of them, if asked, would reply, "I have tried honestly to make my system of relief as satisfactory as I could, but it is far from my ideal." And this is so from another cause. You can never make a *system* of relief good without perfect administration, far-sighted watchfulness in each individual case. (3 –4)

The "far-sighted watchfulness in each individual case" that Hill insists is vital to the success of any social "system" can be provided only by women visitors—not even by the clergy, let alone other "theorists." Of course, what Hill advocates is not that visitors take over the social space; she merely advises that this arena be shared. Her insistence on the mutual need of theorists and visitors for the information only the other can provide, however, constitutes the same pressing claim for women's access to and utility within the social sphere that Gaskell made twenty years earlier in *North and South*.

Although in Hill's—and Gaskell's—formulation, middle-class women visitors are to supply facts about the working class to (presumably) male theorists, the context of Hill's comments is a proposal for official women secretaries to be appointed to supervise and collect information from the visitors and pass it on to the members of the Charity Organization Society. The secretaries, in turn, will be tutored in theory through their attendance at COS meetings and, hence, will be able to use the insights of both theory and practice in their management of the district visitors. Despite their aptitude for the practical, investigative side of social work, some visitors, at least, needed to learn theory as well. In her 1854 *Remarks on the Education of Girls* Bessie Rayner Parkes, the noted feminist and contributor to the National Association for the Promotion of Social Science, declares that young women should most of all study "the Science of Social and Political Economy." This is an important part of their education, contended Parkes, because women are "the sex who are expected more and more to undertake the application of detailed relief for social ills" (12).

Margaret Hale, for her part, disclaims any knowledge of political economy: "I know so little about strikes, and rate of wages, and capital, and labour, that I had better not talk to a political economist like you," she says to Thornton.[16] Margaret's disavowal of theoretical knowledge, however, is ironic; she does go on talking to this "political economist"— and at great length. Her practical knowledge of the workers, she believes, gives her the right to debate with Thornton on equal terms. Further, Gaskell demonstrates that the theoretical concepts Thornton introduces to Margaret are not beyond her comprehension or interest. The need for—and difficulty of—bringing together theory and both direct observation and practice is made apparent in a discussion held in the Hale home after Margaret has discovered the dire need of the Boucher family. Mrs. Hale, Margaret's mother, with "her old Helstone habits of thought prevailing," insists on some Lady Bountiful–like charity. Margaret, her philanthropy now trained by urban experience and Thornton's theory, resists such indiscriminate giving. Convinced, Mrs. Hale, who is not personally acquainted with Boucher, then takes up the side of theory: "After all, we may have been doing wrong. It was only the last time Mr. Thornton was here that he said, those were no true friends who helped to prolong the strike by assisting the turn-outs. And this Boucher-man was a turn-out, was he not?" (158). The contest between the principles of political economy and those of charity is referred to Mr. Hale, whose theoretic certainty, learned from Mr. Thornton, is undermined by Margaret's practical knowledge of the misery the strikers experienced. After raising the debate about the competing claims of theory and practice, Gaskell condones Margaret's actions: as a general rule, Margaret avoids giving money or other donations that would threaten self-help or contradict the other principles of political economy; in an individual case, however, when it is well-examined and thoroughly understood, such principles may be overridden by sympathy and need. The ability to make such distinctions and to administer this compromise between theory and practice is what Gaskell suggests that women visitors had to gain from studying political economy.

It would not be unreasonable to argue that *North and South* is meant to educate women readers—many of whom, of course, were either practicing or potential district visitors—in enlightened political economy. Certainly Harriet Martineau's *Illustrations of Political Economy* had set a precedent for teaching such principles through fiction. When Margaret, who otherwise displays such canny wisdom on matters relating to labor relations, says to Bessy, "Striking is leaving off work till you get your own rate of wages, is it not?" it is hard not to read it as an explanation designed for the woman reader, who might have been unfamiliar with the principles of politics and economics (132). Of course, while Gaskell's novel may be educating her female readers in political economy, it also imparts the visitor's "practical" experience to male "theorists" who may be readers as well, since both groups were to share the terrain of the social.

The argument Hill and Parkes made explicitly and Gaskell implicitly—that women visitors need to be educated in political economy and other theoretical matters pertaining to social relations—is an important one, because it puts visiting in a different category from domestic duty. Even though all three of these writers claimed that women are especially effective at visiting because they are also wives, mothers, and daughters, they did not construe visiting as merely an extension of the home sphere. Visiting that requires theoretical knowledge, however much it may be similar to home duties, is an activity not of the private home but of the social sphere that recasts the home as a public space.

While most people agreed that the personal contacts of women visitors such as Margaret Hale were necessary to harmonious class relations and to the smooth functioning of society, few advocated women's intervention in industrial class relations. Gaskell, however, puts her sympathetic but informed visitor squarely in the middle of a scene of open class hostility. Although Margaret's initial effort to ward off violence by protecting Thornton from the strikers is seen by most of the characters in the book as inappropriate and misguided, in her less public social role as a visitor, Margaret does replace class conflict between Thornton, the factory owner, and Higgins, the union leader, with personal contact. When Gaskell has Margaret teach Thornton that he can initiate such personal contact with his employees in their homes as well as in the workplace, she is not idealizing or romanticizing industrial relations; she is advocating a type of social management, one that women pioneered in the social space of the home and that is based on firsthand knowledge of and practical experience with the poor, in addition to the principles of political economy. Social management based on the personal contacts of women in homes is central to Gaskell's social vision. Margaret Hale's mediations between groups with opposed interests serve as a model of social action not just for women but for both men and women as they operate within the sphere of the social. It is also significant that in Gaskell's novel the female visitor is not under the supervision of male professionals; her mediation is represented as superior to theirs.

Gaskell's Female Visitor and Male Professionals

Visiting the poor, as I have discussed, had long been regarded as the province of ladies. In the nineteenth century, wives and daughters of the landed classes continued the tradition of visiting the poor on their estates and in the surrounding villages to dispense charity, give advice, and exhort the poor to religion.[17] *North and South* idealizes charitable visiting for ladies in the Helstone sections of the novel, and when she has Margaret Hale take up charitable visiting in the industrialized Milton-Northern, Gaskell seems to some critics to urge a return to benevolent paternalism as the solution to urban class conflict.[18] Margaret, however, is not simply an urban Lady Bountiful. For instance in her interactions with the Higgins family, Margaret quickly learns that the role of the benevolent patron is both inappropriate and ineffective in dealing with the urban working classes. As a visitor she cannot merely dispense charity and reinforce deference, but rather she must promote understanding and even intercede to prevent violence between masters and men involved in open class conflict of a kind hardly imagined in the rural south. Keeping the sympathy and sincere interest in the poor that she learned as a rural clergyman's daughter, Margaret modifies her attitudes and adapts her charitable practices to fit the new social circumstances she encounters in the industrial north, exemplifying the principles and possibilities of the revised paternalism advocated by earlier writers such as More, Martineau, Trollope, and Tonna. Learning how to be a model female visitor, Margaret manages to reclaim the mediating role of the traditional Lady Bountiful in an environment where relations between the classes are based on the cash nexus; in other words, she succeeds in commanding a central position in a set of market relations from which, according to the domestic ideology of separate spheres, she should be excluded.

It is significant that Margaret meets and begins visiting in a working-class neighborhood on her own accord. When she visits the Higginses, she does not come as an envoy of the landed gentry or the church, as a Lady Bountiful would; neither also does she visit as an emissary for a philanthropic association. Although some mid-nineteenth-century middle-class women did visit on their own authority, having Margaret do so in *North and South* is critical to the claims Gaskell makes for women's participation in the social sphere. Gaskell's female visitor is exemplary in her expert mediation between masters and men, as we know from the 1856 review addressed at the beginning of this chapter. However, her independent social action does not merely supplement the work of male professionals; rather, Margaret's class mediation complements and, in some cases, threatens to displace male professional contenders for authority in the social realm.

Unlike Margaret Hale, most women visitors, as Hill assumed, were representatives of some organization, either philanthropic or religious. Church-sponsored district visitors were assigned representatives of a parish clergyman, and they were deputed to assist him in carrying out his pastoral duties. In the wake of sweeping reforms that jeopardized the church's established position in English society, the clergy's pastoral duties had taken on a new significance by midcentury. Because the church faced challenges both from a reformed Parliament and from religious controversies within, the traditional gentrified clergy so often portrayed in earlier novels, such as those of Jane Austen, had largely disappeared. They had been replaced by a more professional clergy. Like other professional groups, who were also struggling to consolidate professional power by ousting "amateurs," the clergy shed many of its former practices and clergymen attempted to consolidate their role as religious specialists, or, as one historian expresses it, "the technologists of the sanctuary." In addition, new stress was laid on the pastoral role of the clergy; the traditional allies of the gentry, the clergy came to be seen by many in the nineteenth century as "the main instrument for preserving the stability of the social structure"—in other words, for mediating among classes.[19] As "professional" mediators of class conflict, then, the clergy could be viewed as directly competing with women for this important role within the field of social relations. Since, as Hill pointed out, many middle-class women had the advantage of having more time for pastoral visiting, it became a matter critical to the clergy, not only that women be taught the best way to deal with the poor they visited but also to keep them under the umbrella of the church where they would remain subordinate to and under the supervision of the professional male clergyman.[20]

Margaret Hale, however, is not a district visitor; her visits to the poor in Milton are not under the auspices of the clergy. Even though her father is a former Church of England minister, he no longer holds that office and hence no longer officially directs Margaret's philanthropic activities. Most critics of *North and South* have interpreted Mr. Hale's defection from the church simply as necessary to the plot because it forces the family's removal from southern Helstone to Milton-Northern.[21] Seen in the context of the struggle for access to the social space in which class conflicts are mediated, however, Mr. Hale's resignation from the established church is even more significant because it leaves this contested space clear for his daughter. Trained and advised by her father, Margaret nonetheless visits on her own authority. Margaret, in fact, is shown to be a better class mediator than her father. Although he does well with Higgins after Margaret brings the men together, his efforts toward mediating class tensions are portrayed as slightly ridiculous: agreeing to give a series of lectures for the workingmen's lyceum, Mr. Hale chooses the unlikely subject of "Ecclesiastical Architecture" (141).

Despite his kindly concern for his parishioners and for the working people of Milton, Mr. Hale's often-remarked gentlemanliness allies him more to the paternalistic past of his religious vocation than to the professional present. It is, at least in part, the liturgical emphasis of the newly professionalized clergy that puts Mr. Hale's doubts about the church's authority at issue; those who think of the clergy in the old-fashioned gentlemanly sense—notably his wife and her servant Dixon—cannot understand why such doubts should interfere with his clerical living or even with his promotion to high church office. Their understanding of Mr. Hale's office as primarily to serve as the first gentleman in the community (in the absence of a resident squire) is already at odds with a changing society. To take *North and South*'s depictions of Helstone, even in the early scenes, as its representation of a stable past order is to misread a significant facet of the world Gaskell's characters inhabit—a world complicated by numerous social changes. While some of these characters may indulge in a nostalgic idealization of Helstone and of the land-based economy it represents, such a vision of Margaret's home is relegated to the realm of a romantic fiction—"a village in a tale rather than in real life"—even before Helstone appears as a setting in the novel (12). By the time of Margaret's return to Helstone in one of the final chapters, the displacement of the gentleman clergy by the new-fashioned professional clergy is complete. Mr. Hepworth, the new vicar of Helstone, is a thoroughly modern—and professional—clergyman, renovating the parsonage, modernizing the charity school, and urging temperance on his parishioners.[22]

Mr. Hale is not the only person displaced by a more professional counterpart, however; Margaret finds that she, too, has lost "the important post of only daughter in Helstone parsonage" (6). The school and visiting duties that Margaret and her mother once performed in the Lady Bountiful spirit are now discharged by Mrs. Hepworth, whose busy, self-important, businesslike manner is reminiscent of Dickens's Mrs. Pardiggle and represents what many objected to in the district visitor.[23] Mrs. Hepworth's attitude toward her duties may suggest the concerns some clergymen, including Charles Kingsley in his contribution to *Lectures to Ladies*, expressed about clergy wives seeing pastoral work as a "joint-vocation."[24] If so, the slightly unpleasant Mrs. Hepworth is set up as a figure on which to pin some of the anxieties that women philanthropists posed to professional men—especially the newly professionalized clergy—with whom they competed for ascendancy in the social realm. Pinning these anxieties on Mrs. Hepworth, of course, deflects them from Margaret and hence naturalizes her as the right kind of visitor.

If anxieties about women competing with the clergy for the role of class mediator are represented in the minor figure of Mrs. Hepworth, however, such anxieties are rather hidden. They are more apparent, if also displaced, in a character who plays a somewhat larger role in the plot—Henry Lennox. Although not a clergyman, Lennox is the representative professional man in *North and South*. Lennox is also the male character most insistent on maintaining the separation of private and public spheres and keeping women securely within the home and out of social space. On his first appearance in the text, Lennox insists on the difference between his professional work and the personal, domestic work of women: "Well, I suppose you are all in the depths of business—ladies' business, I mean. Very different to my business, which is the real true law business. Playing with shawls is very different work to drawing up settlements" (10). While this opening remark is satirical—the satire is directed against himself as well as to the ladies—it is consistent with his views throughout the novel. During the scene in which he proposes to Margaret, for instance, Lennox characterizes himself as unromantic, prudent, and worldly; his love for Margaret is "the one outlet which he has formed for the deeper and better feelings of his nature" (30). The "worldly" Lennox is a public man; Margaret, who brings out his "better feelings," is the angelic domestic woman, the repository of values deemed inappropriate to "a struggling barrister." Lennox almost unfailingly identifies himself with strong, professional men—including the new vicar of Helstone, whom he calls "a clever, sensible man, and a thoroughly active clergyman" (380). What he most wants from his prospective wife is dependence—"His eye brightened with exultation. How she was learning to depend upon him!" (433). Lennox desires a relationship in which, although Margaret might continue her London-based charitable visiting (such would be consistent with the role of a professional's wife), she would be supervised and directed by her husband or other male professionals. While she might operate within the social sphere, her role would be an extension of her private role and not an independent role within a social space defined as both private and public.

Margaret does not marry Lennox, however, and her father leaves the church, thus allowing her to enter the social sphere as an autonomous visitor of the poor and, later, as the wife of John Thornton, an entrepreneur who is open to female influence, even female intervention, in his social relations. To solidify her claims for women's access to the social realm, however, Gaskell not only clears away "professional" competitors but also demonstrates the efficacy of women's mediation between opposing interests.

The Mediation of Language

Most nineteenth-century advocates of female visiting, whether they believed in women learning the principles of political economy or assumed that visitors could rely on their "natural" sympathy, agreed that

the woman visitor's most important role was the same as her most significant home duty—she was to use her influence to promote morality and
domestic happiness. While Gaskell would not have discounted the power
of a woman's influence on those she visited, for her and other advocates
of women's social work such as Hill and Parkes the concept of social
mediation went beyond moralizing or giving domestic advice. Mediation, as *North and South* presents it, involves using women to represent
the potentially opposed interests or experiences of different groups to one
another. For Gaskell this means it is women's social duty to manage the
interpretation of signs.[25]

Some critics of *North and South* have observed that "the characters
spend a lot of time arguing about word choices, definitions, and analogies."[26] Their difficulties with language, argues Gallagher, manifest an
"anarchy of signification" that the novel intends but fails to overcome
through the metonymic substitution of family for society in the marriage
of Margaret and Thornton.[27] While Gallagher is right that signification
repeatedly misfires in *North and South,* I assert that it is not Margaret's
marriage but rather her social mediation—which comes about through
philanthropic visiting—that is meant to answer the crisis of signification
that occurs inevitably with rapid social change.

Although Margaret displays most of the characteristics associated
with the ideal lady visitor, as described in numerous manuals, sermons,
and books of advice, she does encounter some difficulties in her inter-
course with the working-class Higgins family. Her troubles arise not from
her lack of sympathy or moral capacity but from her failure to understand
the Higginses' words and gestures. In one of Margaret's interchanges with
Bessy, for instance, Bessy laments that she has sent her father out of the
house and to "the folk that are always ready for to tempt a man, in time
o' strike, to go drink" (136). Margaret responds, with some alarm, "But
does your father drink?" to which Bessy answers, "No—not to say
drink." Margaret automatically associates "drink" with perpetual drunkenness, a sign of the rebellion and spendthrift recklessness of the poor,
and Bessy has to explain to Margaret what drink means in working-class
culture. "Father never was a drunkard," stresses Bessy, "though maybe,
he's got worse for drink, now and then." For Bessy, "drink" is only a
potential hazard, an occasional drink being a normal part of working life.
Although Margaret now understands the working-class distinction be-

tween "drink" and drunkenness, she experiences more difficulty when she in turn must interpret working-class "drink" for her father. When she brings Mr. Higgins home to meet her father immediately after Bessy's death, Margaret, fearing that Mr. Hale will automatically recoil from her friend, tries to explain that Higgins is only partly inebriated. She finds herself at a loss, however, to describe Higgins's exact state to Mr. Hale without calling up the image of the "drunken infidel weaver" (223).

Another example of how crucial it is for Margaret to correctly interpret and value working-class language occurs when Mrs. Hale accuses Margaret of vulgarity because she has adopted "factory slang" (237). Margaret's answer reveals how thoroughly she has come to understand the language of the people she visits: "And if I live in a factory town, I must speak factory language when I want it. Why, mamma, I could astonish you with a great many words you never heard in your life. I don't believe you know what a knobstick is." Margaret's openness to learning language new to her and her willingness to learn additional ways of interpreting signs is key to her success as a mediator of social conflict.

The significance of learning to understand others' language and accurately read their signs is demonstrated in Thornton's description of his social "experiment," a cooperative dining room his employees manage. Thornton explains to Mr. Colthurst, a member of Parliament, that such schemes must be "carried on by that sort of common interest which invariably makes people find means and ways of seeing each other, and becoming acquainted with each other's *characters and persons,* and even tricks of temper and *modes of speech.* We should *understand* each other better, and I'll venture to say we should *like* each other more" (432, emphasis added). Becoming familiar with others, reasons Thornton, teaches one to read the sign systems of their dress, demeanor, gestures, and speech; correctly reading these signs leads to understanding and understanding leads to affection. People who like one another are no longer enemies, are no longer locked in conflict. Thornton, of course, has acquired this "wisdom" through his dialogues with Margaret.

To be a social mediator, Margaret must be able to understand and communicate in both directions. In the various dialogues in the novel, Margaret alternately represents Thornton's opinions to Higgins and Higgins's opinions to Thornton. Margaret is not merely a conduit between the two men, however. Each time she speaks to either of them, she, the "master" of both languages, interprets and translates the men's opinions. The "force connecting public and private life" comes not only from Margaret's moral influence, as Gallagher would have it, but also from her role as ideal reader and interpreter of both personal and public discursive practices. This is a social role informed by and yet more than the personal and domestic.[28] It is often Margaret who brings order to the "anarchy of signification" because she comes to accept and adapt to the social changes registered in language.

Although Margaret serves as an exemplary mediator by translating the languages of men to one another, even she sometimes fails to read or be read properly. The whole Thornton family repeatedly misconstrues Margaret's actions and language, while she sometimes misreads their intentions as well, particularly in the case of Mr. Thornton. Thornton, for instance, takes offense at Margaret's omitting to shake his hand at the conclusion of a visit—a social custom among his set but not hers. When she finally performs this social gesture, he has come to understand it as the mark of intimacy she takes it to be. Margaret and Thornton, after much discussion, finally come to share each other's definition of the word "gentleman." As it does with Thornton and his employees, becoming familiar with each other's language—"characters and persons, and even tricks of temper and modes of speech"—leads Margaret and Thornton finally to understanding and to mutual affection, even love; but they encounter many difficulties along the way. Margaret and Thornton, of course, do not perceive their misreadings of each other; since they lack the language to read the signs correctly, they cannot know about these mistakes until later, when they acquire the requisite information. The reader, however, does recognize these scenes of linguistic misunderstanding. When Margaret fails as a mediator, the novel provides the language that enables the reader to correctly interpret the characters' signs.

Similarly, although the course of Margaret's relationship with the working-class Higginses runs much smoother than it does with Thornton, Margaret sometimes misreads their signs as well—also without knowing it. For instance, on one of Margaret's early visits to the Higginses, she notices that Mary has made a large fireplace fire, despite the hot weather. Margaret assumes that this fire is owing to Bessy's fevered condition; the narrator, however, informs us that the fire is a working-class sign of hospitality meant to welcome Margaret. While Margaret's misreading here does not lead to any consequence, it is an example of something that both occurs repeatedly in the novel and characterizes the narrative structure: the narrator is the model reader of signs, who knows the languages of all the characters and who interprets these signs for the reader. Thus, like Margaret, the narrator mediates among groups who do not understand—and may not like—one another.

To read *North and South* is to read a series of debates, contrasting scenes, and alternated speeches. Each chapter of dialogue between Margaret Hale and Mr. Thornton is placed next to a dialogue between Margaret and Mr. Higgins; each description of Bessy Higgins's illness is followed by a description of Mrs. Hale's illness; the Hales' visit to the Thorntons is contrasted with the Thorntons' visit to the Hales; even Margaret's public appearance at the strike scene is set against Mrs. Thornton's more private intervention in a strike (116). The narrator, like Margaret, presents and interprets all these divergent situations for the reader. Following the model of social mediation that *North and South* offers, we are expected to believe that if the reader becomes familiar with the different signs and languages of class—particularly the working class, but almost as important, the new industrial class—then the reader will understand and like, or feel new interest in and sympathy for, the generators of these signs.[29] Conspicuously, the narrator refrains, for the most part, from taking sides; she presents, she interprets where necessary, and thus she brings the characters together. The solution is provided neither by one side nor the other but always by a moderating position—and this solution is always reached through two vehicles: language and sympathy. While both Thornton and Higgins attempt to handle class conflict with force, such tactics, Gaskell tells us, are doomed to failure. It is only through talk and personal acquaintance that class conflict can be changed into class harmony.

Thus Gaskell's talky novel about the mediation of opposing interests, which are represented in the title of the book, claims access to the social sphere for women visitors and women novelists. Not merely intended for entertainment, to generate tears in the family circle around the fireside, *North and South* presents itself as a novel that not only addresses social problems but enacts the process it recommends. In effect, through its portrayal of an exemplary woman visitor, the novel constructs a social space that is neither wholly private nor wholly public, but it is based on the powerful effects of the control over language—and then it inhabits this space. Gaskell's novel makes claims for its own contribution to the public discourse. Journalists and philosophers become, in a sense, the "theorists" of the writing profession; the sentimental novel occupies the private sphere; but the social-problem novel that joins social theory and personal experience is the ideal discourse of the social sphere. By writing a social-problem novel that functions in the publishing world as does Margaret as a female visitor in her world, Gaskell claims authority for herself and other middle-class women to enter public debates about social and political issues, not despite but because of their position as domestic women. Predictably, however, women's access to the social does not come without cost, one that *North and South* makes evident.

The Marriage of Classes

In the midst of one of *North and South*'s discussions of language—specifically, a dialogue about the use of the parent-child metaphor to represent labor and class relations—Margaret relates an anecdote about a man who for forty years kept his son in a childlike state to protect him from the temptations of the world. "His father," says Margaret, "had made the blunder of bringing him up in ignorance and taking it for innocence; and after fourteen months of riotous living, the city authorities had to take charge of him, in order to save him from starvation" (121). Margaret's analogy inflicts the deathblow to the metaphor they have been arguing over; Thornton complains that Margaret, in this anecdote, has used the parent-child metaphor as a weapon against him, and they henceforth reject it completely as a model for class or labor relations.[30]

Although its narrative method depends on dualities such as that of parent and child, masters and men, and north and south, the novel also rejects, or deconstructs, the polarity of these dualities because, as we have seen, it aspires to construct a ground on which dualities can meet and be mediated. By demolishing the parent-child metaphor, *North and South* argues for adult-to-adult interactions on common ground.[31] Rather than doing away with metaphor, however, Gaskell's novel offers another metaphor to replace the historically loaded metaphor of paternalism. Although it implies a different kind of power relation, one of adult to adult, it is still not a metaphor of equality. The metaphor that *North and South* proposes to replace the paternal model for class relations is, of course, marriage. That it uses this alternative metaphor has implications not only for relations between masters and men but between men and women as well.

The metaphor of marriage as a model for class relations works in Gaskell's novel because of the identification she establishes between women and the working class. This identification underwrites the common claim that women are ideal mediators of class conflict.[32] Women were to serve literally as mediators through personal contact with the working classes in their roles as mistresses of servants and as visitors to the poor, and the concept of women as mediators provided a way to manage middle-class anxieties about the "problem" of the lower classes. Because women were like the working classes, they could stand in for the working class; if women could be managed, the dangerous working classes could also be kept under control.

Like women, the working classes were represented as unruly, ignorant (equated in Margaret's anecdote with "innocence"), and sexual. When Margaret first travels the streets of Milton, she is "very unfortunate in constantly falling in" with the factory workers: "They came rushing along, with bold, fearless faces, and loud laughs and jests, particularly aimed at all those who appeared to be above them in rank or station. The tones of their unrestrained voices, and their carelessness of all common rules of street politeness, frightened Margaret a little at first. . . . [S]he alternately dreaded and fired up against the workmen, who commented not on her dress, but on her looks, in the same open fearless manner" (71). "Bold," "fearless," "loud," "unrestrained," and "careless" are words that call up the figure of uncontrolled female sexuality—the prostitute. The prostitute is the woman who is "unrestrained" and "careless of all common rules"; she is the woman not kept in check within the domestic sphere. Not only are the working-class men frankly sexually aware but their behavior is like the deportment of an unrestrained woman. The "disorderly tumult" that reigns in the working-class streets is contrasted to "the quiet safety of home," where Margaret is not only safe but free of sexual innuendo. Although her position in a middle-class home allows Margaret to deny her sexuality until nearly the last page of the novel, others—Henry Lennox, Mr. Thornton, and Mrs. Thornton and her servants—recognize it. They appreciate that Margaret is a woman, and hence a sexual being, and they also realize that her sexuality has the potential to be unruly and unrestrained. Mrs. Thornton twice interprets as sexually motivated activities Margaret defines as pure and noble (the riot and her walk with her brother, Frederick); and Mr. Thornton has a dream in which he sees Margaret as a lascivious and loose woman, and he reads her lie about her brother as an admission of sexual misconduct. Although Margaret's sexual, and potentially unruly, nature is constantly kept in check by the "common rules" of courtesy, or by the manners and conventions of her class, the only way to ensure her "modesty" is through marriage.[33]

Women's position in marriage entails another likeness to the working class. Like the "hands" in the factory, married women were in a subordinate position—and they were excluded from ownership of property. Since marrying a woman was the socially and legally sanctioned way for middle- and upper-class men to control women's money, labor, and sexuality, marriage was a useful metaphor for representing the management of the lower classes. In *North and South,* the chief power that women and workers have is to refuse to submit to such control—to withhold either their labor (figured as a strike, in the case of the workers) or their sexuality (figured as the refusal to marry, in Margaret's case).[34] Before Margaret yields herself to Thornton in marriage, he reports to her that his men have sent him a "round-robin" pledging their labor to him if he is ever in a position to employ them again (432). Their "round-robin" bears a structural similarity to a marriage vow. A few pages later, Thornton's men and his woman are both pledged to honor and obey him.

It is significant, however, that neither the marriage of man and woman nor of "master" and "hand" are characterized as a complete victory on the one side or as complete submission on the other. Thornton acknowledges that his new relations with his men are not likely to prevent future strikes, but they will only make strikes "respectable." Margaret grabs the Helstone roses (roses are a traditional metaphor for sexuality) from Thornton with "gentle violence" (436). The use of these two oxymorons, "respectable strike" and "gentle violence," marks an important qualification of the work that marriage is supposed to accomplish as a metaphor, because it leaves some power in the hands of the weaker partner. The trope of "gentle violence" would seem more appropriate to the mystification of the power of masters and husbands—masters who call in soldiers to suppress strikes and husbands who possess the legal means to render women powerless; yet Gaskell uses the trope to describe

Margaret's action. Instead of changing laws or overturning existing power structures, Gaskell offers a social vision that tempers power relations with mutual understanding and affection.

Thus, although Margaret's guardian, Mr. Bell, playfully accuses Margaret of being "a democrat, a red republican, a member of the Peace Society, a socialist," Gaskell's novel offers love and marriage instead of revolution, socialism, or feminism (330). Including these politically charged terms in Mr. Bell's jest is a way of rejecting them as absurd alternatives for handling the social problems with which the novel is concerned. Instead, Gaskell uses the conventional novelistic ending—marriage—as a statement of her proposed social agenda. The conventionality of the happy ending serves as a mask that naturalizes what is unconventional in her vision of women's role.

Although the occurrence of a marriage at the end of *North and South* is a novelistic convention, this marriage is not conventional, at least within the terms of the genre. Indeed, the kind of marriage that Margaret and Thornton create is as important to Gaskell's purpose as is the fact of their marriage. While we do not know what exactly their marriage will be like, since the novel ends before the wedding, we do know, presumably, what it will not be like, because at least four different models of marriage are presented—and rejected—in *North and South*. The marriage of General and Mrs. Shaw, for instance, is a marriage of convenience, contracted on the basis of exchange of property and rank. Mrs. Shaw herself rejects this kind of marriage and insists that her daughter Edith marry for love. Margaret, however, finds Edith's society marriage disturbing; she notices disapprovingly that Captain Lennox is "anxiously attentive to Edith's dress and appearance, with a view to her beauty making a sufficient impression on the world" (373). Margaret also rejects her own proposed marriage to Henry Lennox. Although Margaret and Henry share many tastes and sympathies, his vision of marriage rests on the separation of men's and women's spheres and on women's confinement to the domestic. Margaret's parents' marriage is based on love, but Mr. and Mrs. Hale seem unable to communicate with each other on even the most important matters affecting their life together—his leaving the church and her terminal illness. By contrast to these rejected models of marriage, all grounded in the separation of men's and women's spheres, the relationship of Margaret and Thornton follows the formula that *North and South* gives for class harmony—familiarity with the other's language leads to the understanding that leads to affection and cooperation. Further, Thornton's home, where Margaret will presumably live, is not, as were most middle-class homes, removed from the scene of labor and class relations; the home sits on the same ground as the factory, so that Margaret will not inhabit an entirely "separate sphere" from her husband.[35] Similar to the dining room that domesticates the factory, Margaret's home blurs the boundaries between the public and private; presumably her marriage will follow suit.

The happy ending of *North and South* is not merely the lapse into the personal that marks Gaskell's failure to sustain a critique of social relations; it is also not an argument for the "continued isolation of the family from society."[36] The marriage of Margaret, the lady visitor, and Thornton, the progressive industrialist, is Gaskell's metaphor for the newly constructed social sphere. The metaphor demonstrates both the possibilities and the limitations of this space for middle-class women. While by mid-century women such as Gaskell had unquestioned access to the social sphere through writing for publication, visiting, and other philanthropic activities, they did not have full autonomy, even within the sphere. Yet the construction and "feminization" of the social realm, as Denise Riley observes, was a precondition for women's entry into the commercial and political spaces that occurred a few decades later.[37] Because it both portrays women mediating social relations and itself performs an act of mediation, *North and South* looks to the future, and not to the past, of class and gender relations.

6   Educating Women's Desires

The Philanthropic Heroine in the 1860s

IN 1859 BESSIE RAYNER PARKES, the editor of *The English Woman's Journal,* contributed an article entitled "Charity as a Portion of the Public Vocation of Women." Parkes's title challenges the tenets of domestic ideology that limited women to the private sphere of the home and boldly claims for women a "public vocation" that includes, but is not limited to, philanthropic work. Parkes presumes that her readers will accept as normal women's participation in the social sphere that writers such as Anna Jameson and Elizabeth Gaskell helped to carve and define. Parkes challenges any "unprejudiced" observer to deny "that there is a necessity for the employment of women in occupations beyond those attaching to household and domestic duties."[1] Parkes's argument for such occupations, however, does not rest merely on economic or other practical grounds, but rather she focuses on women's right to fulfill their ambitious desires; women, she asserts, are "entitled to share in the inalienable rights of humanity to a free use of every faculty." To this rhetoric of rights Parkes adds the vocabulary of morality: women "possess a moral necessity for action which cannot surely be regarded with impunity" (194). By casting her defense of women's "public vocation" in moral terms, Parkes not only makes women's ambitious desires seem a natural part of their character but also implies that to thwart or restrain such desires may lead to women's immorality: "a consciousness of aspiration for which no available medium of realisation appears" will lead to "deterioration" of the "moral force of character" (195). Women's unrealized aspirations, Parkes threatens, will "become the busy agents of a career of levity or vice" (195).

Like Parkes, many people in mid-Victorian England recognized that women had ambitious desires, or "a consciousness of aspiration," but many also worried about what would happen if such desires were inappropriately channeled. The immoral consequences of women's misdirected desires were often represented in the popular sensation novels so much in vogue in the 1860s, while journal articles and even a few novels tentatively explored the possibility of women fulfilling their (properly selfless) ambitions as artists, actresses, nurses, and writers.[2] Even Parkes, however, who was an ardent advocate of extending occupational opportunities for women, recognized that "to advocate the entry of women into paths of enterprise hitherto monopolized by men, is to assail the very citadel of prejudice" (194). Instead, she suggests a backdoor approach: the "one path of exertion" that is free of "the restraints and prejudices which beset more signal courses of action" is still "the exercise of charity" (195).

While a number of earlier writers, as we have seen, advocated and portrayed women's participation in volunteer philanthropic work, by the end of the 1850s, when Parkes was writing, charitable activity had become in effect "a national pastime" for English women of the leisured classes.[3] Besides the thousands of women who visited the poor and unfortunate on their own, in 1862 there were at least 640 charitable institutions in operation in England, most of them staffed and many of them administered by women.[4] Popular imagination lauded the heroic efforts of nineteenth-century women philanthropists such as Sarah Martin and Elizabeth Fry, who pioneered prison visiting; Hannah More with her Sunday schools and *Cheap Repository Tracts;* Mary Carpenter, whose work with "ragged children" was much celebrated; Louisa Twining, the major force behind the Workhouse Visiting Society; Ellen Ranyard with her Bible women and district nurses; Octavia Hill and her urban housing schemes; writers such as Anna Jameson, Mary Bayly, and Frances Power Cobbe; and, most prominent of all, Florence Nightingale, whose career "gave the lie to arguments about women's natural limitations; she proved beyond a doubt that women could work in the public sphere." [5]

Along with these historical philanthropic heroines, it became commonplace in the 1860s for novelists to deploy the figure of the noble philanthropic woman. As we have seen, novelists as far back as the early eighteenth century had featured heroines who performed charitable acts, while writers such as Mary Astell and Sarah Scott had represented philanthropy as an alternative vocation to marriage for wealthy women, and Hannah More had urged women of both the middle and upper classes to engage in reasoned, religiously motivated charitable work. The earlier nineteenth-century writers I have already discussed went further by helping to define and claim a social sphere in which women philanthropists could play a role in mediating class difference and performing social service. Gaskell's *North and South,* as we have seen, featured a philanthropic woman visitor as its protagonist. Many other familiar nineteenth-century romantic heroines, including George Eliot's Janet Dempster, Romola, and Gwendolyn Harleth Grandcourt, turn to charitable work when their romances fail, while for others, such as Dickens's Esther Summerson and Charlotte Brontë's Caroline Helstone, it is (at least in part) the heroine's charitable works that win her a heroic husband. Even in many novels in which the heroine does not engage directly in charitable work, minor characters—especially older unmarried women—do. [6] By the late 1850s, however, women's philanthropy often became the central focus of novels about young women, with titles such as *The Sister of Charity* (1857), *Charity Helstone* (1866), *A Maiden of our Own Day* (1862), *The Clever Woman of the Family* (1865), and *The Vicar's Daughter* (1872). This figure becomes so common during the period that the "philanthropic heroine" could be said to rival the traditional "romantic heroine" as a literary convention. [7]

The philanthropic heroine of these novels differed from the traditional romantic heroine not only because her devotion to philanthropic works carried her into the social sphere beyond the home but also because she had ambitious desires that were at least as strong as her erotic ones. Curiously, most discussions of women's desires, even now, equate the word "desire" with sexual passion or longings. Although first published in 1981, Nancy K. Miller's "Emphasis Added: Plots and Plausibilities in Women's Fiction" is still one of the few serious explorations of women's nonsexual desires as manifested in literature. Miller's essay contrasts ambitious desires with the erotic desires to which Freud limited women.[8] What is most likely to be repressed in the works of women writers, Miller suggests, are "not erotic impulses, but an impulse to power: a fantasy of power that would revise the social grammar in which women are never defined as subjects; a fantasy of power that disdains a sexual exchange in which women can participate only as objects of circulation" (348). Reading British women's novels of the 1860s, however, complicates Miller's theory of the repression of women's ambitious desires. By the 1860s women's right to ambitious desires was either explicitly or implicitly upheld in the novels featuring philanthropic heroines; in a philanthropic heroine, such desires, with all that they imply, were not repressed but manifest. In mid-nineteenth-century England it was possible not only to imagine but even to expect women to want to "do something" besides marry a hero and live happily ever after as his "angel in the house." After all, not only novelistic heroines but actual women had by this time performed heroic acts and been featured in the public spotlight without tarnishing their image as properly feminine women.

Women's Desires

Societal concern about women's desires became prominent in the 1860s partly because of the dramatic increase in leisure time enjoyed by women, particularly of the middle classes, as employing servants to perform household duties became more and more the norm for even lower-middle-class families. It was primarily during the late 1850s and 1860s that the middle-class woman's complaint of "nothing to do" became a pressing part of "the woman question." During the 1850s Florence Nightingale, for instance, wrote that "it is the hardest slavery [for a woman], either to take the chance of a man whom she knows *so little,* or to vegetate at home, her life consumed by *ennui* as by a cancer."[9] Similarly, Dinah Mulock Craik's 1863 *A Woman's Thoughts About Women* declares that "the chief canker at the root of women's lives is the want of something to do" (11), while Lucy F. March Phillips published a popular book in 1860 entitled *My Life and What Shall I Do With It? A Question for Young Gentlewomen.* The problem was especially acute for unmarried middle-class women without family duties, as we have seen in the writings of Jameson, but, as the example of Nightingale shows, even young women of marriageable age could have ambitious, as well as erotic or romantic, desires that demanded fulfillment. Otherwise their energies might "rust," suggested Nightingale (215)—or be turned to something worse, as Parkes had threatened.

Of course, interest in women's ambitious desires was bound up with concerns about their erotic desires. Since historically women had been valued primarily for their reproductive capacities, controlling their erotic desires had long been an issue. The sexual sin of Eve is the foundational myth of both Christianity and Judaism, and marriage has always been regarded to be the natural and divinely instituted antidote to women's potentially unruly desires. The "redundant woman problem," triggered by the 1851 census that counted more women than men in the British population, made it apparent that not all women's desires could be channeled into marriage. What was redundant about single women was, in large part, their unchanneled erotic desires, which needed to be directed somewhere or they would be either wasted or acted on in harmful ways. Writers such as Parkes thus argued that women needed work, not only for economic reasons but also as an outlet for their extra energies. Work, however, whether for pay or not, might give rise to what nineteenth-century commentators called aspirations, or what Freud would later term ambitious desires, because it necessarily took women into the more public social sphere. Such desires, if they led to defeminizing women, disrupting the "natural" course of family life, or competing with men for jobs and salaries, were potentially as dangerous as uncontrolled erotic desires, which led to coquetry, adultery, and prostitution. Like unfulfilled erotic desires, however, unused ambitious desires might lead to illness and hysteria, or they might be directed toward trivial and petty concerns with gossip, dress, or accomplishments that would ultimately also lead to the destruction of a happy home life. Whether women could have—and especially act on—both erotic and ambitious desires became an especially troubling question once the existence of female ambitious desires had been granted.

Thus, while representations of female philanthropists as heroines might implicitly endorse women's ambitious desires, they were by no means without anxiety about what unleashing these desires might mean. It is significant that legitimating ambitious desires in women changed the accepted definition of women as nondesiring angels, wanting only what

their husbands wanted, and defined them as autonomous subjects. However noble and altruistic the philanthropic projects in which the heroine
engaged, and no matter how feminine and selfless she might appear, the
notion of a woman with her own desires and dreams was unsettling.
Thus, if women were to be allowed to have and act on ambitious desires
and to have access to the developing space of the social sphere, it seemed
crucial that they be rightly educated, both in terms of the work they
intended to accomplish and the proper limits that should be imposed on
this work. Women who were not allowed "legitimate" aims for the exercise of their ambitious desires might channel these desires into immoral
or, at best, frivolous activities, as the attractive but wayward female vil-
lains of sensation novels did; but women who did find an outlet for their
aspirations and energies through philanthropy also had to be carefully
regulated and contained to keep these energies within acceptable boundaries. Therefore, the philanthropic heroine novels, like the sensation novels, redefined women as having both erotic and ambitious desires, with
energies that might be channeled toward one or the other or both. The
problem was to reconcile and discipline both kinds of desires.

Ambitious Heroines

Just as most discussions of female desires assume that these desires are
sexual, most previous discussions of novelistic heroines have taken for
granted that female protagonists function only in love plots. Several
feminist critics have paid careful attention to the implications of the
nineteenth-century heroine's subversive use of or resistance to "the
totalizing ideology of romance," and a few have noted the conflict in
some Victorian novels between "a woman's desire for autonomous self-
fulfillment" and "her need for emotional enrichment."[10] However, only
Patricia Thomson's 1956 *The Victorian Heroine: A Changing Ideal* comments specifically on the emergence of a new kind of heroine who is not
limited to the confines of a love story. Certainly many of the popular
novels of the 1860s complicate the assumption that the romantic heroine
was "the only model of femininity which was officially approved" in Victorian England.[11]

Since the novel had from its beginning been a vehicle for legitimizing
and training women's erotic desires, it also provided a likely avenue for
educating women in how to use their recently acknowledged ambitious

desires. If romantic novels taught women that the only way to discipline and purify erotic desires was to channel them into an appropriate marriage, the philanthropic novels showed them that their ambitious desires could and should be exercised in properly conducted philanthropy. While none of these novels ignore or discount women's desires for love and marriage, their focus is on the conflict between or need to reconcile the heroine's ambitious and erotic desires, and the erotic desires do not always win; not all the novels end in marriage, and many of those that do are careful to portray marriages that still allow the heroine to fulfill her ambitious desires through philanthropy. Significantly, the philanthropic heroines of these novels were not seen as subversive, radical, or even (in most cases) strong-minded. In fact, the philanthropic heroine most often appeared in highly religious, didactic novels aimed at the average female reader of circulating library fiction.[12]

Philanthropic heroines were not seen as subversive, of course, because their activities could be made to seem a natural extension of the duties of the domestic sphere. Like the female heroes Lee R. Edwards describes, they stood "at the border between domestic and public life," inherently challenging that border with their ambitious desires to make something happen in the world beyond their homes.[13] It was because they were acknowledged to have ambitious desires that they could appear in these novels—to have these desires disciplined, trained, and properly directed. The plots of these novels are designed to teach their ambitious heroines—and their readers—how to preserve their femininity, submit to (usually male professional) supervision, and circumscribe their desires within the limits allowed to women. While other forms of philanthropic discourse, including lectures such as those of Anna Jameson and F. D. Maurice and his colleagues; instruction manuals directed to district visitors, workhouse visitors, "ragged" school directors, prison visitors, sanitary workers, and so forth; and even novels such as Gaskell's *North and South,* treated the specifics of how women anxious to engage in philanthropy should go about dealing with the working classes and their problems, the philanthropic heroine novels were more concerned with managing women's own desires. Once these lessons are learned, the heroines are allowed to escape their "entrapment in the heroine's plot" by refusing marriage or by combining the emotional fulfillment of marriage with a philanthropic vocation.[14]

A New Kind of Fairy Princess

One of the most representative of the philanthropic heroine novels of the 1860s is Mrs. Carey Brock's *Charity Helstone,* published in 1866. Subtitled *A Tale,* Brock's novel features a heroine whom another character labels "a fairy princess."[15] Yet, unlike the beautiful princesses in most fairy tales, Charity does not marry the great lord who courts her; she also does not marry her poorer childhood sweetheart. The trials Charity goes through are the disciplining of her desires, both erotic and ambitious, and the happy ending of her fairy tale is to inherit a fortune and spend her life as a paternalist landlord and philanthropist, unmarried and independent.

The eponymous heroine's name in Brock's novel calls up another, somewhat more familiar, orphaned heroine who anticipates a single life devoted to philanthropy, Charlotte Brontë's Caroline Helstone in *Shirley* (1849). Whereas Brontë's heroine goes into a serious depression at the prospect of such a life, for Brock's heroine it is presented as a reward for undergoing the training and subduing of her unruly desires. Intentionally or not, Brock seems to be answering Brontë's dismissal of philanthropy as an outlet for women's aspirations. Bewailing her "impotence" in the face of society's willful ignorance of the plight of single women, Caroline exclaims, "Existence never was originally meant to be that useless, blank, pale, slow-trailing thing it often becomes to many, and is becoming to me, among the rest. . . . The brothers of these girls are every one in business or in professions; they have something to do: their sisters have no earthly employment, but household work and sewing; no earthly pleasure, but an unprofitable visiting; and no hope, in all their life to come, of anything better."[16] Charity's single life, by contrast, is described in glowing terms: " 'Mrs. Charity Helstone,' as in time she came to be called, often gave rise to much speculating wonder amongst strangers. That one so rich, and so singularly beautiful, should pass the whole of a long life in quiet bliss amongst the Huntley Tower turrets, seemed very extraordinary to those who, not knowing anything of the beginning of her life, naturally could not understand the end. But to those who had known the beginning, the end seemed very natural, simple, and beautiful" (352). Where Brontë forcefully describes the limitations of narrow education and expectations for women, especially women unable to marry, Brock, writing almost twenty years later, can blithely imagine a "natural, simple, and beautiful" life of "bliss" for her unmarried philanthropic heroine. Much of the difference, of course, comes from Brontë's greater intellectual complexity and skill as a writer, but, those differences aside, it is important to recognize that by 1866 a new model of positive female endeavor was available to provide some outlet for the wasted energies Brontë's character laments.

Before Charity Helstone can assume her role as a modern "fairy princess," however, she must go through a rigorous program of training and subduing her desires. Orphaned at birth, Charity is given her name and adopted by Mrs. Dorothy Helstone. Mrs. Dorothy, or Aunt Dorothy as she is called by most of the villagers, is reminiscent of Hannah More's model widow, Mrs. Jones, in "The Sunday School." [17] Although of relatively limited means, she has managed through her philanthropic influence to befriend and reform the parish. It is important that while cooperating with the clergyman, Mrs. Dorothy has taken on her own definite role in the community, approved but not directed by him. Mrs. Dorothy is also an example of the kind of philanthropic heroine who has chosen charitable works following the ruin of her erotic and romantic dreams; her husband, like many characters in sensation novels, turned out to be a bigamist and deserted her, leaving her to find her way back to England from America. Childless, Mrs. Dorothy adopts Charity and raises the child to fit her name—and to repress her erotic desires for worthless but attractive men such as Mrs. Dorothy's husband.

Charity, the new generation of philanthropic heroine, with her symbolic name, is full of pride, wit, and strong will, which have to be tamed and chastened. Early in the novel, Mrs. Dorothy's servant Betsy describes a conversation she has had with the local miller in which he likened the child Charity to a colt:

> it was every one that said what a pretty creature she was, and so clever to talk to, and so good to the poor. If she was a bit self-willed, why, that would right itself with time. She would be like his young colt, that was standing so quietly outside then, with the sacks across her back; the time was, and not so very long ago either, when there wasn't any way at all of doing anything with her, for the play and spirit she'd got in her, but one was just

obliged to let her have out her run: but now, why, bless you!
she'd come to know the hand that held her, and the work she
was wanted to do, and there wasn't a better than she in all the
country—no, nor as good an one; for she was all the more valuable for the go she'd got in her by nature. Now she was a bit
trained and taught, he'd warrant her against any of the slow-
paced things that were to be seen about here, that had no sense
or life in them. (33–34)

Pretty and clever but, like a lively young horse, controlled by curiosity
and strong instincts, Charity must be taught to harness her desires and
energies and to stand quietly "with the sacks across her back." The "hand
that [holds] her," however, does not turn out to be a husband, and the
"work she [is] wanted to do" is not bearing and raising children, as one
might expect. Rather, her only master turns out to be God and the work
she is destined to do is to fulfill her early promise of being "good to
the poor."

To be "trained and taught," Charity is sent away to a boarding school
in London, where she is persecuted for being a charity case, as was Betsy,
the rescued workhouse servant. At school, Charity comes under the tutelage of the Reverend Mr. Morton, who sets her to study 1 Corinthians,
the scriptural passage from which her name is taken. In preparation for
her confirmation, Charity goes through trials appropriate to each of the
qualities of her name—"charity suffereth long," "charity envieth not,"
"charity is not puffed up," "charity does not behave itself unseemly,"
and, perhaps most important, "charity seeketh not her own." [18] Master-
ing herself and her desires, Charity earns the respect and love of her
schoolmates and, through Rev. Morton and the requisite novelistic co-
incidences, discovers that she is not a nameless foundling but is really
Mrs. Dorothy's only surviving relative and legal heir. When Charity turns
down the marriage proposal of her childhood sweetheart, Edward Saville, despite her love for him, because he is irreligious and profligate,
she finally proves that she has mastered her desires, and she takes over
Mrs. Dorothy's role as almoner and adviser to the community as well as
that of Lord Huntley, the model paternalist landlord.

Like so many other literary representations of female philanthropists,
Charity Helstone relies on a revised paternalism to preserve and enhance

the influence and authority of the middle-class woman. Charity's story, however, does not follow what Rosemarie Bodenheimer calls the "romance of the female paternalist"; her "most resounding success" does not come in "the form of symbolic romance" in which her marriage serves as a "revised model of social government."[19] Instead of marrying her heroine to Lord Huntley, a reform-minded politician reminiscent of the historical Lord Shaftesbury, and making her his (subordinate) partner, Brock has Charity inherit a fortune (from her tyrannical paternalist grandfather) that enables her to buy Huntley Tower and literally replace the benevolent male paternalist.[20] It is because Charity is destined to take over a traditionally male position that her desires must be so carefully trained and managed. Since as a large landholder she controls both the physical resources and the social structure of the community, it is important to the social vision of the novel that Charity's aspirations all be directed outward, devoted to others and not to herself—or even, it is implied, to her family. Only then can she be trusted with the power over other people's lives and fortunes traditionally vested in, but often misused by, wealthy men such as her grandfather. While Mrs. Dorothy is an example of the authority middle-class women can exercise as modern versions of the traditional paternalistic Lady Bountiful, as Hannah More advocated, Charity takes the feminization of paternalism a step further; she becomes the paternal figure.

It is interesting that although *Charity Helstone* is the fairy tale of a philanthropic heroine, it spends little time describing Charity's charitable activities. She is praised for being "so good to the poor" and we are told that she devotes her life and newly inherited fortune to philanthropic endeavors, but we never see any of it. The closest we come to seeing philanthropy in action is a chapter describing Lord Huntley's improvements and the gratitude of his tenants and the villagers. Charity, of course, later takes over and improves on all these projects, we are told, but we do not see her doing it. What we do see, at length, is the training and curbing of her desires—both her erotic and ambitious ones. Charity learns that she must be selfless, kind, and humble, and not seek prizes or recognition, despite her intelligence and beauty; she learns to forgive insult and to be tolerant of others' weakness and faults; and, most of all, she learns to curb her impulses, submitting her will and voice to the rule of Christian principle. Her most important teacher, after Mrs. Dorothy, is

Mr. Morton, the clergyman, and the importance of his role in the female protagonist's life is reinforced by the author having dedicated the novel to a clergyman, the Reverend Daniel Moore, from "one of his earliest catechumens." However, once Charity has imbibed Morton's teachings, displacing or repressing any selfish desires and internalizing the principles of Christian paternalism, the heroine is granted a new and powerful position, along with the freedom to act independently, manage her own resources, and make her own decisions without external supervision.

By portraying both Mrs. Dorothy, a Hannah More–like philanthropic widow, and Charity, a newly styled philanthropic heroine, Brock's novel represents the widening possibilities philanthropy offered for women in the 1860s, showing women acting independently on their ambitious desires and even filling traditionally male positions. However, the novel's distrust of men—virtually all men except clergymen—and its requirement that both Mrs. Dorothy and Charity give up any romantic dreams of erotic fulfillment reenact the tension between ambitious and erotic desires that so many previous representations of female philanthropists revealed. The fulfillment of Charity's ambitious desires comes at the cost of displacing all her erotic and ambitious energies into a rural, paternal form of philanthropy that gives her independence and authority but preserves her femininity by keeping her in "quiet bliss." She is removed from the public eye—she does not, after all, take up the political half of Lord Huntley's career—and her power and influence are exercised from a position of near seclusion. She may be a fairy princess, but she is walled up by choice behind the walls of Huntley Tower, never to be rescued into marriage.

Ambitious versus Erotic Desires

Like Charity Helstone, Brock's fairy princess, most historical women who took up philanthropic careers in the nineteenth century either did not marry or at least had no children. While performing casual acts of charity might seem compatible with, or even an expected part of, the role of a married woman belonging to the gentry or professional classes, it seemed impossible to most people for women to devote themselves to a philanthropic career and still perform the duties of a mother and wife. Thus portraying women who were able to fulfill both their ambitious and erotic desires was a knotty problem for the philanthropic heroine novels. Some, such as *Charity Helstone,* showed the heroine repressing or sacrificing her erotic desires for the sake of her philanthropic vocation; others presented the heroine fulfilling both kinds of desires but sequentially; and a few, especially those written toward the end of the decade, attempted to reconcile the desires through a new kind of marriage in which erotic and ambitious desires grew out of and were fulfilled by each other.

Like *Charity Helstone,* for instance, Charlotte M. Yonge's *The Daisy Chain,* published in 1856 and subtitled *Aspirations,* tells the story of a heroine who gives up her one chance of erotic fulfillment to care for her aging father and fulfill her philanthropic dream of Christianizing a wild village. Yonge's protagonist, Ethel May, was "a new kind of girls' heroine: battling against her innate dislike of household organization, and the worldly temptations of intellectual pride and sexual attraction."[21] Like the other philanthropic heroines, Ethel, of course, learns to discipline her desires, which for her means giving up both her scholarly pursuits, for which she shows aptitude, and her cousin Norman Ogilvie, to whom she is attracted. Both sacrifices are required—to prove that all her desires are fully disciplined—before she is allowed to become a philanthropic heroine and accomplish the aspirations of the subtitle.

Even by 1867, Eliza Lynn Linton's *Sowing the Wind* is unable to imagine reconciling ambitious and erotic desires in the same woman at the same time. In Linton's novel, ambitious desires are the driving force behind the strong-minded journalist Jane Osborn, who is ridiculed both by other characters and, to some extent, by the narrator's descriptions, for her lack of femininity and unconventional behavior. Yet Linton makes Jane successful in her profession and always describes her as noble, giving, kind, and full of integrity. She even has erotic desires, although she is not allowed to fulfill them. Like her ambitious desires, they are portrayed ambivalently as misguided and somewhat ridiculous, although inherently praiseworthy. Success in achieving ambitious desires, especially through a paid profession, seems to come only at the cost of all femininity and erotic fulfillment.

The novel's heroine Isola Aylott, by contrast, is a model of femininity with no desires except those of her husband—until she meets Jane Osborn. Awakening Isola's ambitious desires, Jane tries to make her beautiful cousin into a philanthropic heroine. The attempt fails; Isola's husband is so upset at the idea of her having any desires that their marriage rapidly crumbles, and the rest of the novel is taken up with describing its disintegration. Although her fledgling efforts at philanthropy are thwarted both by her husband and her naiveté, Isola's erotic desires are finally fulfilled when, after severe trials of her virtue and forbearance (and the death of her now insane husband), she marries the hero Gilbert Holmes. Thus the notion of women having ambitious as well as erotic desires, is, if not taken for granted, at least defended and ambivalently endorsed. Neither of the female protagonists, however, is allowed the reconciliation that philanthropy seems to promise; Jane's financial necessity compels her to channel her ambitious desires into paid employment and give up her femininity and her erotic desires, while Isola proves her true womanhood and fulfills all her romantic wishes but is prevented from fulfilling her ambitious desires.

Two other philanthropic heroine novels, which both achieved popularity, took up even more directly the vexed question of fulfilling both erotic and ambitious desires. A later Charlotte M. Yonge novel, *The Clever Woman of the Family* (1865), and Rhoda Broughton's *Not Wisely But Too Well* (1867) represent different subgenres of the novel. Yonge, a conservative High Church Anglican, wrote this novel, like *The Daisy Chain,* to promulgate her Tractarian religious views, while Broughton's novel is usually classed as one of the racy sensation novels. Both novels, however, portray their heroines participating in organized philanthropic work as a full-time vocation. Despite their different genres and styles, each of the novels also reveals similar anxieties about what limits should be set for the ambitious desires that such work potentially unleashes, and each forces the heroine to choose between love and philanthropy.

Rachel Curtis, the philanthropic heroine of Yonge's *The Clever Woman of the Family,* is a "strong-minded" young woman whose ambitious desires are so evident that they must be mocked, punished, and finally tamed before she is allowed a conventional happy ending. The epigraph to the first chapter makes the novel's moral clear:

> Thou didst refuse the daily round
>   Of useful, patient love,
> And longedst for some great emprise
>   Thy spirit high to prove.[22]

The chapter title, "In Search of a Mission," also makes apparent Rachel's ambitious desires, as well as placing her in the context of midcentury debates about women's work, as June Sturrock notices.[23] Rachel has "thrown herself into the process of self-education with all her natural energy, and carried on her favourite studies by every means within her reach," until she "considerably surpassed in acquirements and reflection all the persons with whom she came in frequent contact" (6). She is contrasted with her older sister, Grace, who has "contented herself with the ordinary course of *unambitious* feminine life" (6, emphasis added). Isolated within her "homely neighbourhood" from "the great progressive world, where, however, Rachel's sympathies all lay," she finds "the quiet Lady Bountiful duties that had sufficed her mother and sister . . . too small and easy to satisfy a soul burning at the report of the great cry going up to heaven from a world of sin and woe." Recalling Girard's model of imitative desire, the narrator tells us that "The examples of successful workers" had "*stimulated [Rachel's] longings* to be up and doing" (6, emphasis added).[24]

The satiric tone of the narrator as she describes Rachel's education and the desires it has produced, however, casts doubt on the probable efficacy of Rachel's fledgling philanthropic efforts. In fact, Rachel is not a sympathetic character for the first third of the novel, as characters and narrator alike ridicule her intellectual, literary, and philanthropic intentions. When, for instance, Rachel founds a school to educate and retrain child lace-makers, the initials of the subscription society she sets up to raise funds are F.U.L.E. Alick Keith, the man who eventually becomes Rachel's husband, catches the pun and has the name changed, but this is only the beginning of the troubles that the school causes. Before long we learn that Rachel has been duped and cheated by a swindler and his mistress; the children she tried to help have been beaten and forced to do even more lacework than they were before being "helped"; her favorite protégé has died of diphtheria; and Rachel, along with several members of her family, is also near death from the disease. After a series of humiliating experiences, culminating in a public trial exposing her gullibility and foolishness, along with a mortifying rumor that she hoped to marry the criminal who has swindled her, Rachel is finally chastened and redeemed by the love of Alick and the tutelage of his blind uncle, the rector Mr. Clare. Yonge ends the novel with Rachel admitting that "I am not fit to be anything but an ordinary married woman, with an Alick to take care of me" (345).

This brief plot summary would seem to squash any notion of women having laudable ambitious desires; however, the novel's effect is not so much to disparage all such desires as it is to denounce the way Rachel goes about fulfilling them—to critique her improper education, her naive pretensions, and, most of all, her irreligion. The novel sets up a rival "clever woman" in the modest, wise, and successful journalist Ermine Williams, and it allows Rachel to meet one of the admirable London female philanthropists she might have become "if [she] had been sensible" (345). Thus the novel still holds out the ideal of the philanthropic heroine as a possibility for middle-class women, but it establishes domestic virtues as primary and subordination to male authority as necessary to the proper exercise of any ambitious aspirations. It also clearly represents the tension between acting on these aspirations and gaining erotic fulfillment.

It is not only Rachel's ambitious desires that are mocked, subdued, and finally rewarded in Yonge's novel, however. Rachel's erotic desires, too, are portrayed as misguided and self-seeking. At first, Rachel claims not to feel any such desires; all her energies are directed toward her "mission." Demonstrating once again both her naiveté and vanity, Rachel mistakenly comes to believe that Colonel Colin Keith, Ermine's longtime lover, is in love with her, because he pays attention to her and listens to her opinions (at Ermine's request). Finally corrected in her mistaken assumption, Rachel undergoes the humiliation of widespread rumors that she loves the profligate and unscrupulous Mauleverer, the sham clergyman-philanthropist who has tricked and swindled her. Thus Rachel's erotic desires, like her ambitious ones, are submitted to a course of chastening and regulation before she is allowed their fulfillment in the love of a man described as a true hero. It is significant, however, that Alick loves Rachel not despite but because of her earnest qualities and her aspirations. To him, her lack of frivolity and coquetry are marks of real womanhood, as distinguished from the false femininity of his sister, Bessie, whose ambitious desires, recalling sensation novel heroines such as Lady Audley, are channeled into a social-climbing marriage with a wealthy and titled older man she does not love.[25] Although all Rachel's desires undergo thorough chastening, the desires themselves are not condemned or denied. Once

she has experienced a religious conversion, developed her motherly instincts, yielded to male direction, and learned to dress better, Rachel is
allowed to love as well as enjoy the possibility of acting on some of her
ambitious desires: Alick mentions to Rachel that there are opportunities
for philanthropy in his regiment (269).[26] Thus, while the novel may seem
to castigate female desires, especially ambitious ones, it holds out promise for fulfilling both erotic and ambitious desires—once they are thoroughly reined in, that is.

Probably written at about the same time as *The Clever Woman of the
Family,* Broughton's sensational *Not Wisely But Too Well* portrays a different kind of philanthropic heroine. Kate Chester, orphaned, outspoken,
passionate, and sexually alluring, seems to have no particular ambitious
desires. Rather, her desires, as she meets and falls in love with the dashing
Dare Stamer, are openly and shockingly (for the 1860s) sexual. She turns
to philanthropy only after she discovers that Dare is already married and
refuses to run away with him. She engages in her first charitable efforts as
a district visitor in a London suburb with reluctance and even fear. Under
the direction of the selfless and devoted curate James Stanley, who "saves"
her the second time she is tempted to run away with Dare, Kate becomes a professional and successful philanthropist, managing a fever hospital during an epidemic and finally joining a Protestant sisterhood after
the deaths of both James and Dare. Thus, while Kate, unlike Rachel Curtis, is allowed a professional career as a philanthropist, she turns to the
work as a substitute for, or displacement of, her sexual desires. Kate's
philanthropy is represented as her way of atoning for her unchaste and
unholy desires, even though she never acted on these desires.

While all the philanthropic heroine novels attempt to deal with the
problem of reconciling women's erotic and ambitious desires, in *Not
Wisely But Too Well* the relationship between these two kinds of desire is
particularly problematic. One of the novel's most recent critics, Pamela K.
Gilbert, claims that Kate's "change of direction" from passion to philanthropy is not really a change; "sex and religion," Gilbert contends, "are
equated as feverish obsessions," both "illicit and unhealthy."[27] As Gilbert
points out, both contemporary critics and other characters in the novel
are as uncomfortable with Kate's philanthropy as with her fervent love
for Dare. It would be a mistake, however, to take the self-satisfied opinion of Kate's middle-class relatives as the measure of the novel's attitude

toward her efforts at relieving and educating the lower class, especially considering the approbation given to the character of the saintly James Stanley, Kate's philanthropic mentor. James contrasts her philanthropic work with the "mad surfeit of brief pleasures," which is how he characterizes her feelings for Dare (272). As with other philanthropic heroines, Kate's trial is to school her too-violent erotic desires by the self-sacrifice and discipline that her philanthropic work provides.

To suggest that Kate's devotion to philanthropy is as obsessive as are her erotic desires for Dare is to echo mid-Victorian suspicions of Protestant sisterhoods.[28] Although some commentators, such as Jameson, supported and defended sisterhoods as a workable compromise between paid professional employment and amateur charitable work, others were outspoken in their denunciations of institutions that both smacked of popery and encouraged women to substitute fulfillment of their vocational aspirations for "natural" devotion to husbands and families.[29] Broughton's portrayal of Kate Chester is reminiscent of European novels that allowed deviant women to enter Catholic convents in lieu of dying, a plot alternative not previously available to English Protestant novelists. The serial version of *Not Wisely But Too Well* follows the more traditional plotline; unable to fulfill her erotic desires honorably by marrying Dare, Kate dies at his hand.[30] The book version, by contrast, takes advantage of a new plot—the philanthropic heroine plot—to rescue not only the heroine but the validity of her desires. Stripped of selfishness and self-aggrandizement, Kate is permitted to live on as an autonomous desiring subject, substituting a community of like-minded women for a conventional family and reasonable ambitious desires for uncontrolled erotic ones.

Unlike many of the other philanthropic heroine novels of the 1860s, *Not Wisely But Too Well* also describes in detail Kate's encounters with the poor. This is important because it suggests that to be allowed to act on their ambitious desires and succeed at a philanthropic vocation, women must learn not only to discipline their desires and submit to male supervision but also to perform their charitable acts in the right way. While some of these novels, such as *Charity Helstone,* seem to assume that a self-regulated and sympathetic middle-class woman will naturally know how to bridge class differences and offer appropriate assistance to the poor, Broughton's implicit suggestion that women need training is more in line with historical developments in philanthropic practice in the 1860s. Many reformers, political economists, philanthropists, and even novelists had already complained about ineffective, even harmful, philanthropic efforts, sometimes despite the best intentions. Dickens's Mrs. Pardiggle, for instance, is ridiculed for indulging her ambitious desires for authority and activity outside the home at the expense of her family, but she is also chastised for alienating the working-class people she is supposedly trying to aid and educate. A number of official organizations, including the Charity Organization Society and the National Association for the Promotion of Social Science, were committed to rationalizing and professionalizing philanthropic social work so that it would be both efficient and effective in dealing with social ills. The kind of casual charity that benevolent but amateurish women traditionally exercised was often portrayed as the antithesis of reasoned and scientific philanthropy, likely to do more harm than good by "pauperizing" the poor; and the term "Lady Bountiful" had by this time become pejorative, even for many women who advocated the revised paternalism More propounded and Brock demonstrated in *Charity Helstone*. Thus when Broughton's novel follows Kate into the slums she visits and describes her education in dealing with the people she meets there, it suggests that womanly sympathy and disciplined desires are not enough to qualify women for the kind of work that will fulfill their aspirations. In the course of her district visiting, Kate learns to treat working-class people as equals, to respect their privacy and not preach to them, to avoid indiscriminately handing out money, and, most of all, not to be afraid of them but to recognize their common humanity. The people Kate meets are portrayed frankly and unsentimentally, while she is gently mocked for her uninformed presuppositions about their lives and attitudes as well as her expectations of deferential treatment from them. Once she learns, partly from James and partly from experience, how to work effectively in her district, Kate is allowed to move on to greater undertakings, such as running the fever hospital during an epidemic, a feat obviously reminiscent of that most famous historical philanthropic heroine, Florence Nightingale.

Hence Broughton's "sensation novel" recognizes, implicitly endorses, and attempts to train women's ambitious as well as erotic desires by using the model of the philanthropic heroine plot. The novel rejects the notion that marriage is the only possible or appropriate vocation for women and that erotic desires, however strong and compelling, are all that women are capable of feeling, although the heroine must act on her desires sequentially rather than simultaneously. Even though the novel gives this qualified endorsement of women having and acting on ambitious desires, however, it suggests that fulfilling one's erotic desires would be better and more natural; Kate's philanthropic career, admirable as it is, seems somewhat anticlimactic, and the chastened Sister of Mercy is but a shadow of the vibrant heroine of the first half of the novel. It is significant that Broughton raises the possibility of Kate being allowed to have a philanthropic vocation and marriage. James Stanley, the philanthropic curate who directs her desires into charitable work, does fall in love with her and she does respond, although certainly with less fervor than she feels toward Dare. James, however, soon dies in the fever epidemic, repressing his erotic desires to the last and hence forcing Kate to do the same. Some philanthropic heroine novels, however, did experiment with permitting the heroine to fulfill both erotic and ambitious desires at the same time—as long as both, of course, are properly channeled, disciplined, and trained.

The Philanthropic Marriage

Two philanthropic heroine novels that do allow the heroine to satisfy both ambitious and erotic desires were modeled in part on historical popular philanthropic heroines who did not both marry and fulfill their philanthropic vocations. Mrs. Annie Emma Challice's *The Sister of Charity; Or From Bermondsey to Belgravia* (1857) utilizes Florence Nightingale's famous nursing experiences in the Crimea, while George MacDonald's *The Vicar's Daughter* (1872) uses ideas about helping the poor and the housing scheme Octavia Hill developed. In both these novels, the philanthropic heroine is allowed to marry and continue her philanthropic vocation, because her philanthropic desires are presented as part of the same desires that lead to marriage and domestic life. To do this, their authors, like Jameson and Gaskell, must represent as another version of the home the social sphere into which the heroine's ambitious desires take her.

Beatrice Lester, the title character of *The Sister of Charity,* is meant to be an exemplary philanthropic heroine. Although she eventually takes on a Nightingale-like role as a Crimean nurse, Beatrice is unlike the historical Nightingale in that she does not turn to philanthropy out of ambition or the need of "something to do"; she also does not embark on a philanthropic career because of a failed romance. Beatrice's philanthropic works instead grow out of her feminine character. Raised in almost complete isolation by a misanthropic and miserly uncle, Beatrice's devotion to aiding the poor, her antipathy to utilitarianism, and her commitment to liberal, nonsectarian religion and to Carlylean individuality seem somehow to belong naturally to her. She does not have to be tamed as was Charity Helstone, humiliated as was Rachel Curtis, or thwarted as was Kate Chester in order to become a philanthropic heroine; Beatrice Lester already is one when she first appears in the novel as an adult.

Like the "fairy princess" Charity Helstone, Beatrice inherits the fortune that enables her widespread generosity, as well as her social triumphs in Belgravia, but she inherits it at the outset of her philanthropic career in the novel not after a preparatory ordeal. It is the philanthropic work in Bermondsey that she is already engaged in, under the direction of the progressive slum doctor, Dr. M——, that brings her into contact with both the hero, the artist Eustace Neville, and her friend and ward Amy Lyle. Not only do Beatrice's charitable activities seem a natural manifestation of her domestic feminine character but they do not detract from her success as a belle of the London season; Beatrice is able to balance her visits to the slums of Bermondsey with carriage rides chaperoned by her fashionable friend, the Duchess of Ayrton, and attendance at all the major balls of the season, where she naturally creates a sensation because of her beauty, charm—and fortune. While her ambitious desires are already selfless, properly channeled, and under appropriate male professional supervision, however, Beatrice does go through a regimen in which she learns to discipline her erotic desires. She must recognize and reject the materialistic motives of the sexually attractive Major Percival, giving up her fortune but not her self to his demands, and she also represses her love for Eustace when she discovers that Amy also loves him. Stripped of her fortune and her love, Beatrice heads for the Crimea with the Sisters of Charity and becomes a heroic "angel with a lamp," the most romantic of philanthropic heroines. Eventually, after nursing the now-married but dying Amy Neville, along with soldiers from Bermondsey and Belgravia, Beatrice regains her fortune and marries Eustace—after completing her term as a war nurse—and continues her career as a philanthropist and general benefactor.

Although John Sutherland, almost the only recent critic who has mentioned Challice's novel, characterizes it as modeled on the career of Florence Nightingale, only the last fourth of the novel bears much relation to the historical Nightingale and this only to the romanticized, idealized image of the "angel with the lamp." [31] Challice's heroine is unlike the Nightingale recent biographers and scholars describe—the assertive administrator who solved supply problems, restored discipline and order to the hospital at Scutari, and waged a lifelong battle for sanitary and nursing reform. [32] Challice's Beatrice is not even portrayed as the leader of the expedition but only as one of the nurses. Thus, rather than being based on the actual life of Nightingale, the novel capitalizes on the idealized image of Nightingale as heroine that was promulgated in the periodical press, enabling the author to make her philanthropic heroine as romantic as any novelistic heroine who marries a hero and lives happily ever after.

It is significant that Beatrice never encounters the disillusionment or nitty-gritty of dealing with the poor as do the heroines in *The Clever Woman of the Family* and *Not Wisely But Too Well,* and she does not encounter squalor or chaos, even in the hospital at Scutari. The main service Beatrice renders in the military hospital is providing sympathy and listening to the stories of the wounded soldiers. When she works with the poor, she already knows how to tactfully gain their confidence and meet their needs. Challice never portrays Beatrice facing the frustration and discouragement Kate Chester experiences, and does not need to learn another dialect or to understand the social customs of the poor, as Margaret Hale must in *North and South.* While Challice's novel argues for women's independence and ability to move in spheres outside the domestic, by downplaying both the administrative and the seamy aspects of philanthropy and romanticizing the role of the heroine, it re-inscribes a rigid separate spheres model for the social sphere. Charity, linked with the purity that results from the repression of erotic desire, is part of woman's nature; female philanthropists are to be womanly and not interfere with or take over from just male authority, but their influence is crucial at all levels, from the family to the social sphere to national politics and, as repeated references in Challice's novel suggest, to empire.

Although Beatrice's natural sympathy and feminine nature are presented as her principal qualifications for the role of philanthropic heroine, she does have strong opinions and an education to back them up. Like other philanthropic heroines, she begins her career as a benevolent rural paternalist, following the direction of a model clergyman, the Reverend Mr. Lyle. Rev. Lyle, a poor but socially conscious rector, has labored for years to bring light to the Cornwall miners and to defuse their rebellious sentiments, caused by the neglect and parsimony of Beatrice's miserly uncle Sir Richard Leicester, who owns the mines and the lands on which they live. After the deaths of both Sir Richard and Mr. Lyle, Beatrice continues the work of Mr. Lyle by selecting an appropriate successor, hiring two curates to help him, and providing the money for their charitable and educational endeavors. She, however, does not remain in rural seclusion as a female paternalist, but instead she moves to London where she can more fully use her sympathy and influence to combat the rampant materialism and utilitarianism she sees as causing England's social ills. Knowledgeable about political economy, domestic and international politics, art, and religion, Beatrice freely (although sweetly) expresses her opinions, exercising sway with political and governmental sources as well as with social reform workers such as Dr. M——. Notably, it is the male villain of *The Sister of Charity,* Major Percival, who spouts the most traditional views about women's role and objects to Beatrice's opinions, believing she needs to be "tamed." Percival's views about women's role are discredited, however, not only by the exemplary Beatrice but also by the major's ultimate fate. Revealed as the disgraced and disreputable son of Sir Richard Leicester, Percival takes over his father's estate from Beatrice, abolishes all her reforms there and becomes the worst kind of tyrannical landlord and mine owner, and is finally murdered by his own accomplice. His death, however, restores her fortune and her more enlightened management of the property, and it validates her rejection of him and all his principles.

However, while Beatrice is represented as having informed opinions and great influence, her main contribution to the social sphere is still limited to her womanly influence. She inspires her future husband, the artist Eustace Neville, to develop his talent and to refuse to compromise his artistic integrity; she sacrifices her own happiness for her friend and ward Amy Lyle; she feels sympathy for destitute women, especially seamstresses and governesses, as well as the miners' wives; and she finds work and homes for individuals in need and supports institutions such as a "ragged" school and a humane insane asylum. But Beatrice does not take part in the administration of these activities and institutions; her sympathetic nursing in the Crimea heals old emotional wounds, as well as war-induced physical ones, but it does not lead her into administrative wrangling or direct intervention in official circles. When the novel ends and Beatrice finally marries the now-widowed Eustace, who has also unexpectedly inherited a fortune and a title, she enters a philanthropic partnership with him in which she fills the role of wife literally and figuratively. Thus Challice's philanthropic heroine is allowed both a philanthropic vocation and a happy romantic ending, but it is at the cost of remaining in a romanticized separate sphere, despite her informed opinions and nominal expeditions into public spaces such as Bermondsey and Scutari.

Published fifteen years later and written by a male author, George MacDonald's *The Vicar's Daughter* also uses the achievements of a historical female philanthropist as part of its fictional plot about a philanthropic heroine. As is the case with Challice's *The Sister of Charity,* however, MacDonald's novel is not based on the life of the well-known philanthropist Octavia Hill, but rather it borrows the idea of her rent collection scheme to solve the dilemma of how to combine his heroine's philanthropic vocation with marriage to the man she (apparently) loves. In other words, Hill's housing project provides MacDonald with a mechanism for simultaneously fulfilling his heroine's ambitious and erotic desires. That MacDonald, a male author and a clergyman, chose to depict an unsupervised independent woman who devotes her life to work among the poor is an indication of how acceptable the philanthropic heroine had become by the end of the 1860s, while his attempt to reconcile her ambitious and erotic desires suggests that his audience felt more comfortable with the notion of women having both kinds of desires.

Like *The Sister of Charity, The Vicar's Daughter* does not portray a heroine who needs to be trained, tamed, or supervised. Marion Clare, the philanthropic heroine of the novel, is a model that all the other characters admire and follow. Not even trained by a clergyman, although she does refer difficult cases to one occasionally, Marion is a child when she enters her philanthropic vocation. By the time the novel opens, she is already established as "Granny," a mediator, counselor, mentor, nurse, and spiritual adviser in a neighborhood so low that she is fired from a job as music teacher to a "good" family merely for living there. She seems to have neither erotic nor ambitious desires to be disciplined but to live purely for the sake of doing good, without recognition or reward.

While Marion Clare needs no training or disciplining, however, the novel's readers presumably do. MacDonald uses his philanthropic heroine to teach by example how women can be most effective in the social sphere. Although the biographical details are not at all similar, Marion is an embodiment of the principles on which Octavia Hill built her philanthropic career—exercising influence among the poor by entering into "close and healthy communication" with them as "hard-working neighbours," rather than as charitable visitors, and promoting "self-help" rather than giving alms. "My only notion of reform," wrote Hill, "is that of living side by side with people, till all that one believes becomes clear to them." [33] Like Hill, with whom MacDonald was acquainted and whom he much admired, Marion's relations with her neighbors are based on the "moral power" of "deeds which speak louder than words" and "just governing more than helping" (Hill, 27, 18). For instance, when Marion resolves quarrels among other boarders in the house where she resides, her understanding and action recall Hill's advice to would-be rent collectors or visitors:

> Consider under such a rule what deadly quarrels spring up and deepen and widen between families compelled to live very near one another, to use many things in common, whose uneducated minds brood over and over the same slight offences, when there is no one either compulsorily to separate them, or to say some soothing word of reconciliation before the quarrel grows too serious. I have received a letter from an Irish tenant actually boasting that he "would have taken a more manly way of settling a dispute," but that his neighbour "showed the white feather and retired." I have seen that man's whole face light up and break into a smile when I suggested that a little willing kindness would be a more manly way still. (Hill, 20)

Similarly, when Marion solves a domestic dispute between a man and his wife by taking them on a visit to the National Gallery, she fulfills Hill's injunction to "develop the love of beauty" among the poor (Hill, 29).

While MacDonald's Marion Clare works according to Octavia Hill's principles, as expressed in Hill's work and published writings, he does not stress the feeling of power and authority Hill claims to have found in her work. Hill repeatedly uses a vocabulary of empowerment in describing the work she advocates: she finds herself "empowered" by her role as rent collector (18); landladies have "power either of life or death, physical and spiritual" (20); she experiences an "awed sense of joy" from being "conscious of having the power to set [a rental property], even partially, in order" (27); she is a "recognized authority" (36); her court is "a wild, lawless, desolate little kingdom [she has] come to rule over" (41); and she believes herself "somewhat like an officer at the head of a well-controlled little regiment, or, more accurately, like a country proprietor with a moderate number of well-ordered tenants" (34). Hill's language calls attention to the way philanthropic work can fulfill women's ambitious desires, and her numerous published articles on her work not only promoted her ideas but also brought her into the public eye.

The narrator of MacDonald's novel, however, is not comfortable with the idea of women having ambitious desires for notoriety in the public sphere. Subtitled *An Autobiographical Story,* the first chapter of *The Vicar's Daughter* is devoted to a scene of three male professionals—the narrator Ethelwynn (Wynnie) Percivale's father and husband as well as her father's publisher—trying to overcome Wynnie's reluctance to writing the book, which is to be a sequel to her father's *The Seaboard Parish* (an earlier MacDonald novel, published in 1868). MacDonald goes to some lengths to show that Wynnie, a young wife and mother, has no desire to put herself into the public eye and that she believes she has nothing to write about. Once convinced by the three men, however, she discovers that she does have a story worth telling; besides her experiences as the wife of a promising young artist (and the kidnapping of her child by gypsies), Wynnie's narrative focuses primarily on her friend Marion Clare. Having Wynnie tell Marion's story has the effect of relieving both female characters from the problem of compromising their femininity by seeming to assert themselves, while still giving both women an outlet for properly disciplined and restrained ambitious desires.

For most of his novel, MacDonald also deflects all erotic desires onto Wynnie, a wife devoted to her husband and her children. The details MacDonald gives of Wynnie and Percivale's married life form a relatively frank and intimate (although not sexual) picture of wedded love. Late in the novel, however, he takes on the problem of Marion's erotic desires as well. Even though her energies are all devoted to her "grandchildren," Marion is the object of desire for two men in the novel, Wynnie's brother-in-law Roger Percivale and the Reverend Mr. Blackstone, a philanthropic urban clergyman who occasionally assists Marion in her work. At first Marion refuses both Roger and Mr. Blackstone because she is so immersed in her work. Like many of the philanthropic heroines, she denies having any erotic desires, and she asserts the primacy of her philanthropic vocation. In her initial refusal to Roger, Marion writes:

> If even I loved you in the way you love me, I should yet make everything yield to the duties I have undertaken. In listening to you, I should be undermining the whole of my past labours, and the very idea of becoming less of a friend to my friends is horrible to me. . . . I thank God if I have been of the smallest service to you; but I should be quite unworthy of that honour, were I for any reason to admit even the thought of abandoning the work which has been growing up around me for so many years, and is so peculiarly mine that it could be transferred to no one else.[34]

Admitting erotic desires as only a hypothetical possibility, Marion stresses the conventional opposition between "her work" and marriage. To avoid the image of the philanthropic heroine as a nun, however, MacDonald must make his heroine susceptible. Her letter and her sad demeanor suggest that, after all, she may be a real woman—one who loves a man. "Could my angel be in love?" asks Wynnie, "and with some mortal mere? The very idea was a shock, simply from its strangeness. Of course, being a woman, she *might* be in love; but the two ideas, *Marion* and *love*, refused to coalesce" (354). Like a model young Victorian lady, Marion's erotic desires are not aroused until after a man falls in love with her, but because she is a woman she must respond to a man's love, no matter how angelically asexual and devoted to her metaphorical family of "grandchildren" she may seem.

If readers wonder why Marion must choose between her work and marriage to Roger, Wynnie provides the reason: "as a married woman, she might be compelled to forsake her friends more or less, for there might arise other and paramount claims on her self-devotion. In a word, if she were to have children, she would have no choice in respect of whose welfare should constitute the main business of her life; and it even became a question whether she would have a right to place them in circumstances so unfavourable for growth and education" (365). Characterizing a woman's philanthropic vocation as "self-devotion," Wynnie reminds the reader that a woman's real duties are to her children, not only to provide for and nurture them but to raise them with the advantages due to their inherited class position.

To keep his heroine from having to make such an agonizing decision—between her "self-devoted" philanthropy and the "main business of her life," the welfare of her future children—MacDonald provides a self-proclaimed deus ex machina. In a chapter entitled "The Dea Ex," the novel's other female philanthropist, Lady Bernard (also purportedly modeled on a historical woman, the philanthropic Lady Byron),[35] solves Marion's dilemma by constructing new housing units modeled on Octavia Hill's, a solution that both provides better housing for Marion's "friends" and allows Marion to live among them with her family (in a larger house) and continue her work as a benevolent rent collector. A married Marion turns out to be an even better influence on the working classes than Marion the single woman: "what amount of her personal ministration would be turned aside from them by the necessities of her new position," explains Lady Bernard, "would be far more than made up to them by the presence among them of a whole well-ordered and growing family, instead of a single woman only" (374).

The deus ex machina MacDonald borrowed from a real-life philanthropic project designed according to the latest principles of scientific philanthropy thus permits his heroine not only to fulfill her erotic desires but to use her reproductive capacity and domestic skills to the fullest in the service of her ambitious desires. MacDonald's solution, however, still reveals the central ambivalence about women's desires that the other philanthropic heroine novels share. Octavia Hill never did marry; most of the other historical philanthropic heroines on whose lives the novels were more or less loosely based did not marry, either. Thus novels such as MacDonald's were attempting to resolve imaginatively a dilemma that most historical women in mid-Victorian England found impossible to solve: how to satisfy both erotic and ambitious desires at once, given the strictures of domestic ideology by which their lives were still in large part governed.

MacDonald's solution, that the philanthropic heroine marry and join forces with a man she meets and learns to love through her charitable work, was one that Florence Nightingale recommended:

> When two meet each other at work upon an object interesting to both,—should not this be their introduction to love? . . . There are spiritual, affectional, mental, and physical attractions. It is plain that great and even good men have had physical attractions to little and not good women. In some minds exists an attraction to great talent, without the feelings being affected. To some the affections (no other part) are attracted. *All* these attractions should meet in the two who are to be peculiarly united, but it is daily experience that it is not so. If it were, and if, though there were differences in character, there was interest for the same work, and *that good* work, then would there be a real independence for these two. They would together devote themselves to God and man, to the universe. This would secure them *all* sympathies, in the course of eternity.[36]

Nightingale's vision of an ideal marriage as based on mutual aspirations, instead of despite them, was shared by Hill and other historical women who devoted their lives to social work, but none of them seem to have been able fully to put it into practice; some were married but almost none had children.[37] That MacDonald must resort to a "dea ex" to resolve this impasse is symptomatic; while both nonliterary and novelistic representations could now recognize and even endorse female ambitious desires, the fundamental conflict between these desires and women's more "natural" erotic desires was inherent in Victorian definitions of women.

While the mid-Victorian novels that used the new convention of the philanthropic heroine show great variety in their use of that figure, all of them share this concern with how women's newly acknowledged ambitious desires could be reconciled with their presumed natural desires for love and family that legitimated their enclosure in the separate domestic sphere that underwrote the Victorian economy, as well as its political, religious, and legal systems. The convention of the philanthropic heroine endorsed women's ambitious desires, but only if these were kept within certain well-defined limits. Most of the novels countered the anxieties sparked by acknowledging these desires by demonstrating how they should be disciplined, subdued, and channeled into acceptably feminine and selfless directions. Many warned that fulfilling ambitious desires would mean the sacrifice of erotic ones, while others held out the somewhat illusory promise of fulfilling both simultaneously. However much they may argue, alongside Bessie Rayner Parkes, that women have an "inalienable right" to use all their faculties, none go so far as to suggest that men and women are equal or that women should step out of the domestic sphere to exercise these rights and faculties. The domestic sphere may be redefined and enlarged to include the space of the social and to give women a wifely and motherly role through charitable work, but the philanthropic heroine never challenges the concept of separate spheres for women and men. Nonetheless, by endorsing women's ambitious desires, however restrained and limited, public acceptance of the figure of the philanthropic heroine signaled an important shift in the definition of woman's nature that paved the way for more systemic changes in the future.

7 George Eliot's *Middlemarch*

The Failure of the Philanthropic Heroine

IN A FREQUENTLY QUOTED 1873 review of George Eliot's *Middlemarch* (1872), Florence Nightingale took the author to task for creating a noble, idealistic heroine but giving her nothing to do: "Indeed it is past telling the mischief that is done in thus putting down youthful ideals. There are not too many to begin with. There are few indeed to end with— even without such a gratuitous impulse as this to end them." [1] Nightingale's comments call attention to *Middlemarch*'s participation in the mid-nineteenth-century debate over what middle- and upper-class women properly could and should do with their time and energies. While writers such as Jameson, Maurice and his fellow lecturers, Gaskell, and the philanthropic heroine novelists of the 1860s argued explicitly or implicitly for an expanded role for middle- and upper-class women in a social sphere that included but also extended outside the home, Eliot's acclaimed novel rejects such a role for its heroine, and, as Nightingale observed, it discourages such ambitious desires on the part of young women such as Dorothea Brooke. Nightingale's criticism, however, oversimplifies Eliot's exploration of women's desires and potential occupations. By setting her novel not in the present (late 1860s and early 1870s) but in the past (early 1830s), Eliot was able to represent both the need for expanded opportunities for women and the obstacles to and limitations of her contemporaries' attempts to extend women's role into the social sphere through philanthropic social work. It is ironic that while *Middlemarch* may be Eliot's most successful novel, it chronicles the failure of the ideal represented by the philanthropic heroine Nightingale represents and Dorothea Brooke aspires to become.

In her *Middlemarch* review, Nightingale offers a philanthropic model worthy of the youthful female heroism available to Eliot in the person of her friend Octavia Hill:

> Yet close at hand, in actual life, was a woman . . . and, if we mistake not, a connection of the author's, who has managed to make her ideal very real indeed. By taking charge of blocks of buildings in poorest London, while making herself the rent-collector, she found work for those who could not find work themselves; she organised a system of visitors—real visitors; of referees—real referees; and thus obtaining actual insight into the moral or immoral, industrial or non-industrial conduct of those who seemed almost past helping . . . , she brought sympathy and education to bear from individual to individual. . . . Could not the heroine, the "sweet sad enthusiast," have been set to some such work as this?[2]

While Dorothea Brooke's plans for building cottages for agricultural laborers are suggestive of Octavia Hill's housing schemes, the fictional Dorothea is not allowed the heroic "real" work Nightingale extols—although there was ample precedent for it in novels from the previous decade. In *Middlemarch* Eliot ultimately rejects the newly available and popular philanthropic heroine Nightingale would have her choose in favor of the traditional literary romantic heroine who ends up marrying the man she loves. But by representing her romantic heroine's ambitious desires, as well as her erotic ones, in the context of male professionals' struggle for vocation, Eliot records both the possibility and the problems of using philanthropy as a solution to women's predicament.

The Philanthropic Heroine

In the late 1860s, when George Eliot began to write *Middlemarch,* the philanthropic heroine was an available convention, as we have seen, in novels and in representations of the lives of real women. Although such a model of womanhood would not have been so widely at hand and acceptable forty years earlier—during the period in which *Middlemarch* is set—the ideal of the philanthropic heroine is available to Dorothea Brooke. Dorothea, whom the narrator proclaims a victim of the "stifling oppression of [the] gentlewoman's world," experiences what by midcentury was the "fashionable feminine complaint of occupational vacuity"—she has "nothing to do."[3] Attributing such desires to a character whose present is late 1829, and who therefore lacks the possibilities for fulfilling her ambitions that were available to later women such as Octavia Hill, marks the progress midcentury feminists claimed in opportunities for women by the 1860s, a progress made possible largely through women's entry into the social sphere as philanthropic workers.[4] By mildly poking fun at what Celia Brooke calls Dorothea's "fads," however, *Middlemarch* suggests that the philanthropic heroine could become as romanticized and illusory as the beautiful romantic heroine traditionally was. Further, by forcing its heroine to choose between her philanthropic ambitions and erotic fulfillment, Eliot's novel demonstrates that as long as women are poorly educated, bound by domestic conventions, and legally powerless, philanthropy is an inadequate solution to the problems domestic ideology posed to women.

Readers often notice the way that Dorothea's "fads"—that is, her idealistic philanthropic plans—are gently mocked, especially in the first book of *Middlemarch*. No one has remarked, however, that what the young Dorothea is attempting to do is to become a philanthropic heroine—a woman whose ambitious, as well as erotic, desires are fulfilled. The prelude to *Middlemarch,* with its focus on Saint Theresa, sets up this model of a different kind of heroine, one whose heart is "beating to a national idea" until it is met by "domestic reality." The "ardour" of "later-born Theresas," we are told, "alternated between a vague ideal and the common yearning of womanhood." Throughout the prelude, language suggesting women's ambitious desires—a "national idea," a "vague ideal," an "epic life," "some long-recognisable deed"—is set against "domestic reality" and "the common yearning of womanhood"—terms that propose the fulfillment of women's erotic desires through marriage. It is ironic that while the prelude laments the modern Saint Theresa, "foundress of nothing," by 1870 England had seen the rise of a number of new Saint Theresas, including not only heroines such as Florence Nightingale and Octavia Hill but also members of Protestant sisterhoods, which were modeled on the religious communities that supposedly provided the outlet for the ambitious desires of the real Saint Theresa. When Eliot aligns women's erotic desires with "many-volumed romances of chivalry and the social conquests of a brilliant girl,"⁵ however, she may be suggesting something else—not that noble deeds are impossible for nineteenth-century women but that the ambitious desires symbolized in the story of Saint Theresa are as romanticized and as far beyond the ordinary life of most women as are chivalric romances with their brilliant, beautiful, and accomplished heroines.

Other writers at midcentury also recognized the fascination that the noble philanthropic heroine held for young women. For instance, in a book whose title—*My Life and What Shall I Do With It?*—obviously engages the question of women's vocation, Lucy F. March Phillips gives her reason for writing:

> I have read a good many of the works written on this subject, and some of them, especially the three I have named [Jameson's *Sisters of Charity, Catholic and Protestant, and The Communion of Labor,* and Maurice's *Lectures to Ladies*], with great interest and thankfulness. But when I have asked myself: If I had read these books at twenty, when I was desiring to do something for my poorer neighbours, would they have helped me? I have thought they would not; that rather they would then have set me dreaming,—not about the dull and rather dirty old woman with her chronic and incurable rheumatism who lived in the lane near,—but about the hospital of Kaiserwerth [*sic*], or the prison school of Nendorf. That the practical lectures would have crushed my wish under despair; just because they are so truly practical, whilst the work they propose would have been as much beyond my powers, as the help they offer was out of my reach. And at twenty it is hard to endure a bathos; one cannot bear to be forced back from the noble ideal to the petty reality, from saving lives and restoring hope and happiness to ideal homes, from reforming hundreds,—to making a few shy and awkward attempts to recommend neatness to one or two unteachable housewives, or

teaching half-a-dozen children to spell "cat" and "bat" week after week.[6]

Rather than choosing a sixteenth-century Catholic woman as her model
heroine, Phillips used contemporary philanthropic heroines such as Florence Nightingale and Anna Jameson. But Phillips's 20-year-old is much
like *Middlemarch*'s Dorothea Brooke, yearning after noble deeds but learning in a climactic moment that "the objects of her rescue were not to be
sought by her fancy"; instead, they lay close by in her ordinary woman's
existence (544).

   It is also significant that the projects Dorothea attempts, but fails, to
initiate in *Middlemarch* are associated with historical philanthropic heroines of the 1850s and 1860s, not the 1820s and 1830s when the novel is
set. Her interest in providing better housing for the poor is, as I have
mentioned, reminiscent of Octavia Hill's urban housing projects. But the
1850s and 1860s saw a general concern over improving nationwide housing conditions for the poor. An 1859 letter to *The English Woman's Journal,* for instance, entitled "Cottage Habitations," addresses the issue of
housing agricultural rather than urban laborers:

> Certainly the homes of our people are not the sacred and beloved
> spots they used to be; or that we, through tradition, assume they
> were. How should they be so, springing up as they do in a few
> weeks, as slightly built as the law allows; inhabited, and then
> changing their occupants, all in the course of a few months: no
> household memories can by any possibility linger about them.
> The majority present a totally different idea of a home to those
> cottages we sometimes, though rarely meet with, where an old
> man and his wife may have lived between fifty and sixty years
> in one dwelling, where all their children had been born, from
> whence they were married, or it might be buried; and where
> even their children's grandchildren come back to climb the good
> man's knee! I knew of one such here, and a more holy quiet
> seemed to come with the sunshine through that latticed window,
> framed as it was in summertime by its mantling vine, and played
> about the aged heads within. But the new railway will soon pass
> over the site of that cottage.[7]

The author of this letter identifies two factors in what she sees as the decline of cottage living—cheaply built and poorly designed new cottages as well as the coming of the railroad, which destroyed old cottages. Both are also brought up in *Middlemarch,* with Dorothea's concern for well-designed cottages and the incident of the laborers trying to stop the railroad surveyors. The author of the letter goes on to describe the moral and sanitary benefits she believes will accrue from improved, affordable cottages, and she includes detailed plans with cost estimates for building such cottages. Dorothea also draws up plans (based on a book not yet published at the time she supposedly works from it),[8] and the thoughts the narrator attributes to her suggest both high-flung ideals and the sentimentalizing of poverty revealed in the above letter: "Dorothea was in the best temper now. Sir James, as brother-in-law, building model cottages on his estate, and then, perhaps others being built at Lowick, and more and more elsewhere in imitation—it would be as if the spirit of Oberlin had passed over the parishes to make the life of poverty beautiful!" (20). Connecting Dorothea's ideas for cottages with her misreading of Sir James's motives also reinforces the visionary idealization in which the character indulges.

The facts that later in the novel Sir James does build some cottages, without an erotic or matrimonial motivation, and that the land manager and builder Caleb Garth approves of Dorothea's designs indicate that, separated from their entanglement with romantic attachments and romanticized ideals, Dorothea's plans have practical merit. Such plans were not uncommon beginning in the 1840s, following the investigations surrounding the implementation of the New Poor Law of 1834, and by the 1860s a number of women, Octavia Hill being only the most well publicized, were becoming involved in planning and building housing for the poor in both urban and rural areas. By allowing Dorothea's cottage plans to be implemented, Eliot avoids condemning women's concerns with housing. Yet by portraying Dorothea's plans in the first section of the novel as idealistic, romanticized, and entangled with a potential erotic encounter, she is also able to represent the kind of impractical youthful dreaming Phillips identified as a common effect of idealizing female philanthropists as heroines.

Another of Dorothea's projects that would have cast her as a philanthropic heroine is thwarted by the "practical" counsel of Sir James, after he has become her brother-in-law and "masculine adviser" (524). Dorothea describes her "delightful plan": "I should like to take a great deal of land, and drain it, and make a little colony, where everybody should work, and all the work should be done well. I should know every one of the people and be their friend" (380). This plan is reminiscent of the social experiments of visionaries such as Robert Owen. Eliot's readers would have known that most such experiments, including Owen's in New Harmony, Indiana, had failed. Elizabeth Barrett Browning's *Aurora Leigh* (1856), for instance, had represented the failure of such a utopian community, with the "people" turning on their philanthropic "friend," burning his ancestral home, and blinding him. But the *Middlemarch* passage makes evident Dorothea's ambitious, although altruistic, desires; she wants to "know every one of the people and be their friend." [9] When Sir James comments that "It is a pity she was not a queen" (370), he names the powerful, commanding, but benevolent heroine that Dorothea's desires call up. But, pity or no, Dorothea is not and cannot be a queen, nor can she—in the context of a novel set in 1829–30—fulfill her ambitious desires by adopting a philanthropic vocation; as Lucy F. March Phillips indicated, neither could most women even by 1870, despite the fact that many philanthropic heroines were by then available food for fantasy. In other words, although by 1870 women could act out their ambitious desires in a symbolic economy that included novels and nonfictional representations of philanthropic heroines, the fulfillment of such desires was still almost as impossible in the material economy of the 1860s as it was in 1830.

The prelude to *Middlemarch* gives several reasons for the heroine's failure to fulfill her ambitious wishes. "Domestic reality" "in the shape of uncles" suggests the constraints nineteenth-century Englishwomen, especially of the middle and upper classes, faced in their position as dependents in families headed by male relatives—fathers, husbands, brothers, or uncles. In Dorothea's case, first her uncle, then her husband, and finally her brother-in-law discourage her "plans." In an effort to be sympathetic, Celia offers the hope that "perhaps little Arthur will like plans when he grows up, and then he can help you" (380). Celia's assumption, of course, is that Dorothea must have a man—preferably a male relative—to "help" her act on her plans. When, as a young unmarried woman, Dorothea wants to build cottages, she cannot because her uncle is unwilling to spend the money on his estate. After her marriage to Mr. Casaubon, she is again prevented from building cottages or implementing other philanthropic projects because her husband either disapproves or lacks interest. Even when, as a widow, Dorothea controls her money, she is hampered by her lack of business experience as well as by the social conventions that prevent her from traveling and conducting real estate transactions by herself—despite Caleb Garth's assertion that "Mrs. Casaubon had a head for business most uncommon in a woman" (381). Sir James and her uncle "convince" Dorothea that her plan for a village and school of industry will involve too much risk (528), even though she has formed an apparently well-considered and reasonable plan.

For Dorothea to engage in "business" puts her at risk of stepping out of her place as a woman, even though Caleb Garth defines business as "skillful application of labour" rather than as financial transactions. Merely from hearing Dorothea's cottage plans mentioned, the strong and competent Mrs. Garth "half suspects" that "Mrs. Casaubon might not hold the true principle of subordination" (381). Mrs. Cadwallader, recognizing Dorothea's inclinations, suggests that by marrying the philanthropist Lord Triton she could fulfill some of her benevolent dreams (371). But whether Dorothea is allowed to act on her desires as she wishes always depends on the permission and support of her male relatives. Except as a widow, she has no control over her money (and even then, she seems to have very little); she has no training or experience in managing money or business transactions; and, by convention, she cannot with propriety by herself undertake philanthropic projects on a large scale. Further, although she attempts it, Dorothea has no grasp of the principles of political economy that in the early 1830s would result in the New Poor Law and that by the 1870s would dominate all discussions of and plans for aiding the poor through philanthropy.

The prelude also suggests that "these later-born Theresas were helped by no coherent social faith and order which could perform the function of knowledge for the ardently willing soul" (xiii). The "coherent social faith and order" here refers to Catholicism and the opportunities it had traditionally provided to women by offering a definite sphere of action and an alternative to marriage, despite lack of education or professional skills. In other words, the "coherent social faith" Catholicism's institutions granted women could substitute for the "knowledge" that enabled men to act on their ambitious desires. Dorothea is repeatedly compared to female Catholic saints in *Middlemarch,* not only Saint Theresa but also Santa Clara (150), Saint Catherine (369), and the Virgin Mary (530); the painter Naumann declares that Dorothea "should be dressed as a nun" (131). As I have suggested, the reference alludes to a midcentury phenomenon, the advent of Protestant sisterhoods.[10] Instituted primarily by High Church Anglicans, the sisterhoods were meant to offer Englishwomen the same opportunities for active service available to Catholic Sisters of Charity on the continent. The sisterhoods, however, were controversial and did not increase in number sufficiently to be an attraction to large numbers of Englishwomen. Both Nightingale and Jameson had visited and studied the work going on in Kaiserswerth and other Catholic institutions in Europe, but despite many lessons learned, neither woman advocated founding the same sort of institution in England. Even by 1870 most Englishwomen had "no coherent social faith and order" that would conveniently answer for them the question of what to do or substitute for the knowledge and skills they lacked. Rather, like Dorothea, they might feel desires to do good and to take action in the world, but they might be baffled as to how to begin or what to do. As Phillips put it:

> One enthusiastic leader bids young gentlewomen "go out into the world to work and be independent, and trust their own hearts to tell them what is womanly and pure." Now I say that such advice given to young women of average ability is simply absurd: where is the world? how are they to get into it? what shall they do when they are there worth doing? And if they were there would not the (disgracefully childish, but still somewhat pertinent) question rise up, "Were it not as well to go home again, by the dressing bell?" The fact is, they are not independent either in character or in fortune."[11]

Although dependent in character and fortune as well as regulated by "domestic reality" "in the shape of uncles" and without a "coherent social faith and order" to give form and substance to their ambitious desires, most women even in 1870 were no more in a position to become philanthropic heroines such as Saint Theresa or even Florence Nightingale than Dorothea is, and so their "vague" ideals were most often "disapproved as extravagance" (xiii).

A third obstacle to becoming a philanthropic heroine, according to the prelude, is "the common yearning of womanhood," or, as I read it, erotic desires that lead women to choose marriage and motherhood over other ambitions. The difficulty of combining active heroic philanthropy with marriage and motherhood is evident in the tradition of nuns serving as Sisters of Charity. Protestant women who sought to establish communities of philanthropic women, such as the one Sarah Scott described in *Millenium Hall,* had to deny or at least hide their sexuality in order to devote themselves exclusively to charitable works. Although Hannah More recommended charity as a vocation for married women as well, the charitable system she suggests for them is primarily a local, Lady Bountiful–like charity on a small scale; women who achieve philanthropic heroine status, like More did, were most often unmarried. And, as we have seen, most of the well-known female philanthropists at midcentury were unmarried (or at least childless).

Many nineteenth-century novelists recognized and represented the conflict between romantic, passionate desires and the ambitious desire to accomplish positive good through philanthropy. Besides the philanthropic heroines discussed in the previous chapters in this study, Charlotte Brontë's heroine in *Jane Eyre* faces the choice of marrying Rochester or becoming a missionary, and her erotic desires at last prevail. In some of the philanthropic novels of the 1860s the heroine chooses philanthropy over marriage; in others she decides to forego her philanthropic dreams to marry her hero. In a few novels, especially those written in the 1870s and later, the heroine is able to combine her erotic and ambitious desires by marrying a like-minded man or by finding a mission as a result of her marriage. Gaskell's *North and South,* with its heavily weighted marriage, allows the heroine to combine social action with marriage, although she is still subject to the rule of "uncles."

Dorothea gives up her "plans"—along with the bulk of her fortune—upon her second marriage to Will Ladislaw, sacrificing them, we are to assume, to "the common yearning of womanhood." *Middlemarch* is not so simple, however. On the one hand, using Saint Theresa, instead of some other female saint, as the model against which modern women are to be judged, is particularly suggestive, for Saint Theresa is perhaps even better known for her erotic devotion to God than she is for her work with Catholic sisterhoods. The reference to Saint Theresa, then, implies that, at least for Catholic women, becoming a philanthropic heroine could involve satisfying both ambitious and erotic desires—or that ambitious desires could themselves be erotic. The language used in Eliot's prelude to describe Saint Theresa is transparently erotic: "Theresa's passionate, ideal nature demanded an epic life: what were many-volumed romances of chivalry and the social conquests of a brilliant girl to her? Her flame quickly burned up that light fuel; and, fed from within, soared after some illimitable satisfaction, some object which would never justify weariness, which would reconcile self-despair with the rapturous consciousness of life beyond self" (xiii). Likewise, Dorothea's "ardour" carries a hint of passion, erotic desire, and pleasure. She seeks at first to fuse her erotic and ambitious desires by marrying a Miltonic husband, Casaubon, but this, of course, fails miserably. Yet because Dorothea never finds out "what to do," never discovers the object, the "plan," that she could carry out in such a way as to satisfy her "ardour," she still chooses finally to satisfy her erotic desires by marrying the man she loves.

Marrying Will Ladislaw, however, is also a complicated choice that can be read as in some sense combining ambitious and erotic desires. Because Ladislaw finally finds his vocation as a politician working for reformist causes, Dorothea has allied herself to a large, national "plan." Pat Jalland shows, for instance, how active and influential political wives were becoming in the 1860s. Wives of political figures became important to the political process by serving as managers of households from which politically involved husbands and fathers were often absent, by acting as political hostesses, by using their influence as confidantes, by working actively in election campaigns, and eventually by becoming political figures themselves. According to Jalland, the additional functions beyond being wives and mothers of women married to politicians "carried social status as well as responsibility and a sense of public usefulness."[12] Emilia Dilke, the former Frances Pattison, for instance, who some think served as one of Eliot's models for Dorothea, began by marrying a scholar much older than herself. She later married, under somewhat scandalous conditions, an important political reformer, and she became a substantial and well-known figure.[13] Although Dilke's second marriage and later notoriety occurred after *Middlemarch* was written, the coincidence illustrates the potential inherent in the position of the political wife, as *Middlemarch*'s readers would have recognized.

Read in the context of the dialectic of female desires in *Middlemarch,* Dorothea's marriage to Will Ladislaw can also be interpreted in another way. If Dorothea's progress through the novel is characterized by her search for a vocation that will fulfill her ambitious desires, as well as her erotic ones, then so is Will Ladislaw's. By displacing Dorothea's failed vocational desires onto Will, a feminized male figure who finally finds his vocation, and then marrying the two, *Middlemarch* marks the failure of volunteer philanthropy to satisfy women's needs in the face of the nineteenth-century drive toward professionalized social work, while at the same time it preserves the category of benevolent charity as a social virtue removed from the market.

The Conflict over Vocation

In the nineteenth century the major change in philanthropic practice that posed a challenge to women's traditional charitable prerogatives was the gradual professionalization of the social work that had been the province of philanthropy. Both Anna Jameson's philanthropic writings and Elizabeth Gaskell's novel *North and South* worked to construct the social sphere in such a way that women would have access to and authority within it; as we have seen, however, women's efforts were always contested by male professionals who also wanted to dominate social spaces and practices and who attempted to exclude, or at least exert control over, female philanthropists. Crucial to this struggle was the concept of vocation.

The term "vocation," from the Latin "to call," was initially a religious term connoting a divine call to a religious life or mission. Under Catholicism, with its monasteries and convents, either men or women could have a vocation. Although the term also early took on a secular meaning, applying to any sort of occupation or employment, it still carried the sense of work pursued not simply for money but rather from some inner sense of mission. By the nineteenth century the term vocation was closely linked to the idea of a profession. For instance, Hannah More used the words "vocation" and "profession" interchangeably in claiming charity as a proper occupation for women.

Recent sociologists identify the notion of vocation as key to the formation of the modern professions during the nineteenth-century. "The vocational orientation," writes Magali Larson, includes "a sense of work as self-realization and a sense of duty to one's calling deeper than just compliance with a set of standards." An occupation with a "vocational orientation," claims Larson, is one that is relatively freely chosen, as well as interesting and creative; hence it suggests that the work itself has an intrinsic value. The idea of work as a calling, connected to an "ideal of service," functioned to distinguish the professional from other occupational groups perceived to work primarily for wages or profit. Thus emphasizing the ideology of vocation enabled the professional to achieve status and wealth while appearing to be antimarket, or outside of the market economy.[14]

Numerous critics of *Middlemarch* have noticed the significance of vocational struggles in the novel. Mary Ellen Doyle documents the religious language surrounding Mr. Lydgate's "call" to a medical vocation; she concludes that since Dorothea's aims, although equally noble, are less specific and therefore less believable, her failure to achieve them is not tragic, whereas Lydgate's failure is.[15] Although several others address the issue of vocation in the novel, only Alan Mintz's *George Eliot and the Novel of Vocation* contains a fully elaborated historical treatment of the nineteenth-century notion of vocation and its manifestation in Eliot's fiction. Mintz focuses on Eliot's "spiritualization of work" as "a secularized version of the Puritan beliefs that a man is called by God to a specific worldly vocation and that his success in it is a token of salvation." Mintz also considers the notion of vocational professionalism in the time in which *Middlemarch* is set:

> What attracted George Eliot was the thought that at a certain moment in history—on the eve of reform—there existed the possibility that vast reservoirs of ambitious energy and practical knowledge could be released on behalf of the great causes of the age: scientific discovery, philanthropy and benevolence, political reform and humanistic learning. If a man could undertake the methodical yet ambitious pursuit of one of these high goals, then the emerging specialized forms of work did indeed hold out promise.

Mintz's analysis of the way vocation works in *Middlemarch* is astute, and he makes an attempt to consider how gender functions in relation to vocation as well. "Ironically," he writes, "the character who stands firmly at the symbolic center of the novel has no profession whatever. As a woman, Dorothea is not allowed the direct access to the world possible for men." But, concludes Mintz, "Dorothea's womanhood, instead of being an anomaly, is simply the most extreme example of the variety of constraints and contingencies that frustrate the urge to alter the world." I contend, however, that Dorothea is not merely an "extreme example" of the ways anyone's vocational desires may be frustrated by social constraints; I argue instead that, given the context of nineteenth-century struggles for professionalism, Dorothea's—and other women's—vocational desires had to be suppressed in order for male professionals to consolidate their economic and class positions.[16]

N. N. Feltes gives an even more sophisticated and historically informed reading of *Middlemarch*. In his *Modes of Production of Victorian Novels,* Feltes recognizes that by the middle of the nineteenth century, "vocation" had been subsumed by "profession," which now signified, in effect, a set of "organizational ideological practices." He demonstrates on the basis of Eliot's notebooks and her treatment of Lydgate that she was aware of the nature of the internal struggle within the medical profession. However, claims Feltes, Eliot emphasized the vocation or sense-of-calling aspect in her treatment of Lydgate and the medical profession in *Middlemarch* in order to "ignore those historical features which would deny and prevent [the] equivalency" of Dorothea's vocational quest. Feltes here identifies a strategy that was used not only by Eliot but also by Octavia Hill and numerous other nineteenth-century female philanthropists as well as by male professionals.[17]

Stressing the spiritual element of their work enabled female philanthropists to extend their activities into the public spaces of the social sphere without seeming to assert themselves. Hill, for instance, who served alongside a number of male professionals as the only female council member for the Charity Organization Society, always insisted that she was "called" to her work. Using the religious sense of vocation to characterize philanthropic work that was becoming more and more professionalized, Hill, Nightingale, and many other female philanthropists capitalized on the double sense of the word "vocation." Likewise, however, male professionals such as F. D. Maurice and his associates also approached their work with "huge moral seriousness," emphasizing the spiritual and altruistic side of their paid professional work.[18] It was necessary for professionals to insist on this "ideal of service," explains Larson, because professionals were selling services rather than products. In the absence of tangible products, professional practitioners needed to convince the public they could be trusted to control the terms of their own work. In other words, since it was difficult for professionals to prove "good results," patients, clients, and parishioners needed to believe that the professional was more interested in their welfare than their money.[19] Of course service untainted by market values was also supposedly the chief characteristic of women in the home and in the social spaces they inhabited as charitable workers. Thus both unpaid but serious female philanthropists and paid male professionals had important reasons to claim the concept of vocation for themselves.

In *Middlemarch,* however, it is the professional's wife who tries to taint the service ideal with market values. While Lydgate sees his profession in terms of the people he can help and the scientific discoveries he can make, his wife, Rosamond, views his professional skill as a commodity to be traded for wealth and status. Rather than depicting his rise to wealth and position on the basis of his professional expertise, *Middlemarch* portrays Lydgate as losing both money and social prestige. By projecting the desire to capitalize on a professional vocation onto the daughter of a wealthy tradesman, Eliot's novel ensures the purity of Lydgate's "calling" and blames the acquisitive middle-class Rosamond for his professional failure. Rosamond imagines that by refusing to share Lydgate's financial woes and keeping scientific equipment out of her home, she fulfills her domestic role of preserving the home from the market. Instead, of course, she attempts to barter Lydgate's professional status to improve her economic and social standing. Had Lydgate married Dorothea with her "pure" ambitious desires, *Middlemarch* implies, he could have realized his professional aspirations to achieve professional and scientific eminence. Even though Dorothea has her own sense of vocation, she does not represent a threat to Lydgate or any other male professional because her feminine ambitious desires, unlike Rosamond's, are characterized as exclusively selfless and altruistic. Just as important, however, are the facts that Dorothea does not have (and cannot seem to get) professional training and that she is repeatedly hampered in her efforts to devote herself to philanthropic activities on any regular, systematic basis; nor, of course, could she hope to be paid for her services. Dorothea is, therefore, an amateur not a professional.

As the many critics who equate Dorothea's and Lydgate's quest for vocation continue to demonstrate, it was difficult to tell the difference between the spiritualized vocation considered appropriate to women and the professionalized sense of vocation that male professionals claimed. Feltes posits that Eliot fudged the difference (at least partly) deliberately.[20] If male professionals' vocation looked so much like women philanthropists', his argument suggests, male professionals needed another way to distinguish themselves in order to consolidate their monopoly over the social sphere. Even if women could claim vocation, they could still be classed as amateurs. Thus for professionals engaged in the struggle to prove their superior authority and worth over other, "nonprofessional," practitioners, it became critical to exclude amateurs, especially unpaid female philanthropists, from professionalized vocations.

Amateurs and Professionals

Middlemarch's Dorothea, as we have seen, then, is an amateur in search of a vocation that will make her a philanthropic heroine similar to the professionalized female philanthropists that Nightingale and Hill represented. Although Feltes brings up the issue of the amateur in relation to the women writers against whom Eliot needed to position herself to be considered a professional author, he does not consider the way Dorothea's amateurish philanthropic activities are positioned not only against the male professionals in *Middlemarch* but also implicitly against a new breed of professionalized female philanthropists, as Nightingale's linking of Dorothea and Octavia Hill suggests.

Octavia Hill can be called a professionalized philanthropist because she made her philanthropic projects her full-time occupation; she took pains to train herself; she held herself and the volunteers who worked with her to strict standards; and she came to be recognized as an expert in an identifiable field of social work. As we have seen, Hill believed that women who were to engage in philanthropic work should study political economy. Jane Lewis observes that Hill "felt that she was espousing a radically different approach and attitude towards the poor although in *practice* there were significant continuities between the well-off-lady-doing-good and Octavia Hill's visitors." Hence Hill had "a contempt for the traditional amateurism of ladies. It mattered not that her workers were volunteers, they were expected to develop expertise in the law relating to housing and the complexities of the London rating system, as well as in keeping accounts."[21]

Dorothea's search for "something to do" includes some of the conventional Lady Bountiful charitable activities against which Hill positioned herself. She visits and prays with the sick (3), founds an infant school in Tipton (4), pays charitable visits to the village school in Lowick (555), arranges for and purchases a new bell for the school (341, 534), and provides sympathy and flannel to the cottagers (555). All these activities are characteristic of the traditional Lady Bountiful, and, pursued regularly, with a system, they could constitute the "vocation" or "profession" Hannah More recommended to women. Dorothea fits More's prescription for women in several ways, including her plain dress, her worries about vanity, and her "giving up." But *Middlemarch* spurns More's kind of vocation for its heroine:

> With some endowment of stupidity and conceit, she might have thought that a Christian young lady of fortune should find her ideal of life in village charities, patronage of the humbler clergy, the perusal of "Female Scripture Characters," . . . and the care of her soul over her embroidery in her own boudoir—with a background of prospective marriage to a man who, if less strict than herself, as being involved in affairs religiously inexplicable, might be prayed for and seasonably exhorted. From such contentment poor Dorothea was shut out. (17)

"Poor" Dorothea, with her "nature altogether ardent, theoretic, and intellectually consequent," must have something more to do than village charities—particularly because such charities, at least in Lowick, are shown to be superfluous. Dorothea's wish that she had found her new home "in a parish which had a larger share of the world's misery, so that she might have had more active duties in it" (17) is reminiscent of Lucy Aikin's comments on the influence of Hannah More's advocating charity as a woman's profession: "a positive demand for misery was created by the incessant eagerness manifested to relieve it."[22]

Using the adjective "poor" to describe Dorothea is of course ironic, but it has another meaning as well. Dorothea is meant to be pitied not because she is not content with being an underutilized Lady Bountiful but because while she is "enamoured of intensity and greatness" (2), with ambitious desires to be able to "justify by the completest knowledge" "the thing which seemed to her best," she is "struggling in the bands of a narrow teaching" and "hemmed in by a social life which seemed nothing but a labyrinth of petty courses, a walled-in maze of small paths that led no whither" (17). Unlike the training the professionalized female philanthropists of Eliot's day advocated, Dorothea has had a superficial education in accomplishments and "ladies-school literature" (14)—hardly social theory and political economy. By continually naming the books Dorothea has been reading, the narrator emphasizes the amateurish, dilettantish nature of Dorothea's understanding of the social world.

Hence when Dorothea contemplates philanthropic projects on a grander scale than village charities, "everything seems like going on a mission to a people whose language I don't know" (18). Rather than referring to the customs and dialect of the poor, however, as we might expect in Gaskell's *North and South,* the "language" Dorothea does not know is political economy. As a young woman, Dorothea is "twitted with her ignorance of political economy, that never-explained science which was thrust as an extinguisher over all her lights" (10). As a widow, her erotic and romantic desires for Will Ladislaw get in the way of her acquiring an understanding of this key facet of the professionalized philanthropy that could make her a modern philanthropic heroine who accomplishes a "long-recognisable deed":

> there were various subjects that Dorothea was trying to get clear upon, and she resolved to throw herself energetically into the gravest of all. She sat down in the library before her particular little heap of books on political economy and kindred matters, out of which she was trying to get light as to the best way of spending money so as not to injure one's neighbours, or—what comes to the same thing—so as to do them the most good. Here was a weighty subject which, if she could but lay hold of it, would certainly keep her mind steady. Unhappily her mind slipped off it for a whole hour; and at the end she found herself

reading sentences twice over with an intense consciousness of many things, but not of any one thing contained in the text. (555)

The repeated references to Dorothea's ignorance of political economy are not the only parts of *Middlemarch* that pointedly connect her to but also distinguish her from philanthropic heroines such as Octavia Hill. Certain phrases and concepts, for instance, occur both in Hill's writings and in descriptions of Dorothea in *Middlemarch*. In *Homes of the London Poor,* Hill writes of her work with poor tenants as "truly a wild, lawless, desolate little kingdom" she has "come to rule over." [23] Dorothea, too, claims her "little kingdom, where I shall give laws" (253). [24] This sense is reinforced in Dorothea's description of her planned utopian community, which she describes as "a little colony, where everybody should work, and all the work should be done well. I should know every one of the people and be their friend" (380). Dorothea's stress on everyone working was, of course, a basic tenet of Hill's social philosophy. It was her practice always to offer work instead of charity to the poor and even to withhold relief if the work was not done. [25] In a letter to Hill, John Ruskin interpreted her stated determination to "raise the poor without gifts" as meaning not "to stop the current of charity but to direct that current to the giving of employment." [26]

Further, Dorothea's goal of knowing "every one of the people [so as to] be their friend" is straight out of Hill's teachings: "For, firstly, my people are numbered; not merely counted, but known, man, woman, and child. . . . Think of what this mere fact of *being known* is to the poor!" writes Hill in *Homes of the London Poor*. Once the poor are known, "there is the individual *friendship* which has grown up from intimate knowledge, and from a sense of dependence and protection" (emphasis added). In an 1871 essay, Hill also explained that her goal was to make the management of urban courtyards like the relation of the landlord, "who holds dominion over the neat cottage, with its well-stocked garden; over the comfortable farm-house; over broad, sloping parks, and rich farm-lands" and who would "think it shameful to receive the rents from his well-managed estates in the country, year by year, without some slight recognition of his tenantry—at least on birthdays or at Christmas." The one reform Dorothea does succeed in is convincing her uncle Brooke to become such a landlord to the tenants she "knows" in the way Hill recommends. While these beliefs and practices were by no means unique to Hill, the similarities are enough to situate Dorothea's efforts at finding a philanthropic vocation within the context of the projects accomplished by the female philanthropists of Eliot's day. Yet Dorothea, with the "right" aims and methods, succeeds at almost nothing.[27]

Despite Dorothea's noted failures to implement her "plans," however, one of her philanthropic projects does at least come close to fruition; she nearly replaces Mr. Bulstrode as the sponsor and codirector of the New Hospital. This project is worth noting because, more than any of Dorothea's other, more forward-looking schemes, it has a connection with traditional women's philanthropy that makes it seem acceptable to Middlemarch society. Even before the eighteenth century, wealthy women had frequently endowed hospitals, almshouses, and similar institutions, and they had exercised some control in their direction. In *Middlemarch,* of course, Bulstrode has made his position as the largest donor one of considerable power in the town. Although as a woman Dorothea would not succeed to all Bulstrode's directorial positions, presumably she would, as chief benefactress, still have a say in the direction of the hospital. Even before she is asked to become the hospital's primary contributor, Dorothea makes a substantial subscription and visits there often. By becoming a hospital visitor—another common nineteenth-century female philanthropic practice—Dorothea presumably could promote cleanliness and morality as well as exercise (benevolent) power over the poor patients.[28]

Not only is the position of benefactor to the hospital a potentially powerful one but it would also involve Dorothea in one of the newest and most important philanthropic movements—sanitation. As the narrator comments dryly, *Middlemarch* is set in "that unsanitary period" (165) before the cholera epidemics of the 1830s and 1840s led to extensive sanitary reforms—to which many female philanthropists contributed. The New Fever Hospital, as Lydgate and Bulstrode have conceived it, is designed as a measure to help prepare for a cholera epidemic (441). The reader, aware of the history of the sanitation movement, might well predict a grand philanthropic career for Dorothea as the benefactor of this hospital.

However, as with all her other projects, Dorothea is finally unable to act on her benevolent plan for hospital reform, because of Lydgate's professional failure. Since as a woman she does not have the professional education and expertise Lydgate has, she can aspire to being no more than "an amateur in medicine," similar to Mrs. Cadwallader (61). To realize the farseeing goals she and Lydgate have discussed, Dorothea must depend on Lydgate as medical director for the hospital. In other words, Dorothea's potential vocation is preempted by a man's vocational failure. Once again, "domestic reality" "in the shape of uncles" has appeared to thwart the philanthropic heroine and to reinforce her status as an amateur, or a dabbler. As she explains to Will Ladislaw, "knowledge passing into feeling" (156)—instead of into poems or other products of vocational desires—is what she experiences in all her attempts to accomplish some kind of noteworthy good. "I have never carried out any plan yet" (566) is Dorothea's summary of her search for vocation.

Will Ladislaw

If Dorothea is made an amateur in comparison both to male professionals such as Lydgate and, implicitly, to the professionalized female philanthropists of Eliot's day, so is, throughout much of the novel, Will Ladislaw. Although Dorothea (and the reader for her) experiences frustration at not being able to find a vocation, *Middlemarch* is unequivocal about the need for men to have work to define themselves. Along with Fred Vincy, Ladislaw is the one young man in the novel who has not yet had his "moment of vocation" (98), and he is characterized as "dilettantish and amateurish" (132). To be a dilettante and an amateur in the world of Middlemarch is also to be feminized. As Dorothea's uncle Mr. Brooke says (with unintended irony aimed at himself), "there is a lightness about the feminine mind—a touch and go—music, the fine arts, that kind of thing—they should study those up to a certain point, women should; but in a light way, you know" (43).

Many critics have noticed, with scorn, disappointment, or approval, that Will Ladislaw is a feminized hero. Karen Chase details the textual evidence for his feminization:

> What informs so much of the common recoiling from Will is that he fails to be an impressive man. The question one might ask, only half facetiously, is how he impresses as a woman. In the

manuscript George Eliot had written that his "curves of lip and chin were scarcely shaded by hair even of the shaven sort," and in the published novel, Will is referred to as the "slim young fellow with his girl's complexion." Dorothea defends him as "a creature who entered into every one's feelings, and could take the pressure of their thought instead of urging his own with iron resistance." Will, in other words, is valued as a receptacle for Dorothea's energies, and quite apart from the startling sexual imagery, it is clear that Will—in his various "attitudes of receptivity"—often plays a role that had traditionally been reserved for the heroine of fiction.

Chase also points out that "it is Will's descent through 'two generations of rebellious women,' his 'matrilineal genealogy,' that determines his most important personal inheritance." Dorothea "blends his image with the image of his grandmother Julia that survives in a miniature, and if this does not sufficiently confuse the boundaries of gender, we may recall that Julia has been said to have a 'masculine' face." "It seems clear that George Eliot is wilfully *dissolving* a traditional sexual typology," concludes Chase.[29]

It is ironic, however, that the feminized dilettante Ladislaw finally does find his vocation through his work for that other ridiculous dilettante, Mr. Brooke. Chase explains the similarity between the two men as an example of "the process of evolution."[30] However, there is a key difference between them that complicates Chase's reading—the difference of class. Mr. Brooke, of course, belongs to the landed gentry and so is the one category of man in *Middlemarch*—the category to which Fred Vincy believes he is most qualified to belong—that does not strictly need to be professional. While Casaubon might be said to have two professions, clergyman and scholar, and Sir James is arguably working to become something of an agricultural professional, for them a profession, if not a vocation, is optional. So while Mr. Brooke's dilettantism is portrayed as rather ridiculous, it does not take away from his stature in the community or, most important, from his authority as a father figure and landowner. By contrast, Ladislaw's marginal class status is, if anything, overdetermined. Without any income except through the charity of Casaubon, descended from corrupt, possibly Jewish entrepreneurs on one side and from a Polish music master on the other, Will has only his education—and his potential profession—to qualify him as a gentleman.[31]

While Will's feminine characteristics suggest a difficulty with finding a vocation, however, his relative classlessness allies him with the new professional man, as his friendship with Lydgate suggests. According to Larson's analysis, a "move by merit against birth and patronage" characterizes the rise of the professional class and "was closely connected to the political fortunes of the middle classes and, in England, to the electoral reform of 1832."[32] Thus Will Ladislaw is in a sense a perfect representative of the new professional, a classless man who finds a place through merit rather than birth, a place that specifically involves him in attaining political power for himself and for other "classless" men, meaning, of course, men not of the landed class.

George Eliot's readers would also have known that Ladislaw's choice of profession, as writer, politician, and reformer, would involve him in a movement that would lead not only to the 1832 Reform Bill but also to the 1867 Reform Bill that enfranchised working-class men as well. And, since there was an important attempt to include women's suffrage in the 1867 Reform Bill, some readers might also associate Will's career as a professional reformer with the cause of women. Additionally under the umbrella of reform, of course, would be the social causes for which women philanthropists worked throughout the century. So, in one sense, Will is at least connected to the philanthropic heroines Dorothea is not allowed to become.

Will Ladislaw, then, is similar to Dorothea because he is a feminized dilettante and is allowed to find the vocation she is not permitted. When I suggest that Dorothea's vocational desires are displaced onto Will, I am articulating something Dorothea is represented as doing throughout *Middlemarch*. After her first meeting with Ladislaw, she is already defending his inability to decide on a profession in terms that suggest she is thinking as much of her own search as of his: "'Perhaps he has conscientious scruples founded on his own unfitness,' said Dorothea, who was interesting herself in finding a favourable explanation. 'Because the law and medicine should be very serious professions to undertake, should they not? People's lives and fortunes depend on them'" (54). The focus on "conscientious scruples" and the emphasis on moral seriousness are, of course, far more characteristic of Dorothea than they are of Ladislaw at this point; clearly she is projecting her feelings and ideas onto him. Even when they are not discussing vocation, Dorothea perpetually identifies herself with Will: "I notice that you like to put things strongly," she says; "I myself often exaggerate when I speak hastily" (154). Ladislaw is also identified with Dorothea by things he does that Dorothea would like, but is not allowed, to do—such as sorting Mr. Brooke's papers and, especially, "mov[ing] about freely" among the poor (147). Will even has his own utopian philanthropic scheme that he considers pursuing (552). The many ways Dorothea identifies herself and is identified with Ladislaw lend credence to the notion that Ladislaw not only becomes Dorothea's vocation as her husband but also that the text projects her vocational desires onto him.

By projecting Dorothea's ambitious desires onto a rising young political reformer who is, by virtue of both his talent and his "classlessness," representative of the new professional man, *Middlemarch* acknowledges that women's vocational dreams, however "ardent," have little chance of succeeding in a society increasingly dominated by the expert—unless they, too, become experts, as did Nightingale, Hill, and the other mid-century philanthropic heroines. If women become professionalized experts, even as philanthropists, they occupy a masculine position, which in nineteenth-century England threatens the realization of their erotic or romantic desires. The only way the novel can resolve this dilemma is by creating a male character such as Will Ladislaw. Then the heroine's ambitious desires can be projected onto him, while she can still share them by becoming one with him in marriage.

Will Ladislaw is, then, as a number of critics have noticed, a "woman's man."[33] In other words, Ladislaw is neither wholly masculine nor feminine but rather is an undecidable figure on which to pin both the heroine's erotic and her ambitious desires. At the end, purged of ambitious desires, the figure of Dorothea remains the repository of values that are both outside history—"unhistoric acts"—and outside a market economy—"*incalculably* diffusive"; yet they still contribute to the "growing good of the world" (578). By memorializing such "fine issues" in a novel, Eliot makes visible the "hidden life" and takes us to visit the "unvisited tomb" of the many nineteenth-century women who were unable to become philanthropic heroines. In so doing, *Middlemarch* works to preserve the beneficent influence women were believed to exercise through one-to-one contact with family members and the poor, in the face of male professionals' challenge to women's traditional philanthropic prerogatives.

Middlemarch, of course, was not alone in trying to retain a sense of the value of women's one-to-one contacts, even as England increasingly began to turn to professional and legislative, rather than philanthropic, solutions to social problems in the latter half of the nineteenth century. The whole point of Octavia Hill's rent collection scheme, for example, was to use—in an organized system—the influence of educated, refined "ladies" to reform the poor. In 1883, in her "Preface to the First Edition" of *Homes of the London Poor,* Hill reflected on the place of the kind of work she pioneered with her housing projects now that the government seemed likely to take legislative action on the problem of urban housing: "Might I then retire . . . and leave the larger work to statesmen and town councillors and vestrymen? why reprint, now of all times, these sketches of tiny schemes and small personal endeavour?" Answering her own question, Hill writes, "There will be no retreat for you yet, even if all outside buildings were put to rights tomorrow. It would simplify your work; it would not do away with the need of it." She explains: "The peoples' homes are bad, partly because they are badly built and arranged; they are tenfold worse because the tenants' habits and lives are what they are. Transplant them to-morrow to healthy and commodious homes, and they would pollute and destroy them. There needs, and will need for some time, a reformatory work which will demand that loving zeal of individuals which cannot be had for money, and cannot be legislated by Parliament." Like *Middlemarch,* Hill's *Homes of the London Poor* intends to convince the public that there is, and will always be, a need for unpaid, nonprofessional (although organized and partly professionalized) female philanthropic work, even though the separation between professionalized social work and casual acts of charity became wider and more strict as the century wore on and government took over more and more responsibility for social welfare.[34]

Thus, as in Gaskell's *North and South,* the marriage at the end of *Middlemarch* is freighted with consequences for women and their participation in the social sphere. Although the novel represents the difficulty of becoming an idealized philanthropic heroine, by marrying Dorothea to Will Ladislaw, *Middlemarch* still hopes to offer ordinary, nonheroic women a social role of "incalculable" value. But the value of women's influence must remain even more "incalculable" than that of the male professionals' service, which of course is assigned a value. This effectively removes nonprofessional women from competition with male professionals, allowing them to "marry," or work side by side in the social sphere without directly challenging conventional male and female roles but also without accomplishing "long-recognisable deeds."

Hence most readers of the novel have found unsatisfying the marriage that ends *Middlemarch*. This dissatisfaction is even acknowledged in the text, when in the finale we are told that "many who knew [Dorothea] thought it a pity that so substantive and rare a creature should have been absorbed into the life of another. . . . But no one stated exactly what else that was in her power she ought rather to have done" (576). In 1829–30 not much else would have been "in the power" of most women; by 1870 the ideal of the philanthropic heroine was available, but it was still not "in the power" of the majority of women, who continued to lack expert training, freedom to move about freely, control of money, and legal equality. I believe that part of the feeling of dissatisfaction with the ending of *Middlemarch* comes from George Eliot's sense that, in the face of the claim of male professionals to control the social sphere and in the absence of the kind of education, opportunity, and legal status that would allow women to meet those men on equal ground, philanthropy was no longer an adequate solution to the problem of what middle- and upper-class women were to do. Realizing ambitious desires by becoming a philanthropic heroine, although possible, typically involved the sacrifice of erotic fulfillment, while fulfilling erotic desires through marriage most often meant giving up any ambitious desires for "long-recognisable deeds" and settling for "unhistoric acts."

Most feminist critics of *Middlemarch* note that, like Hannah More, Marian Evans, the woman behind the author George Eliot, was able to achieve the public success she denies her heroine. And, unlike More, Evans seems also to have achieved erotic fulfillment through her liaison with George Lewes. Evans was able to do this partly by projecting her professional ambitions onto a created male figure—George Eliot—while assigning her erotic desires to Marian Lewes. Splitting her desires between George Eliot and Marian Lewes, in other words, enabled her to occupy the position of a male professional.[35] But the pseudonym, like the unsatisfying ending of *Middlemarch*, memorializes the difficulty that nineteenth-century women faced in realizing their desires, and it marks the failure of idealizing heroines, romantic or philanthropic, to overcome that difficulty.

Conclusion

As I was finishing the manuscript for this book, our university's theater department staged a production of the English playwright Sarah Daniels's *The Gut Girls* (1989).[1] This play, which is set in turn-of-the-century Deptford, indicates the continuing relevance of my investigation of representations of women philanthropists. The protagonists are four working-class girls employed in the gutting sheds of a large meat-processing operation who are "rescued" by a woman philanthropist who finds them jobs as domestic servants when the sheds are shut down. Literally mired in blood and guts, the "gut girls" work in the worst imaginable conditions and fulfill all the nineteenth-century stereotypes about mill girls: they are loud, vulgar, and aggressive; they wear ludicrous hats but no underwear; they swear and drink; and even men are afraid of them. This late-twentieth-century feminist play makes heroines out of these unlikely characters. Their independence, individuality, streetwise intelligence, and bawdy sexuality are what make them appealing, rather than appalling, to a twentieth-century audience. The end of the play, which shows all the girls reintegrated into more "proper" and passive domestic roles, is meant to provoke a sense of loss and sadness, if not outrage, from the audience.

In Daniels's hands, the philanthropist Lady Helena, unlike the sympathetically portrayed gut girls, becomes almost villainous.[2] Although she is made to appear well-intentioned, Lady Helena is mocked for her naive, snobbish, and self-interested attempts to "help" the working-class heroines. While she does visit them in their horrifying workplace and tries to see them as individuals, her goal is to remake them into a version of respectable middle-class womanhood by teaching them to be "ladylike" and fitting them for the role of domestic servants. The audience, of course, immediately recognizes that to remove the girls from the gutting sheds, however horrible the conditions, is to take from them their autonomy and place them in a subordinate position where their every movement is subject to surveillance. Not only their individuality but also their lively working-class cultural rituals and relationships must be suppressed as they learn to conform to genteel middle-class values.

Daniels's view of the woman philanthropist is, of course, different from the perspective of the eighteenth- and nineteenth-century women writers I have been discussing. Her play does, however, show how philanthropy offered a sense of usefulness and power to middle- and upper-class women. For Lady Helena, one result of her efforts to retrain and mold working- class women is to enhance her own sense of accomplishment and importance. The play does acknowledge her altruistic intentions and her oppression at the hands of men of her own class, but it portrays the woman philanthropist as (unwittingly) abusing the power she holds over other women by virtue of her class position. Daniels is right that the personal gains of women philanthropists were in some ways achieved at the expense of working-class women—and men. My point is, however, that despite the power dynamics of such relationships between charitable women and the less fortunate people they aided and patronized, philanthropy did accomplish something for women even of the working classes. Aside from its specific effects—monetary or material aid or providing jobs (and historically these were often more appreciated than in Daniels's play) for working-class people and affording a sense of power and fulfillment for the female philanthropists—women's philanthropy contributed to British culture a new sense of what women of all classes, cultures, and races desired and were capable of attaining. The sadness one feels at the end of a play such as *Gut Girls* is for the potential missed in the women of all classes. This is a regret generated by the underlying belief that most contemporary viewers, both women and men, have that women do want and need and can achieve success and happiness outside a narrowly defined domestic existence. This assumption, which has come to be self-evident at least among most late-twentieth- and early-twenty-first-century viewers and readers, was in large part created and naturalized by representations of women philanthropists acting in socially useful capacities outside their homes. While Daniels's play makes a different point, its subject matter indicates how current the discussion of women's philanthropy still is; I argue that it is also crucial for a historical understanding of our culture's definitions of and attitudes toward gender and gender roles.

This study has been concerned with questioning what seemed in the nineteenth century a natural connection between the activities of the domestic sphere and volunteer philanthropic work. Examining some of the cultural representations and negotiations that made this connection seem natural has made it possible to account, at least in part, for certain important changes in the way women and their roles were—and are—perceived. Specifically, representations of women's philanthropy helped to naturalize women's ambitious desires and to contest the notion that women could be defined only by their sexuality. Thus, while the domestic ideology of separate spheres for men and women has had enormous force over the past three centuries, these representations of women performing philanthropic work reveal one of the contradictions within this ideology that changed the way it organizes human relations.

Understanding how change occurs—and how literary works contribute to it—has been one of my central concerns in this project. Although feminists for some time now have borne witness to the limitations domestic discourse has imposed on women, the overwhelming majority of women in the eighteenth and nineteenth centuries did not resist or even question its prescriptions—and many still do not. Yet assumptions about what women can and should do have changed over the past three hundred years, despite women's general lack of resistance, partly because cultural representations of women's philanthropy enabled even nonresisting women to imagine possibilities for themselves that transcended the limitations their confinement within a narrow domestic sphere caused.

Both philanthropy and novels were thus essential to the process of changing domestic ideology's definition of women and of social relations generally.

Literary critics in recent years have paid a great deal of attention to the novel's role in establishing the hegemony of the middle-class values that underwrite a capitalist economy. Alongside novelistic discourse, however, grew up a philanthropic discourse that both contributed to and challenged novelistic conventions. Philanthropy, therefore, is important not only as an aspect of social history but as a powerful discourse that helped to shape eighteenth- and nineteenth-century subjectivity as well as literary forms. Philanthropic discourse, which borrowed some of its terms from literature, particularly the novel of sentiment, helped to determine the shape of novelistic plots, the attributes of virtuous characters, and the configuration of relations among people of different social classes. Philanthropic discourse, as we have seen, also provided the terms for representing desires that were in tension with the novel's insistence on marriage as the guarantor of both social and aesthetic resolution.

Although contemporary writers such as Daniels still occasionally find the representation of women philanthropists useful, philanthropic discourse was especially important for women writers in eighteenth- and nineteenth-century England. By the middle of the eighteenth century, writing novels that focused on domestic concerns had come to seem an acceptable and natural occupation for respectable women. Because philanthropic discourse encompassed aspects of the privatized domestic sphere and the public spheres of politics, economics, and social theory, using its terms provided women writers a way of participating in these more public discourses, which in turn contributed to their being taken more seriously as artists and professionals. By retaining the domestic focus of both novelistic and philanthropic discourse, women writers were often able to envision and represent alternative models for society that ensured women's participation. Hannah More's refashioned version of traditional paternalism, for instance, replaced political economy with a woman-driven philanthropic gift economy, while Elizabeth Gaskell imagined a social sphere in which women's personal contacts across classes superseded theoretical abstractions about social organization. Both women were taken seriously as writers and social commentators. However, as my closing chapter on *Middlemarch* indicates, by the latter part of the nineteenth century women writers began to outgrow their need to rely explicitly on philanthropic discourse as a way to represent women's ambitious desires to participate in public activity. This happened because by then women's confinement to a narrowly defined domestic sphere was being challenged not only in the language of philanthropic discourse but also in the terms of legal, professional, and political discourses. Nonetheless, the vocabulary and analogies the conjunction of domestic and philanthropic discourse provided continued to be used in these other cultural debates even after specific representations of women performing philanthropic acts ceased to convey the same cultural challenge.

At the same time that philanthropic discourse began to lose some of its force as a method of challenging the tenets of domestic ideology, women writers began to rely less on the novel as their primary means of contributing to public discourse. As the nineteenth century continued, more women participated in public and platform speaking, in congresses such as the National Association for the Promotion of Social Science, in local government, and especially in the periodical press. Women such as Beatrice Webb and Annie Besant, for instance, became known as important social commentators through their professional writings and public speaking. While women writers continued to write and publish novels in large numbers, the novel also underwent changes in form and content. New Woman and suffrage novels, for instance, addressed head on the issues of women's desires, without relying on the traditional romantic heroine or resorting to the contradictory figure of the philanthropic heroine. Modernist challenges to realist form in the novel also in some ways lessened the genre's focus on overt social criticism.

Throughout the nineteenth century, however, the interpenetration and interaction of novelistic and philanthropic discourses were significant, widespread, and complex. While I have considered the impact of the conjunction of these discourses on domestic ideology's descriptions of and prescriptions for women and, to some extent, on representations of relations among classes (both the relation of the middle to the upper classes and the relation of each to the lower classes), the subject deserves even more attention. Both discourses, for instance, were significantly involved in representing slavery and colonial relations to the English public, and they also had an important impact on changing views of education and political reform. What I am calling for is not merely an exploration of philanthropy as a theme in novels but rather for further analysis of the way philanthropic and novelistic discourses rewrote each other and helped to dictate the terms by which English-speaking audiences perceived and experienced social realities.

Notes

Introduction

1. Dickens, *Bleak House*, 82. See also Dyson, *Casebook*, 50–51, which reprints a review of *Bleak House* that appeared in the 17 September 1853 issue of *The Athenaeum*.
2. Howson, "Deaconesses," 180.
3. Jameson, *Sisters of Charity*, 199.
4. Pope, *Dickens and Charity*, 140.
5. Dickens, *Bleak House*, 151, 158.
6. Elizabeth Kowaleski-Wallace, for instance, characterizes Hannah More's philanthropic work and writings as "patriarchal complicity" in *Their Father's Daughters*. Christine L. Krueger, another recent feminist critic, dismisses women's philanthropy in *Reader's Repentance* (91). Others, such as Susan Zlotnick in *Women, Writing, and the Industrial Revolution*, pay more attention to female philanthropy but still dismiss it as an essentially retrograde response and an inherent (and unquestioned) part of domesticity (142–43, 161–65).
7. Despite his satiric portrayals of women philanthropists, Dickens—and most other writers—praised "proper" women's philanthropy as natural and indispensable. Esther Summerson, the narrator-heroine of *Bleak House*, serves as a model of the kind of sympathetic, intuitive charity to which many wanted to restrict women.
8. Legates, "Cult of Womanhood," 35.
9. Freud, "Creative Writers and Day-Dreaming," 147.
10. Miller, "Emphasis Added."
11. Girard, *Deceit, Desire, and the Novel*, 14, 96.
12. For a discussion of Girard's ideas in relation to other theories of desire, see Livingston, *Models of Desire,* and Weinstein, *Semantics of Desire.* For an analysis of desire as it is embedded in language, see Butler, *Subjects of Desire.*

13. Livingston, *Models of Desire*, 72–73.
14. Girard, *Deceit, Desire, and the Novel*, 5.
15. Observing Arabella's activities, the worldly Miss Glanville sarcastically comments that "you Country Ladies . . . are very fond of visiting your sick Neighbours" (Lennox, *Female Quixote*, 182). Arabella's benevolent nature is frequently remarked on, and one of the adventures she imagines is delivering "some Person" who has met "with a Misfortune" (260).
16. Armstrong, *Desire and Domestic Fiction;* Poovey, *Proper Lady and the Woman Writer* and *Uneven Developments;* Hall, "Early Formation of Domestic Ideology."
17. Several historians have pointed out that with the decline of home production, many women became more economically dependent on their husbands' earning power. See Perry, *Women, Letters, and the Novel*, 35–43; Hall, "Early Formation of Domestic Ideology," 23.
18. See, for instance, Lucinda Cole's reading of Wollstonecraft in "(Anti)Feminist Sympathies," 125–28.
19. See also Yeo, *Contest for Social Science*, 120–47.
20. *Oxford English Dictionary.*
21. The term "Age of Benevolence" comes from Asa Briggs in *Age of Improvement.* David Owen also uses the phrase to designate this period in *English Philanthropy, 1660–1960.*
22. Bettany, "Thomas Guy" 8:833–35.
23. See Carter, *History of the Oxford University Press* 1:95; J. Johnson and Gibson, *Print and Privilege at Oxford to the Year 1700*, 78.
24. Bettany, "Thomas Guy"; Owen, *English Philanthropy*, 44–46.
25. B. K. Gray, *History of English Philanthropy*, x.
26. See ibid., 273; Owen, *English Philanthropy*, 12.
27. W. K. Lowther Clarke, *A History of the S. P. C. K.* (London, 1959), 23, quoted in Owen, *English Philanthropy*, 12.
28. Owen, *English Philanthropy*, 14.
29. Lean, *God's Politician*, 127.
30. Rodgers, *Cloak of Charity*, 2.
31. See, for instance, Newby, "Deferential Dialectic."
32. Andrew, *Philanthropy and Police*, 13, 17.
33. See Pocock, "Mobility of Property."
34. Ibid., 109.
35. Ibid., 112–13.
36. Mullan, *Sentiment and Sociability*, 23, 29–30, 39.
37. A. Smith, *Theory of Moral Sentiments*, 21–23.
38. I deliberately use masculine pronouns here because that is what Smith does. The question of gender and sympathy will be considered shortly.
39. A. Smith, *Theory of Moral Sentiments*, 112–13, 159–60.
40. See Markley, "Sentimentality as Performance," 218.
41. This plot occurs in many eighteenth-century novels, including Samuel Richardson, *Pamela* (1740–42) and *Clarissa* (1747–48); Henry Fielding, *Joseph Andrews* (1742) and *Tom Jones* (1749); Sarah Fielding, *The Adventures of David Simple* (1744); Oliver Goldsmith, *The Vicar of Wakefield* (1766); Henry Mackenzie, *The Man of Feeling* (1771); Fanny Burney, *Evelina* (1778); and Ann Radcliffe, *Mysteries of Udolpho* (1794).

42. Laurence Sterne's *A Sentimental Journey* (1768) is renowned for associating the pleasurable sensations of sensibility with sexual pleasure. There is by now a large body of scholarly work on sensibility. For a good general account, see Todd, *Sensibility*.

43. Sterne's *Sentimental Journey* and Mackenzie's *Man of Feeling* abound in such incidents.

44. John Mullan, for example, denies any connection between novels of sensibility and actual philanthropic practice in *Sentiment and Sociability* (144–46).

45. Layng, *Sermon*, 5, 6, 9, 10–11.

46. Francklin, *Sermon,* 9.

47. See Schneewind, "Philosophical Ideas of Charity."

48. J. Massie attributes the increase in numbers of unemployed poor, thieves, and prostitutes directly to the "Defects of our Poor's-Laws." He cites as economic factors the "Monopolizing of Farms, and the Inclosure of Common Lands; which have likewise decreased the Number of People, and brought our Woollen Manufactures into a precarious State" in *Plan for the Establishment of Charity-Houses,* title page.

49. This was true throughout the eighteenth century, even before the turbulent last decades of the century, argue Lee Davison and the other editors of *Stilling the Grumbling Hive,* xi–liv.

50. Andrew, *Philanthropy and Police*, 20.

51. Markley, "Sentimentality as Performance," 211–12.

52. Armstrong, *Desire and Domestic Fiction*, 4, 92.

53. Barker-Benfield, *Culture of Sensibility*, 12, 141.

54. Ibid., 91–92.

55. Markman Ellis's discussion of the impact of sensibility in *Politics of Sensibility* more nearly anticipates mine because he not only considers the gendering of sensibility but also the way in which the sentimental novel worked in conjunction with practical philanthropy to work an important cultural transformation. Even Ellis, however, somewhat overemphasizes sensibility's association with the feminine. Another important recent discussion of sensibility is Skinner, *Sensibility and Economics in the Novel.*

56. This is true of most of the major historians of philanthropy, especially those that treat philanthropy before the nineteenth century, including Owen, B. K. Gray, and W. K. Jordan. Historians of nineteenth-century philanthropy, particularly Prochaska and Summers, do tend to pay more attention to women's role in philanthropy because by then women's widespread participation is hard to ignore.

57. Andrew, *Philanthropy and Police*, 87, 87 n, app. 203–24.

58. Francklin's sermon, for instance, specifically speaks to women subscribers (10–11), as does Bishop Beilby Porteus's address to the guardians of the Asylum for Female Orphans in *A Sermon preached in the Chapel of the Asylum for Female Orphans, at the Anniversary Meeting of the Guardians of that Charity* (28).

59. Andrew, *Philanthropy and Police*, 201.

60. Gerard, "Lady Bountiful," 186.

61. Lennox, *Female Quixote*, 182.

62. Astell, *Serious Proposal* 1 : 36, 53–54.

63. Francklin, *Sermon*, 10–11.

64. Estimates of the number of women involved in philanthropic activities are necessarily inaccurate, since so much of this activity went unreported. In her 1893 survey, Angela Burdett-Coutts reported that about five hundred thousand women were "continu-

ously" involved in volunteer philanthropy, while up to three hundred thousand worked as part-time volunteers or as paid charitable workers. See Prochaska, *Women and Philanthropy*, 224–25.

1. "An Assured Asylum against Every Evil"

1. Ogle, *Sermon*, 7.
2. B. K. Gray, *History of English Philanthropy*, 79–81.
3. See Andrew, *Philanthropy and Police*, 6–7, 9, 23.
4. Donna T. Andrew notes in *Philanthropy and Police*, for instance, that the thirty-one board members who sat on governing boards of London charitable societies with Jonas Hanway in the late 1750s and early 1760s were all male (76 n). The first charitable society to have women directors and governors that I have been able to identify was the Magdalen Asylum for Female Penitents in Dublin in the late 1760s.
5. One example is Elizabeth Montagu, sister of the author Sarah Scott. Montagu was known for her various charities, including numerous contributions to private individuals in distress, as well as largesse to those on her family's estates. Although Montagu was a regular subscriber to organized philanthropies, she was not on the board of governors or directors for these charities. After her husband's death Montagu became actively involved in running his mines and other business affairs, which led her to organize local charities to aid her employees, demonstrating the connection that often obtained between business and organized charity. See Doran, *Lady of the Last Century*.
6. One article that directly treats issues of philanthropy in *Millenium Hall* is Johanna M. Smith, "Philanthropic Community in *Millenium Hall* and the York Ladies Committee." Smith's Foucauldian reading raises some important issues about upper-class women's philanthropy and the exploitation of women from the classes beneath them. Recent critical readings of *Millenium Hall* as a novel of sensibility include Stoddard, "Politics of Sentiment," Rabb, "Making and Rethinking the Canon," and Haggerty, "'Romantic Friendship' and Patriarchal Narrative." *Millenium Hall* has also been read as an early example of feminist utopian fiction. See especially Dunne, "Mothers and Monsters," and Schnorrenberg, "Paradise Like Eve's."
7. See Climenson, *Elizabeth Montagu, The Queen of the Blue-Stockings*, 5–7.
8. Although there were rumors that Lady "Bab" wrote or coauthored *Millenium Hall*, it seems fairly clear that Scott was the primary, if not sole, author. See Spencer, *Description of Millenium Hall*, ix. For an account of Scott's philanthropic activities, see Rizzo, introduction to the recently issued edition of *The History of Sir George Ellison* by Sarah Scott.
9. Armstrong, *Desire and Domestic Fiction;* Poovey, *Proper Lady and the Woman Writer*.
10. Haggerty argues in "'Romantic Friendship' and Patriarchal Narrative" that *Millenium Hall* is a "lesbian narrative" (119). Susan Sniader Lanser in *Fictions of Authority* gives a more nuanced reading of the novel's "lesbian sensibilities" as part of her examination of communal voice in women's narratives (230).
11. See Spencer, *Description of Millenium Hall*, xi.
12. Other women, notably Mary Astell, had written advocating charitable works for women. Astell's *Serious Proposal,* however, does not go into detail about what charitable projects the women will undertake. It does not purport to contribute to discus-

sions of how philanthropy should be undertaken, nor does it focus on any specific-ally philanthropic institutions such as the houses of charity. Other representations of charitable work as an occupation for women, such as Samuel Richardson's in *Sir Charles Grandison,* also take for granted Lady Bountiful good works without seriously considering what form these works might take or what impact they might have economically or politically.

13. Scott, *Millenium Hall,* 1, 207. Further references are cited parenthetically.

14. Jonas Hanway, plausibly the most famous eighteenth-century philanthropist, often wrote public letters on charitable subjects. See, for instance, *Three Letters on the Subject of the Marine Society* (1758); *Letters to the Guardians of the Infant Poor* (1767); and *Twenty-nine Letters to a Member of Parliament* (1775). Like Scott's narrator, Hanway also sometimes signed his writings "by a gentleman" or "by a merchant."

15. Ellis, in *Politics of Sensibility,* also considers the sentimental novel in connection with philanthropic institutions, specifically the Magdalen Asylum. Ellis's focus, however, is on how the reclaimed prostitutes are constituted by philanthropic discourse as sentimental subjects. He does not specifically comment on the way both philanthropic objects and sentimental heroines were cast as sexualized victims, nor does he consider the impact of women's philanthropic participation.

16. Welch, *Proposal,* 1, 7, 8.

17. J. Massie, for instance, estimated that eight thousand people per year were coming to London from the country. Whether or not his figures have any semblance of accuracy, his estimate indicates the general perception among contemporaries that London was being besieged by displaced country people. Massie points out that men who could not find work could enlist, but for women "their Sex makes them less capable of getting their Living, and more liable to be ruined" (*Plan for the Establishment of Charity-Houses,* 16).

18. Most philanthropic writers express concerns about the health, depravity, extravagance, or idleness of the working classes in their various proposals for charitable projects. See, for instance, Hanbury, *Essay on Planting,* 39−41. Hanbury's unique scheme for promoting industry among the poor, as well as for preserving England's natural heritage, supplying timber for warships, and fostering religious observance, was to establish tree nurseries in every parish. Hanbury believed his plan would prevent the idleness and extravagance he claimed London charities fostered in the poor.

The listing of additional materials appended to Massie's plan for female asylums indicates the connection he perceived between the increased number of prostitutes and the rise in vagrancy caused by inadequate poor laws and enclosures: "Considerations relating to the Poor and the Poor's-Laws of England; Wherein the great Increases of Unemployed Poor, and of Thieves and Prostitutes, are shown to be immediately owing to the Severity, as well as the Defects of our Poor's-Laws; and to be primarily caused by the Monopolizing of Farms, and the Inclosure of Common Lands; which have likewise decreased the Number of People, and brought our Woollen Manufacturies into a precarious State, as it may appear by Extracts from several Laws and other Authorities. Also, A New System of Policy, Most humbly proposed, for Relieving, Employing, and Ordering the Poor of England; Whereby a great Savings may be made in the Charge of Maintaining Them; the Poor's-Rates be kept nearly Equal in all Parishes, as in Equity they ought to be; and every Pretence for wandering about Begging, may be taken away" (*Plan for the Establishment of Charity-Houses,* title page).

19. Welch, *Proposal,* 13 n.
20. Hazeland, *Sermon,* 5–6.
21. Andrew, *Philanthropy and Police,* 54.
22. Armstrong, *Desire and Domestic Fiction,* 5; Poovey, *Proper Lady and the Woman Writer,* 10–11.
23. Armstrong, *Desire and Domestic Fiction.* In most eighteenth-century sentimental novels, for instance, the heroine is a model domestic woman, whether she is a servant (as in Richardson's *Pamela*) or an aristocrat.
24. To say that social fears were translated into gendered ones does not, of course, preclude the possibility of their translation into other vocabularies as well. Another influential set of terms for handling social anxieties, for instance, was that of political economy.
25. Because depositing infants at the Foundling Hospital was done anonymously, it was, of course, possible for married couples to leave legitimate children; it was usually represented, however, as a recourse for unmarried women and their illegitimate children.

   The one major midcentury charity that had nothing to do with women, and, significantly, the one universally acknowledged to be most successful in achieving its aims, was the Marine Society, which rescued abandoned boys and fitted them out as sailors. It was widely considered a model of what efficient, businesslike joint charity could accomplish. The success of this charity seems to be directly related to the fact that, because the sexuality of boys was not a major issue—that is, they did not require protection or isolation, and they did not need to be returned to the family (either as daughters or as servants)—they were not as expensive to reclaim. Also, finding employment that would both support boys and keep them from being (dangerously) idle was obviously not the problem it was for similar projects aimed at helping girls. See Andrew, *Philanthropy and Police,* 119–31.
26. Welch's recommendation for a penitent prostitute asylum, for instance, was published together with "A Letter upon the Subject of Robberies, wrote in the Year 1753" in his *Proposal.* See also J. Massie's title page in *Plan for the Establishment of Charity-Houses.*
27. [Hanway], *Plan for Establishing a Charity-House,* xviii.
28. Ogle, *Sermon,* 10.
29. Ibid., 11.
30. On the history of the term "old maid," see Deegan, *Stereotype of the Single Woman,* 7, and B. Hill, *Women, Work, and Sexual Politics,* 230.
31. Another prominent example of eighteenth-century hostility toward "old maids" may be seen in Daniel Defoe's biting satires in *Applebee's Original Weekly Journal* (1723–24). These include (fictional) letters from an unmarried woman named Anne, complaining about her lot, and the even more biting "Satire on Censorious Old Maids" (324–25, 126).
32. Tucker, *Hospitals and Infirmaries,* 9, 11.
33. [Hanway], *Plan for Establishing a Charity-House,* xxii.
34. Massie, *Plan for the Establishment of Charity-Houses,* 23.
35. [Hanway], *Plan for Establishing a Charity-House,* v.
36. See B. Hill, *Eighteenth-Century Women,* 157.

37. Sarah Scott provided a number of fictionalized examples of dependent spinsters in *The History of Sir George Ellison* (1766), her later novel that is both prequel and sequel to *Millenium Hall*. For a discussion of *Sir George Ellison*'s relation to *Millenium Hall* as prequel and sequel, see Carretta, "Utopia Limited." See also Rizzo, introduction to *Sir George Ellison*.

38. Massie was unusual in stressing that most prostitutes were from the lower classes and that they were driven to prostitution for economic reasons (*Plan for the Establishment of Charity-Houses*, 3). The prostitutes most often used as examples in sermons and prospectuses were young women of the middle or upper classes who fell victim to the seduction of the local squire or some other philandering gentleman.

39. Unlike Richardson's scandalous portrayal of a well-born woman reduced to keeping company with "common" or "low" prostitutes, asylums usually separated prostitutes of higher birth from those of lower origins. Massie's plan, for instance, proposed four separate asylums with distinct rules and procedures for penitent prostitutes of different classes (*Plan for the Establishment of Charity-Houses*, 338–44). Richardson's story, however, demonstrates that despite such distinctions, "fallen" women of all classes were dangerously alike.

40. For a discussion of the domestic woman and sexuality, see V. Jones, *Women in the Eighteenth Century*, 57–59.

41. Hazeland, *Sermon*, 4.

42. Insisting on cleanliness and industry was not unique to charitable institutions for female victims; it was nearly a universal requirement for institutions that treated the poor and unfortunate. Cleanliness and industry were seen as antidotes to all sorts of wayward desires.

43. Secker, *Sermon*, 16.

44. Marshall, *English Poor in the Eighteenth Century*, 2.

45. Andrew, *Philanthropy and Police*, 135.

46. See Marshall, *English Poor in the Eighteenth Century*, 125–60.

47. Hufton, "Women without Men," 361.

48. I do not suggest that *Millenium Hall*'s home for indigent gentlewomen and urban Magdalen asylums are identical; certainly there are key differences, a major one being the difference of class between the women who live in the two types of institutions. What I do point out, however, are the significant similarities in the language and details used to represent them, particularly the way in which both are represented as "asylums." Scott would presumably have been familiar with the details of Magdalen asylums since, according to Ellis, her companion Barbara Montagu had published *The Histories of Some of the Penitents in the Magdalen-House* only two years before the publication of *Millenium Hall*.

49. Fielding and Scott were evidently intimate friends; Fielding may have been a model for one of the *Millenium Hall* ladies. See Crittenden, *Description of Millenium Hall*, 12.

50. See Carretta, "Utopia Limited," 309.

51. Foucault, *Madness and Civilization*, 70; Baldick, *In Frankenstein's Shadow*, 10.

52. Bayly, *Sermon*, 12.

53. Not surprising, there is speculation about the sexual nature of Scott's relationship with Lady Bab, but such speculation is beside the point in reading the gender politics of the novel. The argument that critics such as J. David Macey, Jr., have made, that the "fecundity" of metaphor and description in the novel are evidence of "the rich-

ness of the women's sexual experience in a same-sex community," is too easy and ahistorical ("Eden Revisited," 173 n. 26). Linda Dunne argues, as I do, that both heterosexual and homosexual love must be repressed in order to maintain the female community in *Millenium Hall* ("Mothers and Monsters," 71–72).

54. For a discussion of the nonthreatening, grandfatherly sentimental male, see Todd, *Sign of Angellica*, 182.

55. Haggerty, "'Romantic Friendship' and Patriarchal Narrative," 115.

56. The Italians Mr. d'Avora most resembles are the fashionable opera-singing castrati. For a discussion of ideas about castrati and eunuchs in the eighteenth century, see Wagner, "Discourse on Sex," 56–57.

2. "The Care of the Poor Is Her Profession"

1. Channing and Aikin, *Correspondence*, 396.

2. More's novel-cum-conduct book was extremely popular when it first appeared. Ford K. Brown notes, in *Fathers of the Victorians*, for example, that *Coelebs in Search of a Wife* went through more editions and brought in more profits than Sir Walter Scott's *Waverley* (395 n). Because of its heavy didacticism, the book's genre has always posed problems for critics. Sydney Smith, in an *Edinburgh Review* article, used the suggestive term "dramatic sermon" to describe More's book, while the reviewer for the 30 July 1809 issue of *Monthly Magazine*, criticized it on the grounds that it was inappropriate to introduce religious controversy in a novel (663–64). The reviewer for the *Christian Observer*, by contrast, praised *Coelebs*, writing that he could not "allow this work to be called a novel. . . . [T]he preceptive parts are not choked with incidents" (Quoted in Rosman, *Evangelicals and Culture*, 190). Hannah More, however, intended the book to be read as a novel (M. G. Jones, *Hannah More*, 193).

3. Channing and Aikin, *Correspondence*, 397.

4. For a thorough account of nineteenth-century women's involvement in such philanthropic endeavors, see Prochaska, *Women and Philanthropy*.

5. The title of More's most famous conduct book is *Strictures on the Modern System of Female Education*.

6. Davidoff and Hall, *Family Fortunes*, 149; Poovey, *Proper Lady and the Woman Writer*, 33.

7. Myers, "Reform or Ruin," 202, 204, 209, and "Hannah More's Tracts," 273–74.

8. Kowaleski-Wallace, *Their Fathers' Daughters*, 93. While Kowaleski-Wallace's reading is also historical, her reliance on global, ahistorical categories such as patriarchy, complicity, nature, and various psychoanalytic terms, as well as her rather suspect attempt to psychoanalyze the historical Hannah More is ultimately less convincing than Myers's accounts of More's influence. For instance, Kowaleski-Wallace recognizes "a kind of female empowerment" in middle- and upper-class women's philanthropic work, but her persistent stress on the way "the patriarchal system" or Evangelical men "employ" or "allow" women to further patriarchal aims denies More's (and other women's) agency in claiming, defining, and shaping both accepted female roles and their participation in social activities such as philanthropy (56–58).

9. K. Sutherland, "Hannah More's Counter-Revolutionary Feminism," 46.

10. Krueger, *Reader's Repentance*, 113.

11. For discussion of the Lady Bountiful role in England, see Gerard, "Lady Bountiful." Jessica Gerard explains how this kind of traditional women's philanthropy coexisted

with more institutionalized urban philanthropy well into the nineteenth and even twentieth centuries. For discussion of the way this tradition evolved in other countries, see the essays collected in McCarthy, *Lady Bountiful Revisited*.

12. For a discussion of the bonds of deference, see Newby, "Deferential Dialectic."

13. Perkin, *Origins of Modern English Society*, 31.

14. Harold Perkin claims that the ruling aristocracy itself sought to destroy the paternal system by abolishing the poor laws in favor of laissez-faire capitalism (*Origins of Modern English Society*, 188–92). Wealthy women, by implication, would then lose their role in reinforcing paternalism. Gertrude Himmelfarb suggests that in the eighteenth century, the poor were increasingly seen as the charge of the state, rather than the local church and community, which would also tend to exclude women's traditional role in local charity (*Idea of Poverty*, 4–5, 150). Dorothy Marshall, in *English Poor in the Eighteenth Century*, discusses Gilbert's Act (1782), which first granted parishes the right to form workhouse unions (13–14). Although this was not done on a wide scale until after the passage of the New Poor Law in 1834, Gilbert's Act reflects the kind of thinking that would institutionalize the poor in publicly run establishments. Women were not regularly admitted to workhouses until well into the middle of the nineteenth century.

15. More, *Coelebs in Search of a Wife* 2:20. Further references are cited parenthetically. A particularly vituperative account of More's paternalist sympathies is Richardson, "Sentimental Journey of Hannah More."

16. See Harland, *Hannah More*, 176–77.

17. H. More, *Works* 1:260. Further references to the works of Hannah More are cited parenthetically.

18. Kathryn Sutherland in "Hannah More's Counter-Revolutionary Feminism" makes a similar point about the power More gives to middle-class women in the story of Mrs. Jones (38–40), as does Mitzi Myers in "Hannah More's Tracts for the Times" (275–77). They do not, however, address the way in which Mrs. Jones's reform of her community contributes to the redefinition of paternalism or the desires it is expected to inspire in women readers.

19. Richard D. Altick describes the methods employed for widespread distribution to the lower classes of political pamphlets, especially Paine's *The Rights of Man*. Altick also discusses the *Cheap Repository Tracts*, showing how More and her coworkers "designed the tracts to look like the pamphlets they were intended to supersede" (*English Common Reader*, 74–75). The phenomenal sales figures for More's tracts—over two million were sold the first year—indicate they were successful in achieving their aim, although it is impossible to determine how many laboring people bought or read the tracts because many of them were sold to middle- and upper-class buyers for free distribution to the poor.

20. Harland, *Hannah More*, 172–73.

21. Spinney, "Cheap Repository Tracts," 303.

22. Olivia Smith gives a helpful account of More's innovative use in the *Cheap Repository Tracts* of realistic techniques and of language that is simple but without condescension (*Politics of Language*, 90–94).

23. See M. G. Jones, *Hannah More*, 193.

24. Mauss, *Gift*, 15, 5.

25. In his essay "Wordsworth's 'The Old Cumberland Beggar': The Economy of Charity

in Late Eighteenth-Century Britain," Gary Harrison also discusses charity as a version of a gift exchange economy. In his reading of Wordsworth's poem, the recipient of charity "does not participate fully in the gift exchange that supposedly creates the communal bond of domestic affection" because he "ostensibly returns their favors in an abstract exchange of which he is entirely unaware" (35). In the example of More's gardener, however, her charitable recipient knowingly exchanges his gratitude and service for the material gifts conferred. While More's portrayal of the exchange of gifts also reinforces "paternalistic attitudes" (34), it enlists the poor in maintaining the system that (for More) benefits both the poor and women philanthropists, while contributing to the safety and security of the nation.

26. Gareth Stedman Jones also comments on the "social meaning of charitable gift-giving" and what he calls the "deformation of the gift" in urban class relations, although he does not specifically mention women philanthropists (*Outcast London*, 251–53).

27. David Cheal claims that "the tension between market relationships and personal relationships [that is, gift exchange] is a distinctive characteristic of social life in capitalist societies" (*Gift Economy*, 4).

28. Blau, *Exchange and Power*, 112.

29. In her discussions of More's *Cheap Repository Tracts*, Olivia Smith notes how frequently the tracts portray poor characters who exhibit extraordinary endurance but are unable to get ahead without the intervention of charity; as Smith observes, More "wanted them to endure, but not to manage for themselves" (*Politics of Language*, 93). By representing the poor, however hardworking and virtuous, as still in need of charitable rescuing, More tries to ensure that philanthropists, especially women, will continue to have work to do.

30. Channing and Aikin, *Correspondence*, 90.

31. For an extended discussion of working-class attitudes toward and participation in charitable schools, see Laqueur, *Religion and Respectability*.

32. See M. G. Jones, *Hannah More*, 3.

33. For a summary of arguments that in a gift exchange the "donor's rights are never extinguished" because a gift is not a commodity that can be "alienated," see Cheal, *Gift Economy* 10.

34. Elizabeth Kowaleski-Wallace makes an important point about Evangelical women when she argues that their "supreme bodily self-discipline became the identifying mark of [their] class privilege" (*Their Father's Daughters*, 74).

35. McKendrick et al., *Birth of a Consumer Society*, 9. While Neil McKendrick's description of a consumer "revolution" has been disputed by other historians, there is evidence of rising consumerism throughout the eighteenth century. See Davison and others, "Reactive State," xxv–xxviii.

36. McKendrick et al., *Birth of a Consumer Society*, 15, 16. In the last quotation McKendrick is quoting Appleby, "Ideology and Theory," 515.

37. Mathias, *Transformation of England*, 162.

38. Nancy Armstrong describes the role of husband and wife in the new household domestic economy in this way in *Desire and Domestic Fiction*, 83–88.

39. While earlier in the eighteenth century it was thought that even prostitutes could be reformed and turned into "joyful mothers of children" ([Hanway], *Plan for Establishing a Charity-House*, xxii), by the end of the century attitudes toward "fallen women"

had changed to reflect the growing emphasis on the desexualized "angel" as the norm for women; such women could be helped and protected but not returned to their former place in society (see Andrew, *Philanthropy and Police*, 189). Hannah More would not have wanted to have Lady Melbury commit sexual sin because it would then have been difficult, if not impossible, for More to represent her as the highest exemplar of female virtue.

40. While Beth Fowkes Tobin and others are right that the values More is promoting are those of the emergent middle class, it is not accurate to assume that More is primarily speaking to middle-class women or that she believed aristocratic women had "forfeited to the middle classes the right to occupy supervisory roles" (*Superintending the Poor*, 5). The argument seems reasonable if one looks mostly at the story of Mrs. Jones and the other tales addressed to the middle ranks, but *Coelebs in Search of a Wife* focuses almost exclusively on the gentry and aristocracy. Tobin acknowledges that Lucilla Stanley and Hannah More were tied to the landholding classes, but she still regards them as spokeswomen for the middle classes. While More does criticize landholders' handling of their paternal responsibilities, as Tobin maintains, her aim is to reform, not replace, them; the exemplary middle classes, in More's view, will join, not supplant, the upper class in governing the laboring population.

41. Early in More's career she published a poem called "Sensibility." In the poem, written before her conversion to Evangelicalism, More demonstrates her already ambivalent attitude toward sensibility—she both extols it, cautioning against a "pausing prudence" that might refuse "charity with open hand," and claims such feelings as the special prerogative of women. But she is also careful, even in this early poem, to link both sensibility and charity to religion, the "Love Divine! sole source of Charity!" (*Works* 1:135–55).

42. The most obvious novelistic examples of this kind of heart-rending but pleasurable charity are Sterne, *A Sentimental Journey* (1768) and Mackenzie, *The Man of Feeling* (1771), although most novels of sensibility portray at least a few similar scenes. An example closer to the time of More's novel is Ann Radcliffe, *Mysteries of Udolpho* (1794), where the hero Valancourt gives up nearly his last franc for the pleasure of relieving a shepherd's family (52).

43. Lucinda Cole also discusses More's association of sensibility with "a devotion to a principle of worldly pleasure, as opposed to Christian sacrifice," in "(Anti)Feminist Sympathies," 16.

44. Thomas R. Malthus, *Essay on Population*, 5th ed. (London, 1817), bk. 4, chap. 10, quoted in Owen, *English Philanthropy*, 98.

45. For a discussion of how even benevolent philanthropic men could be perceived as sexually threatening to the victimized object of charity, see chapter 1. The solution to this problem was to employ paid matrons or enlist lady supervisors whose sexual nature was presumably well regulated and safe.

46. For a discussion of the paradox of modesty, see Poovey, *Proper Lady and the Woman Writer*, 22–26.

47. More was opposed to the "epidemical mania" for accomplishments among women of "the middle station," whom she saw as "declining in usefulness" as they rose in "ill-founded pretensions to elegance" (*Strictures* 1:75). Claiming that a "man of sense" would prefer a companion to an artist (*Strictures* 1:112), More advocates a serious education for women instead of a course in such accomplishments. One other

reason for objecting to the widespread pursuit of accomplishments, in More's view, is that practicing takes up time better spent elsewhere (that is, doing philanthropy), and it also puts ladies in the position of competing with professional artists (*Coelebs* 1 : 343).

48. Several other critics have noticed the way More deploys the metaphor of the family as a model for social and political relations. Elizabeth Kowaleski-Wallace, for instance, comments on what she calls a "familial configuration" in the "new alliance between the Evangelical clergy and women" (*Their Father's Daughters*, 60). While I, too, identify a familial model in the organization of Evangelical philanthropic reform projects, I challenge Kowaleski-Wallace's exclusive focus on the "maternal" and "nurturing" role "assigned" to women in philanthropic projects by men (almost unfailingly read as father figures). Her contention that More's settling for "maternal agency" failed to "transcend cultural stereotypes," and hence proved inadequate as a feminist strategy, ignores the ways in which this strategy of organizing the world in domestic terms was useful to women arguing for women's advancement throughout the nineteenth and twentieth centuries (93). Christine L. Krueger also identifies "class and gender interests striving to reconfigure social relations along the lines of a rigidly structured domestic model," but she does not connect this to philanthropy (*Reader's Repentance*, 106 – 7).

49. Armstrong, *Desire and Domestic Fiction*, 84.

50. Along with More, Sarah Trimmer had been active in organizing and directing Sunday schools; Elizabeth Fry is well known for her domestic reform work in early-nineteenth-century prisons. For other examples during the period, see Prochaska, *Women and Philanthropy*.

51. In another place, Mrs. Stanley also refers to her elder daughters as "veterans in their trade" (*Coelebs* 2 : 23).

52. M. More, *Mendip Annals*, 12 – 13.

53. For an account of More's schools, see M. G. Jones, *Hannah More*, 151 – 71, and Hopkins, *Hannah More and Her Circle*, 156 – 84. The primary sources for this information are both Martha More, *Mendip Annals*, and Hannah More, "The Sunday School," a fictional account (*Works* 4 : 358 – 86).

54. Rodgers, *Cloak of Charity*, 144.

55. John Pollock, in *William Wilberforce*, describes one of many other incidents in which More provided the sympathy and the legwork, while Wilberforce and two of his friends supplied money, when it was discovered that the prominent Methodist Charles Wesley's widow and unmarried daughter were in a reduced financial situation (155). Ernest Marshall Howse, in *Saints in Politics*, depicts More as the "appointed agent of Wilberforce and Thornton in their philanthropic activities" (19).

56. Brown, *Fathers of the Victorians*, 135.

57. Spinney, "Cheap Repository Tracts," 302.

58. Bradley, *Call to Seriousness*, 42. For a discussion of new mass-market ventures, see also McKendrick's introduction to *Birth of a Consumer Society*, 31 – 33. Although McKendrick does not mention books or the *Cheap Repository Tracts* as an example, the project in some ways fits in the same category with the "small items of household consumption" he does discuss (31).

59. See, for instance, Kowaleski-Wallace, *Their Father's Daughters*, 57, 64.

60. More's biographers note that by the time of her death she had amassed thirty thou-

sand pounds, a considerable fortune, mostly from her prodigious literary output. See Hopkins, *Hannah More and Her Circle,* 251.

61. M. G. Jones, *Hannah More,* ix. More's most recent biographers tend to echo this sentiment. See Ford, *Hannah More,* xi; Demers, *World of Hannah More,* 22. Robert Hole, the editor of *Selected Writings of Hannah More,* repeats the more typical, one-sided view of More as "traditional and conservative," although he does acknowledge the historical importance of at least her earlier works (vii, xvii).

3. Hannah More's Heirs

1. Martineau, *Cousin Marshall,* in *Illustrations of Political Economy* 3:39. Further references are cited parenthetically.

2. This scenario is predicted in *Cousin Marshall* and is illustrated by the Bells, a working-class family who rely on charity and poor relief rather than their own labor. The Bells are contrasted to the Marshalls, who eschew any kind of relief and exemplify the principles of self-reliance and charity to their peers.

3. See Gerard, "Lady Bountiful."

4. See Engel and King, *Victorian Novel before Victoria,* 14, 116–17.

5. In her study *Harriet Martineau: The Poetics of Moralism,* Shelagh Hunter traces More's influence on Martineau, pointing out that Martineau's first published piece of writing was on More's works of divinity (59–70). Valerie Sanders also comments on More's influence on Martineau in *Reason over Passion,* 54, 194–95.

6. "On National Economy," 403. The author of the review is unidentified, although it may have been William Maginn, the editor of *Fraser's Magazine.*

7. Ibid. Ann Hobart also discusses this passage in "Harriet Martineau's Political Economy of Everyday Life," 225.

8. See Martineau's "Summary of Principles illustrated in this Volume," appended to *Cousin Marshall (Illustrations* 3:130–32).

9. The most famous workhouse visitor in the early nineteenth century was Sarah Martin, who began visiting the Yarmouth workhouse in 1810. Workhouse visiting, however, did not become common until much later in the century. The Workhouse Visiting Society was not formed until the end of the 1850s. See Prochaska, *Women and Philanthropy,* 163–75.

10. Boyd Hilton describes Chalmers's social experiments at St. John's Parish in Glasgow as "a sort of urban feudalism" in *Age of Atonement,* 56.

11. Poovey, *Making a Social Body,* 100–102. Mary Poovey explains the term "disciplinary individualism," coined by Michel Foucault (99).

12. Gillian Thomas, in *Harriet Martineau,* maintains that Martineau's belief in the effectiveness of education as the foundation of social progress is so pervasive that it "underlies the sense of a crusading mission in the tales" (92).

13. Chalmers also insisted on "strict clerical control" in his parochial experiments (Hilton, *Age of Atonement,* 58).

14. On middle-class women's management of servants, see Cohen, *Professional Domesticity,* and Langland, *Nobody's Angels.*

15. See Poovey, *Making a Social Body,* esp. 35–37.

16. Hilton contends that views of evangelical Christian economists such as Chalmers were "more widespread and probably more influential" than the more familiar pro-

fessional economists such as David Ricardo (*Age of Atonement*, 69). While Martineau did not share Chalmers's evangelicalism (she was Unitarian), her version of political economy has much more in common with Chalmers's than with Ricardo's.

17. Martineau, *Deerbrook*, 476. Further references are cited parenthetically.
18. For an excellent discussion of Martineau's career, see Hunter, *Harriet Martineau*.
19. Frances Trollope's *The Life and Adventures of Jonathan Jefferson Whitlaw* (1836) was, according to Helen Heineman, the first novel "to treat the evils of slavery for a wide reading public" (*Frances Trollope*, 59). Trollope published *Jessie Phillips; a Tale of the Present Day* (1844), a novel portraying the ruinous consequences of the New Poor Law beginning in 1842.
20. Some of the major critics to address and identify this genre are Cazamian, *Social Novel in England;* Colby, *Fiction with a Purpose;* Kovacevic, *Fact into Fiction;* Webb, *From Custom to Capital;* Kettle, "Early Victorian Social-Problem Novel"; and Guy, *Victorian Social-Problem Novel.* Dr. K. C. Shrivastava makes some detailed generic distinctions in *Women Novelists,* 11–15.
21. Heineman, *Mrs. Trollope: The Triumphant Feminine,* 172. Pamela Neville-Sington describes the publication rivalry between Trollope's novel and Charles Dickens's *Nicholas Nickleby,* which was published simultaneously in the same format, in *Fanny Trollope* (276–77).
22. Quoted in Chaloner, "Mrs. Trollope and the Early Factory System," 165.
23. On Trollope's fact-finding trip, see Heineman, *Triumphant Feminine,* 169–70, and Chaloner, "Mrs. Trollope and the Early Factory System," 160–64.
24. Joseph A. Kestner points out in *Protest and Reform* that although Trollope's novel portrays conditions from the 1820s and 1830s (particularly in the section decrying the factory apprentice system), she is "dealing with a contemporary subject in a slightly distanced form" (51). The first short-time legislation was not passed until the 1844 Factory Act reduced the hours of women and young people to twelve. The Ten-Hours Bill (also restricting the hours of women and children) was not passed until 1847. See R. Gray, *Factory Question,* 190–91. On state paternalism and the family, see Gallagher, *Industrial Reformation of English Fiction,* 121–25.
25. Rosemarie Bodenheimer makes a similar point in *Politics of Story* (17–18).
26. Susan Zlotnick points out that many reformers tried to define children and women who worked in factories as "unfree agents" in order to reinforce the doctrine of separate spheres and justify protective legislation (*Women, Writing, and the Industrial Revolution,* 139). This is true for children in Trollope's novel, but I argue that she attempts to redeem middle-class women and adult workers from passivity and show them as capable of judging and acting on both their own fates and industrial conditions generally.
27. Zlotnick also focuses on Trollope's (and Charlotte Elizabeth Tonna's) portrayal of the factory, which she describes as "disclosing the massive, sustained concealment of the conditions of production" (*Women, Writing, and the Industrial Revolution,* 127). I concentrate more on the way these authors use these depictions to kindle the physical sensations characteristic of much sentimental fiction.
28. For an excellent discussion of the larger implications of the worker-slave metaphor, see Gallagher, *Industrial Reformation of English Fiction,* 3–35.
29. Tonna makes this point explicitly in *Helen Fleetwood,* 151. Hannah More was one of the most famous women involved in the abolition crusade.

30. See Zlotnick on the way Trollope and Tonna implicate middle-class women in the fate of factory workers through their role as consumers (*Women, Writing, and the Industrial Revolution*, 130–33).

31. Harsh, *Subversive Heroines*, 25.

32. This is not Trollope's worst description of children suffering in the factories. Her depiction of Michael's experiences as a factory apprentice at Deep Valley Mill shows, among other horrific details, children competing with pigs for food in the best of times, while during a fever epidemic at the factory their corpses are buried at night to escape detection by authorities. To counter charges of exaggeration, Trollope footnotes this scene, claiming she is withholding the factory's real name to avoid libel (180). Evidently she based the scene on a pamphlet printed in 1828, called *Memoir of Robert Blincoe*, detailing the experiences of an actual factory worker and attributed to John Brown (see Chaloner, "Mrs. Trollope and the Early Factory System," 164).

33. Although both the first short-time act (the 1844 Factory Act which limited hours to twelve) and the Ten-Hours Bill (1847) reduced hours only for women and children, the historian Robert Gray notes that contemporaries and some earlier historians realized that the use of "protected workers" (that is, children and women) in the rhetoric surrounding the bill was strategic; such workers were "stalking-horses, in campaigns 'really' aimed at shorter hours for the men" as well (*Factory Question*, 8). This view would complicate arguments such as Zlotnick's and Gallagher's that short-time advocates were attempting to reinforce domestic ideology by denying women agency, getting them out of the factories and returning them to the home. See Zlotnick, *Women, Writing, and the Industrial Revolution*, 139–41; Gallagher, *Industrial Reformation of English Fiction*, 127–30.

34. Heineman, *Frances Trollope*, 70, and *Triumphant Feminine*, 170.

35. Harsh, *Subversive Heroines*, 99–101.

36. In *Women, Writing, and the Industrial Revolution*, Susan Zlotnick comments briefly on "the (bourgeois) woman's mission" in Trollope's and Tonna's novels, but she assumes that this is merely an extension of the domestic sphere (142). Zlotnick never explores the origins or implications of this "mission."

37. Heineman, *Frances Trollope*, 67, 208–9.

48. Poovey, *Making a Social Body*, 11.

39. See my article "Servants and Hands."

40. Kovacevic and Kanner, "Blue Book into Novel," 160.

41. See Mary Poovey's work for a theoretical and historical account of how the poor came to be seen as abstractions and how women philanthropists such as Ellen Ranyard resisted the abstracting impulse (*Making a Social Body*, 25–54).

42. Tonna, *Helen Fleetwood*, 95, 97. Further references are cited parenthetically.

43. For a description of contemporary attitudes toward "mill girls" and female factory workers, see Valenze, *First Industrial Woman*, 97–103, and Zlotnick, *Women, Writing, and the Industrial Revolution*, 16–20, 147–51.

44. Deborah Kaplan makes a similar point in "Woman Worker": "The vision of a universal innate femininity realized in a harmonious and orderly hierarchical framework expresses for Tonna not an archaic but an alternative set of values to those conveyed by the exploitative social relations of industrial capitalism" (54).

45. Christine L. Krueger gives a useful discussion of this scene in *Reader's Repentance* (140–41).

46. Hilton, *Age of Atonement*, 87.
47. Harsh, *Subversive Heroines*, 90–91.

4. "The Communion of Labor" and *Lectures to Ladies*

1. Jameson, *Sisters of Charity*, 268. This is the American edition of Mrs. Jameson's lectures. "Sisters of Charity" (under the title *Sisters of Charity, Abroad and at Home*) was first published in England in March 1855; "The Communion of Labor" was added to the 1856 edition. Further references are cited parenthetically.
2. H. More, *Strictures on the Modern System of Female Education*, in *Works* 7 : 173.
3. Prochaska, *Women and Philanthropy*; Summers, "Home from Home."
4. One of the most prominent commentators on the "redundant woman problem" was W. R. Greg, "Why Are Women Redundant?" in 1862.
5. Dickens lampoons district visiting with the figure of Mrs. Pardiggle, his "cast-iron Lady Bountiful" (the phrase comes from the 17 September 1853 review of *Bleak House* in *The Athenaeum*, which is reprinted in Dyson, *Casebook*, 51). He attacks women's participation in philanthropic institutions with his representation of Mrs. Jellyby, who is "always the same, looking off to Borioboola Gha, and looking over the immediate objects which are entitled to her attention and sympathy—a perfect type of the philanthropist by trade" (*Putnam's Magazine* [November 1853], reprinted in Dyson, *Casebook*, 78). Dickens's description of Mrs. Jellyby, her office, and her daughter as covered with writer's ink and littered with paper suggests anxiety about her competition with professional male writers, particularly writers of "social problem" novels (*Bleak House*, 85).
6. For a discussion of the social work male professionals and female philanthropists undertook in the nineteenth century, see Yeo, *Contest for Social Science*. Eileen Janes Yeo, however, tends to represent the relations between these two groups as cooperative, while I see more evidence of (submerged) conflict.
7. A number of recent critics have also pointed out that the public and private spheres were never as separate or autonomous as nineteenth-century thinkers assumed they were. Monica F. Cohen, for example, describes how novelists blurred the distinction between public and private by using the terms of professionalism and the Puritan work ethic to characterize domesticity as professional, in *Professional Domesticity*. See also Gallagher, *Industrial Reformation of English Fiction*, and Bodenheimer, *Politics of Story*, whose arguments are discussed in chapter 5.
8. For an in-depth discussion of the formation of the "social domain," see Poovey, *Making a Social Body*.
9. Riley, *"Am I That Name?"* 49.
10. Only two years after the publication of Jameson's lectures, the National Association for the Promotion of Social Science (NAPSS) was founded. A number of liberal thinkers and reformers participated in its annual congresses. Women played a conspicuous role in the meetings and in the association's publications. Frances Power Cobbe defended women's participation in the new field in "Social Science Congresses, and Women's Part in Them," an 1861 article for *Macmillan's Magazine*. For an excellent discussion of the NAPSS and women's role in it, see Yeo, *Contest for Social Science*, 148–82.
11. Riley claims that the social sphere was inherently feminized (*"Am I That Name?"* 50).

To make this claim, however, Riley conflates the positions of the masculinized expert and the feminized object of social observation. When women took up the position of expert, they were taking up a masculinized position. Although Riley is right to observe that women had easier access to the social sphere because the object of investigation was feminized, her assumption that this sphere was "doubly feminized" obscures the struggle between male professionals and middle-class women for social authority.

12. For a discussion of Jameson's other writings on the "woman question," see Rendell, *Origins of Modern Feminism*, 130, 339 n. Jameson's "Woman's Mission" and "Woman's Position" are reprinted in her 1846 *Memoirs and Essays*. See also Johnston, *Anna Jameson*, a biography.

13. For a discussion of the construction of the public image of Florence Nightingale as a competent but domestic heroine, see Poovey, *Uneven Developments*, 164–98.

14. Macpherson, *Memoirs*, 288.

15. Besides extensive personal study, Nightingale had spent three months learning nursing from the Protestant deaconesses in Kaiserswerth, Germany, which she followed with hospital training at the Catholic Maison de la Providence in Paris. See Boyd, *Three Victorian Women*, 179–82.

16. For instance, Ernest Marshall Howse rather self-consciously classes More with the "great men" of the Clapham group in *Saints in Politics* (166).

17. Wood, *Frederick Denison Maurice*, 135.

18. Maurice, *Lectures to Ladies*, 2. Further references are cited parenthetically.

19. "I am indebted," says Maurice, "to Mrs. Jameson's book on Sisters of Charity for so many hints, that it is superfluous to confess any particular plagiarism." The "great and pregnant truths" he learned from reading her book, he continues, "and the inference from them, that we are not to cheat a whole sex of its appointed tasks and blessings" are "precisely the one[s] which I should wish to be expressed and carried out in our College" (*Lectures*, 15–16).

20. The idea was, however, mistakenly attributed to Nightingale rather than Jameson by a reviewer for the *Edinburgh Review* in January 1856.

21. Larson, *Rise of Professionalism*, xvi, 49, 69.

22. Ibid., 58.

23. Review of *Lectures to Ladies*, 149.

24. Kingsley's language is reminiscent of an amusing comment Jameson's friend Mrs. Procter made in response to negative reviews of Jameson's *Winter Studies and Summer Rambles* (1838): "A fig for reviewers. The men . . . are much alarmed by certain speculations about women; and, . . . well they may be, for when the horse and ass begin to think and argue, adieu to riding and driving" (Quoted in Macpherson, *Memoirs*, 49–50).

25. Erskine, *Letters*, 285; Macpherson, *Memoirs*, 291.

26. Poovey, *Uneven Developments*, 126–28.

27. Jameson wrote at least one essay about the plight of governesses (see Macpherson, *Memoirs*). She had been a governess prior to her unhappy marriage; her experience no doubt contributed to her interest in the predicament of women who needed to support themselves (see Kunitz, *British Authors*, 325).

28. For a description of Maurice's involvement with Queen's College, especially his

opening address in which he "set out to raise the governess' standard of self-respect" (134), see Wood, *Frederick Denison Maurice*, 134–35.

29. Larson, *Rise of Professionalism*, 61. See chapter 7 for a more complete discussion of vocation.

30. On Protestant sisterhoods in England, see Heeney, *Women's Movement in the Church of England;* B. Hill, "Refuge from Men"; Malmgreen, *Religion in the Lives of English Women;* Vicinus, *Independent Women;* and Anson, *Call of the Cloister.*

31. J. Harrison, *History of the Working Men's College*, 110.

32. Rendell, *Origins of Modern Feminism*, 71; Macpherson, *Memoirs*, 292–94.

33. Parkes, "A Review of the Last Six Years" is reprinted in Lacey, *Barbara Bodichon*, 216. See also Parkes, "What Can Educated Women Do?" reprinted in Lacey, *Barbara Leigh Smith Bodichon*, 151–54; Parkes, "A Year's Experience in Woman's Work," *Transactions of the NAPSS*, 815–16; as well as Bodichon, "Women and Work," which is reprinted in Lacey, *Barbara Leigh Smith Bodichon*, 62–63.

34. Frederick Maurice devotes one paragraph to this venture in his biography, *Life of Frederick Denison Maurice.* Wood, in *Frederick Denison Maurice,* does not mention it at all, although he discusses Maurice's involvement with Queen's College and the Working Men's College. Stanley J. Kunitz does not mention either the *Lectures* or the classes in his biographical sketch of Maurice in *British Authors.* Kingsley's wife quotes part of Kingsley's lecture in *Charles Kingsley: His Letters and Memories of His Life* but only to illustrate "the human and humane rules by which he worked in his parish" (223). She does not mention the classes for women. Brenda Colloms in *Charles Kingsley: The Lion of Eversley* gives Kingsley's lecture one line. J. F. C. Harrison in *History of the Working Men's College* gives a paragraph to the *Lectures* and another page to the later history of the Working Women's College, but he does not discuss the original classes or their result.

5. The Female Visitor and the Marriage of Classes in Elizabeth Gaskell's *North and South*

1. Review of *Lectures to Ladies,* 150, 151. Further references are cited parenthetically.

2. The most well-known Marxist readings of *North and South* are Kettle, "Early Victorian Social-Problem Novel," and Williams, *Culture and Society.* Other critics who read *North and South* primarily in terms of the social problems of class and industrialization include Lansbury, *Elizabeth Gaskell;* Brantlinger, *Spirit of Reform;* and Kestner, *Protest and Reform.* For examples of feminist readings, see Basch, *Relative Creatures;* David, *Fictions of Resolution;* Nestor, *Female Friendships and Communities;* Stoneman, *Elizabeth Gaskell;* Morgan, *Sisters in Time;* and Davis, "Feminist Critics and Literary Mothers."

3. Lucas, *Literature of Change,* xiv; Minogue, "Gender and Class," 76.

4. Gallagher, *Industrial Reformation of English Fiction,* 178.

5. Schor, *Scheherazade in the Marketplace,* 144.

6. Bodenheimer, *Politics of Story,* 67.

7. "A Memoir of Mr. Justice Talfourd," *Law Magazine* n.s. 20 (1854): 323.

8. For an account of the 1850s strikes, especially the Preston Strike, see Dutton and King, *"Ten Per Cent and No Surrender."*

9. For more extended discussion of Gaskell and the Preston Strike, see Carnall, "Dick-

ens, Mrs. Gaskell, and the Preston Strike," as well as Brantlinger, "Case against Trade Unions."

10. Ashworth, *Preston Strike*, 15–16.

11. See J. Harrison, *History of the Working Men's College*.

12. Manuals and other published advice to visitors often equate middle-class women's influence on servants in their own homes and their influence in the homes of the poor, although their relative position in the two situations is quite different. See, for instance, the popular lecture by Charles Kingsley, "The Country Parish" in *Lectures to Ladies*, 53–66. Visiting, in some cases, was taken up as part of a program of finding or training good servants. See Gerard, "Lady Bountiful," 199; Horn, *Rise and Fall of the Victorian Servant*, 36–37. For a discussion of middle-class women as mediators of class through their relations with servants, see Summers, "Home from Home."

13. *District Visitor's Manual*, 31.

14. Eileen Janes Yeo, in *Contest for Social Science*, makes a similar point (127–28).

15. O. Hill, *District Visiting*, 4–5. Further references are cited parenthetically.

16. Gaskell, *North and South*, 118. Further references are cited parenthetically.

17. Gerard discusses the way in which the traditional rural Lady Bountiful role had a renewed ideological significance in the nineteenth century. "In their role as Lady Bountiful," she writes, "women in the nineteenth century gentry and aristocracy reinforced the landed classes' rule over the rural poor, implementing paternalism and enforcing deference. . . . They made the personal contacts so crucial for maintaining the system of patriarchal control and deference" ("Lady Bountiful," 183–84).

18. For instance, Ivan Melada's thesis in *The Captain of Industry in English Fiction* is that nineteenth-century industrial novels chart the progress of industrialists in assimilating the principles of paternalism.

19. Anthony Russell discusses the changing role of the clergy during the nineteenth century in *Clerical Profession*, 40, 166, see esp. 162–66.

20. The clergy's attempts to keep women's visiting under their control have been noted by most commentators on visiting and on the clergy. That this control was deemed essential is also readily apparent in virtually all the nineteenth-century manuals for district visitors. Both *The District Visitor's Manual* and *Hints to District Visitors*, for instance, include excerpts from "A Charge of the Late Bishop of London" (1830) that exhort the clergyman not to relinquish authority to women visitors:

> [I]t is incumbent upon me to caution the Parochial Clergy against relinquishing the superintendence and direction of these auxiliary laborers; and against delegating to *them* their own peculiar functions and duties, as the Commissioned Interpreters of Scripture, as the LORD's Remembrancers for His people, and as the appointed Guides of their devotion.
>
> There is a special promise of blessing annexed to ministerial service, and the sense of that speciality ought never to be effaced from the minds of our flocks, by the permitted intrusion of laymen however pious or zealous, into that which belongs to our own peculiar office. (*Hints*, ii)

For a discussion of the attempt of the clergy to subordinate women visitors as part of their move toward professionalization, see Heeney, *Women's Movement in the Church of England*. Beth Fowkes Tobin also finds evidence of this conflict between women visitors of the poor and the established clergy in Hannah More's works from early in the century, in her chapter "Women, the Clergy, and the Battle for the Superintendency of the Poor" in *Superintending the Poor*, 98–128.

21. Suzy Clarkson Holstein reads Mr. Hale's renunciation as Gaskell's challenge to patriarchal authority, in "A 'Root Deeper Than All Change.'" Patsy Stoneman, in *Elizabeth Gaskell*, offers a similar reading.

22. Russell, in *Clerical Profession*, cites all these activities as characteristic of the new professional clergy.

23. Anthony Russell identifies a stereotype that Gaskell apparently utilizes in the Hepworths: "The picture of the managing clergyman and his formidable wife ruling the local community dates from this period" (*Clerical Profession*, 178). However, as Jessica Gerard indicates, in "Lady Bountiful," rural Lady Bountifuls also arguably played a revitalized role in promoting the interests of the gentry during the mid-nineteenth century.

The "bad" or "dangerous" female visitor was perhaps best represented to the nineteenth-century popular imagination in Dickens's Mrs. Pardiggle. The response of the working man Mrs. Pardiggle visits indicates the negative effect on class relations that the wrong kind of visitor was feared to have: "'make it easy for her!' growled the man upon the floor. 'I wants it done, and over. I wants an end of these liberties took with my place. I wants an end of being drawed like a badger. Now you're a-going to poll-pry and question according to custom—I know what you're a-going to be up to. Well! You haven't got no occasion to be up to it'" (*Bleak House*, 158). Margaret Hale, unlike Mrs. Pardiggle, always treats the Higginses with respect, courtesy, and gentle friendliness, always fearing to intrude and never prying or pushing advice on them. Margaret's interactions with the Higginses are always exemplary, and her character serves as an antidote to Dickens's negative caricature of the female visitor.

24. Kingsley writes, "It is said that a clergyman's wife ought to consider the parish as *her* flock as well as her husband's. It may be so: I believe the dogma to be much overstated just now" (*Lectures to Ladies*, 55–56).

25. Hilary M. Schor, in *Scheherazade in the Marketplace*, also discusses Margaret's role as "textual transmitter," to a somewhat different purpose (121).

26. P. E. Johnson, "Role of the Middle-Class Woman," 143.

27. Gallagher, *Industrial Reformation of English Fiction*, 181, 183.

28. Ibid., 168.

29. Schor makes a similar point when she suggests that the novel "posit[s] the literary text as the object that moves between masters and men, that will lead them to the sympathy that in turn brings about reform" (*Scheherazade in the Marketplace*, 137).

30. Bodenheimer, *Politics of Story*, 57–58, and Gallagher, *Industrial Reformation of English Fiction*, 167–68, also point to this rejection of the parent-child metaphor as a rejection of paternalism.

31. Mr. Hale tries to suggest adolescence as a substitute for the child half of the paternalist analogy for class relations, but this, too, is rejected because, as Margaret claims, adolescence is still childhood in the sense that the parent, however much independence is granted, continues to hold all the power.

32. Rosemarie Bodenheimer makes a similar argument about a number of industrial novels: "The middle-class heroine is also in a structurally double relation to working-

class characters, figuring the latent social power of both classes while robbing it of its destructive power" (*Politics of Story*, 18). Joseph A. Kestner offers a more literal connection by claiming that "women identified [themselves] with the disenfranchised working classes" (*Protest and Reform*, 3).

33. On Victorian women and modesty, see Yeazell, "Why Political Novels Have Heroines," as well as her *Fictions of Modesty*.

34. In the eighteenth century, it was sexuality rather than labor that the working classes were represented as withholding. The major fear was that the laborers would not have enough children to stoke the nation's economic prosperity and military strength, rather than the fear that the laborers would not work.

35. A letter Gaskell wrote during the composition of *North and South* indicates she thought of having Thornton's mill and house burn so that Margaret "need not go & live there when she's married." For whatever reason, Gaskell did not, however, make this change, and thus presumably Margaret does need to "go & live there" following her marriage (Elizabeth Gaskell to Catherine Winkworth, 11 to 14 Oct. 1854, *Letters*, no. 211, p. 310).

36. Gallagher, *Industrial Reformation of English Fiction*, 148.

37. Riley, *"Am I That Name?"* 48, 54–55.

6. Educating Women's Desires

1. Parkes, "Charity as a Portion of the Public Vocation of Women," 193. Further references are cited parenthetically.

2. Some relevant studies of the sensation novel include Brantlinger, "What Is 'Sensational' about the 'Sensation Novel'?"; Dalke, "Shameless Woman Is the Worst of Men"; Nenadic, "Illegitimacy, Insanity, and Insolvency"; Briganti, "Gothic Maidens and Sensation Women"; J. Sutherland, "Wilkie Collins and the Origins of the Sensation Novel"; Huskey, "No Name"; Tromp, *Private Rod;* and Tromp et al., *Beyond Sensation*.

   Mid-Victorian novels that represented women as professional artists, actresses, and so forth include Anne Brontë, *The Tenant of Wildfell Hall* (1848); Dinah Mulock Craik, *Olive* (1850); Geraldine Jewsbury, *The Half Sisters* (1848); Frances Trollope, *Mabel's Progress* (1867); Eliza Lynn Linton, *Sowing the Wind* (1967); Charles Reade, *A Woman-Hater* (1877); and Elizabeth Barrett Browning, *Aurora Leigh* (1857), a novel-length poem.

3. Thomson, *Victorian Heroine*, 18.

4. Ibid., 28.

5. Poovey, *Uneven Developments*, 198. For an account of the work and writings of these female philanthropists, see Prochaska, *Women and Philanthropy*.

6. For more examples, see Thomson, *Victorian Heroine*, 25.

7. An important study of the romantic heroine is Brownstein, *Becoming a Heroine*.

8. Freud, "Creative Writers and Day-Dreaming," 147.

9. Nightingale, *Cassandra*, 66.

10. Ardis, *New Women, New Novels*, 61; Foster, *Victorian Women's Fiction*, 14. Other feminist critics who discuss the role of the heroine in the nineteenth-century novel include Basch, *Relative Creatures;* Edwards, *Psyche as Hero;* Rabine, *Reading the Romantic Heroine;* Morgan, *Sisters in Time;* and Reynolds and Humble, *Victorian Heroines*. Jo-

seph Allen Boone also assesses at length the ideological implications of the marriage plot in *Tradition Counter Tradition*.

11. Reynolds and Humble, *Victorian Heroines*, 3.

12. See R. C. Terry's account of his survey of the circulation figures for Mudie's Select Library in *Victorian Popular Fiction* (11–23).

13. Edwards, *Psyche as Hero*, 5.

14. Ibid., 23.

15. Brock, *Charity Helstone*, 353. Further references are cited parenthetically.

16. Brontë, *Shirley*, 390–91.

17. Mrs. Jones appears in two of Hannah More's *Cheap Repository Tracts* addressed to "persons of the middle ranks": "A Cure for Melancholy" and "The Sunday School" in *Works*, vol. 4. See chapter 2 for a discussion of the tracts.

18. 1 Cor. 13:4–7.

19. Bodenheimer, *Politics of Story*, 22, 23.

20. Beth Fowkes Tobin discusses the issue of middle-class women replacing paternalist landlords who have failed to live up to their duties to the poor in *Superintending the Poor*.

21. Sanders, *Eve's Renegades*, 64.

22. Attributed to "C. M. N." Yonge, *Clever Woman of the Family*, 5. Further references are cited parenthetically.

23. Sturrock, "Heaven and Home," 48–73.

24. Girard, *Deceit, Desire, and the Novel*. See the introduction to this study for a discussion of Girard's theory and its relation to the generation of women's ambitious desires.

25. Braddon, *Lady Audley's Secret*.

26. Alick's proposal is reminiscent of a pamphlet outlining philanthropic opportunities for women in military regiments, entitled *Work While It is Day. An Appeal to the Women of the United Kingdom (Especially those personally connected with the British Army) on Behalf of our Gallant Soldiers, by One of Themselves*, which praises a Mrs. Sherwood as the first woman to do what she could in her husband's regiment.

27. P. K. Gilbert, *Disease, Desire, and the Body*, 122, 123.

28. See Craik, "On Sisterhoods." Margaret Goodman, *Experiences of an English Sister of Mercy* (1862) is another contemporary representation. Several other philanthropic heroine novels flirt with the possibility of the heroine joining a Protestant sisterhood, including Lady Georgiana Fullerton, *Mrs. Gerald's Niece* (1869), an Anglo-Catholic novel; Annie Emma Challice, *The Sister of Charity* (1857), in which the heroine travels to the Crimea with a sisterhood but apparently does not take vows; Frances Trollope, *Mabel's Progress* (1867), in which the heroine's home backs onto a sisterhood; and Elizabeth Gaskell, *North and South* (1855), chap. 5.

29. For Jameson's views on sisterhoods, see chap. 4.

30. The serial version of *Not Wisely But Too Well* was published in the *Dublin University Magazine*, Aug. 1865–July 1866. I am indebted to Helen Debenham for calling my attention to the differences between the serial and the book, which many other critics fail to notice.

31. J. Sutherland, *Stanford Companion to Victorian Fiction*, 112.

32. See Poovey, *Uneven Developments*, 164–98; Judd, *Bedside Seductions*.

33. O. Hill, *Homes of the London Poor*, 15, 36. The chapter from which these quotes are taken was originally published as an essay in the *Fortnightly Review* in November 1866

under the title "Cottage Property in London." Further references are cited parenthetically.

34. MacDonald, *Vicar's Daughter*, 367. Further references are cited parenthetically.
35. Thomson, *Victorian Heroine*, 34.
36. Nightingale, *Cassandra*, 188−89.
37. See Lewis, *Women and Social Action*, 18−19.

7. George Eliot's *Middlemarch*

1. Nightingale, "A 'Note' of Interrogation," 567.
2. Ibid.
3. Thomson, *Victorian Heroine*, 18.
4. Jerome Beaty dates the setting of the novel from 30 September 1829 through the end of May 1832 in "History by Indirection" (173). Gillian Beer notes that the time difference between the setting and writing of the novel "register[s] some changes in women's circumstances, but rather small change in the actual conditions of women's lives" in *George Eliot* (170). Beer does not, however, take into account the crucial role of women's philanthropy in any consideration of women's opportunities in the nineteenth century.
5. Eliot, *Middlemarch,* xiii. Further references are cited parenthetically.
6. [Phillips], *My Life and What Shall I Do With It?* 6−7.
7. M. M., "Cottage Habitations," 73.
8. See Eliot, *Middlemarch,* 19 n.
9. Alan Mintz comments on the "entanglement of private need with public task" in Dorothea's "fantasies of the good" in *George Eliot and the Novel of Vocation* (108). While Mintz is right that Dorothea's plans involve paternalistic control over those she intends to aid, he implies that such a wish is more objectionable in a woman such as Dorothea than it would be if she were a man.
10. On Protestant sisterhoods, see Heeney, *Women's Movement in the Church of England,* 63−74; Prelinger, "Female Diaconate in the Anglican Church"; and Anson, *Call of the Cloister.*
11. [Phillips], *My Life and What Shall I Do With It?* 8−9.
12. Jalland, *Women, Marriage and Politics,* 189.
13. See Kali Israel's excellent biography of Emilia Dilke, *Names and Stories.*
14. Larson, *Rise of Professionalism,* 62, 61.
15. Doyle, *Sympathetic Response.*
16. Mintz, *George Eliot and the Novel of Vocation,* 3, 17, 60. Other critics who write on vocation in *Middlemarch* include Greenstein, "Question of Vocation"; Barrett, *Vocation and Desire;* and Blake, "*Middlemarch* and the Woman Question."
17. Feltes, *Modes of Production,* 44, 52−54, 56. Although it receives somewhat less attention, *Middlemarch* represents the same kind of professional struggle going on in the clerical profession as well as in the medical. See Lovesey, *Clerical Character,* 84−95.
18. Lewis, *Women and Social Action,* 20, 11.
19. Larson, *Rise of Professionalism,* 57.
20. Feltes, *Modes of Production,* 55−56.
21. Lewis, *Women and Social Action,* 36, 65.
22. Channing and Aikin, *Correspondence,* 90.

23. O. Hill, *Homes of the London Poor*, 41. Although *Homes* was not published until 1875, after the publication of *Middlemarch*, it deals with her housing and rent collection projects, which date from the 1860s. Much of *Homes* consists of reprinted newspaper and periodical essays Hill wrote in the 1860s.

24. Although in the particular context, the "little kingdom" Dorothea wishes to rule is Will Ladislaw, the phrase also carries the implication that she wishes to rule him because her efforts to "rule beneficently" in other areas have been frustrated.

25. Bell, *Octavia Hill*, 109.

26. Maurice, *Octavia Hill*, 179–80.

27. O. Hill, *Homes of the London Poor*, 34, 35, 23, 38, 39.

28. Hill frequently dwelt on the sense of power she experienced in working with the poor as a "friend"—that is, as a rent collector and district visitor. For a description of Catherine Cappe's gaining entry for female visitors to a hospital by getting wealthy women to subscribe when the hospital was short of funds in 1813, see Prochaska, *Women and Philanthropy*, 141–42.

29. Chase, *Middlemarch*, 64.

30. Ibid., 70.

31. Will's character is associated with even more marginalizing traits than I have mentioned. He is compared several times with Wilkie Collins's villainous Count Fosco, the "Italian with white mice" (see Bates, "Italian with White Mice," and Kurata, "Italians with White Mice Again"). Another critic asserts that Will's Polishness links him with the radical working-class movement of the 1860s (see Malcolm, "What Is a Pole Doing in *Middlemarch*?").

32. Larson, *Rise of Professionalism*, 5.

33. See Henry James's unsigned review in *Galaxy* in 1873. Sandra Gilbert and Susan Gubar give a positive feminist reading to James's disparaging remark (see *Madwoman in the Attic*, 528–29).

34. O. Hill, *Homes of the London Poor*, 10.

35. See Feltes for a discussion of Marian Evans's relation to the pseudonym George Eliot (*Modes of Production*, 40).

Conclusion

1. *The Gut Girls* was performed in 1988 in London in a production directed by Teddy Kiendl at the Albany Empire Theatre. It was then copyrighted and published in 1989. The production I witnessed was directed by Delores Ringer for the University of Kansas Theatre in April 1999.

2. Susan C. Haedicke writes that "Lady Helena, while representing a point of view opposing that of Daniels, is not a monster determined to break the gut girls, and her sympathetic portrayal intensifies the conflicts both author and audience feel about the enforced conformity she imposes on the gut girls" ("Doing the Dirty Work," 79). In the production I viewed, however, Lady Helena was not portrayed as particularly sympathetic.

Bibliography

Primary Sources

Ashworth, Henry. *The Preston Strike, an Enquiry into its Causes and Consequences.* Manchester, 1854.

Astell, Mary. *A Serious Proposal to the Ladies, for the Advancement of Their True and Greatest Interest.* Pt. 1 1694. Pt. 2 1697. 4th ed. London: R. Wilkin, 1701.

Austen, Jane. *Emma.* 1816. Edited by Stephen M. Parrish. 2nd ed. New York: Norton, 1993.

Bayly, Edward. *A Sermon Preached on the Opening of the New Chapel of the Magdalen Asylum in Leeson-Street, Dublin.* Dublin: Josiah Sheppard, 1770.

Benson, Christopher. "A Sermon Preached in Behalf of the General Society for Promoting District Visiting." In *The District Visitor's Manual.* 2nd ed. London, 1840.

Bodichon, Barbara Leigh Smith. *Women and Work.* 1857. New York: C. S. Francis, 1859. Reprinted in *Barbara Leigh Smith Bodichon and the Langham Place Group,* edited by Candida Ann Lacey, 36–73. New York: Routledge, 1987.

Braddon, Mary Elizabeth. *Lady Audley's Secret,* 1862. Oxford: Oxford University Press, 1987.

Brock, Mrs. Carey. *Charity Helstone: A Tale.* London: Seeley, Jackson, and Halliday, 1866.

Brontë, Charlotte. *Shirley.* 1849. Oxford: Oxford University Press, 1979.

Broughton, Rhoda. *Not Wisely But Too Well.* 1867. Dover, N.H.: Alan Sutton, 1993.

Browning, Elizabeth Barrett. *Aurora Leigh.* 1856. Athens: Ohio University Press, 1992.

Burdett-Coutts, The Baroness [Angela], ed. *Woman's Mission: A Series of Congress Papers on the Philanthropic Work of Women by Eminent Writers.* New York: Charles Scribner's; London: Sampson and Low, Marston, and Co., 1893.

Challice, Mrs. [Annie Emma]. *The Sister of Charity; Or From Bermondsey to Belgravia.* London: Richard Bentley, 1857.

Chalmers, Thomas. *The Christian and Civil Economy of Large Towns.* Glasgow: Chalmers and Collins, 1821.

Channing, William Ellery, and Lucy Aikin. *The Correspondence of William Ellery Channing, D. D. and Lucy Aikin.* Edited by Anna Letitia le Breton. London, 1874.

"A Charge of the Late Bishop of London." London, 1830.

Cobbe, Frances Power. "Social Science Congresses, and Women's Part in Them." *Macmillan's Magazine* 5 (1861): 81–94. Reprint, In *Free and Ennobled: Source Readings in the Development of Victorian Feminism,* edited by Carol Bauer and Lawrence Ritt, 84–88. Oxford: Pergamon, 1979.

Craik, Dinah Mulock. "On Sisterhoods." 1883. Reprint, edited by Elaine Showalter, New York: New York University Press, 1993.

———. *A Woman's Thoughts About Women.* New York: Rudd and Carleton, 1863.

Daniels, Sarah. *The Gut Girls.* London: Methuen, 1989.

Defoe, Daniel. *Applebee's Original Weekly Journal.* 1723–24. Reprinted in *Daniel Defoe: His Life, and Recently Discovered Writings,* edited by William Lee. London: John Camden Hotten, 1869.

Dickens, Charles. *Bleak House.* Edited by Norman Page. New York: Penguin, 1971.

The District Visitor's Manual. 2nd ed. London, 1840.

Doran, Dr. John. *A Lady of the Last Century (Mrs. Elizabeth Montagu).* 1873. Reprint, New York: AMS Press, 1973.

Eliot, George. *Middlemarch.* 1871–72. Edited by Bert G. Hornback. New York: Norton, 1977.

Erskine, Mrs. Steuart, ed. *Anna Jameson: Letters and Friendships (1812–1860).* London: T. Fisher Unwin, 1915.

"A Fear for the Future, That Women Will Cease to Be Womanly." *Fraser's Magazine* 59 (Feb. 1859): 243–48.

Fielding, Sarah. *The Adventures of David Simple.* 1744. Oxford: Oxford University Press, 1987.

Francklin, Thomas. *A Sermon preached in the Chapel of the Asylum for Female Orphans, at the Anniversary Meeting of the Guardians on Monday the Sixteenth of May, 1768.* London: W. Bunce, 1768.

Freud, Sigmund. "Creative Writers and Day-Dreaming." *The Standard Edition of the Complete Psychological Works of Sigmund Freud.* Edited by James Strachey, 141–53. Vol. 9 London: Hogarth, 1959.

Gaskell, Elizabeth. *The Letters of Mrs. Gaskell.* Edited by J. A. V. Chapple and Arthur Pollard. Cambridge: Harvard University Press, 1967.

———. *North and South.* 1855. Edited by Angus Easson. Oxford: Oxford University Press, 1973; New York: World's Classics, 1982.

Greg, W. R. "Why Are Women Redundant?" *National Review* 14 (April 1862): 434–60.

Hanbury, William. *An Essay on Planting and a Scheme for Making it conducive to the Glory of God and the Advantage of Society.* Oxford: S. Parker, 1758.

Hanway, Jonas. *Letters to the Guardians of the Infant Poor.* London: A. Millar and T. Cadell; C. Marsh and G. Woodfall, 1767.

[———]. *A Plan for Establishing a Charity-House, or Charity-Houses, for the Reception of Repenting Prostitutes, to be called the Magdalen Charity.* London, 1758.

———. *Three Letters on the Subject of the Marine Society.* London, 1758.

————. *Twenty-nine Letters to a Member of Parliament*. London: J. Dodsley; and Brotherton and Sewell, 1775.

Hazeland, William. *A Sermon Preached in the Chapel of the Asylum, near Westminster Bridge, on the Sunday before Christmas-Day, 1760*. London: J. Beecroft, 1761.

Hill, Octavia. *District Visiting*. London, 1877.

————. *Homes of the London Poor*. 1875. Reprint, London: Macmillan, 1883.

Hints to District Visitors, Followed by a Few Prayers suggested for their Use. London: Sheffington, 1858.

Howson, J. H. "Deaconesses." *Quarterly Review* 108 (Oct. 1860): 179–203.

James, Henry. Unsigned review of *Middlemarch. Galaxy* xv (March 1873): 424–29. Reprinted in *George Eliot: The Critical Heritage*, edited by David Carroll. London: Routledge, 1971.

Jameson, Mrs. [Anna Brownell Murphy]. *Memoirs and Essays, Illustrative of Art, Literature and Social Morals*. London, 1846.

————. *Sisters of Charity, Catholic and Protestant, and The Communion of Labor*. Boston: Ticknor and Fields, 1857.

Kingsley, Charles. *Charles Kingsley: His Letters and Memories of His Life*. Edited by His Wife. Abridged ed. New York: Scribner and Armstrong, 1877.

————. "The Country Parish." In *Lectures to Ladies on Practical Subjects*, edited by F. D. Maurice, 53–66. 2nd ed. Cambridge: Macmillan, 1856.

Layng, Henry. *A Sermon preached in the Parish-Church of All-Saints in Northampton, before the President and Governors of the County Infirmary for Sick and Lame Poor*. Northampton: William Dicey, 1746.

Lennox, Charlotte. *The Female Quixote*. 1752. Oxford: Oxford University Press, 1989.

Linton, E[liza] Lynn. *Sowing the Wind*. London: Tinsley Bros., 1867.

MacDonald, George. *The Vicar's Daughter: An Autobiographical Story*. 1872. Philadelphia: David McKay, 1911.

Macpherson, Geraldine. *Memoirs of the Life of Anna Jameson*. Boston: Roberts, 1878.

Martineau, Harriet. *Cousin Marshall*. In *Illustrations of Political Economy*. Vol. 3. 1832.

————. *Deerbrook*. 1839. London: John Murray, 1892.

————. *Illustrations of Political Economy*. 9 vols. 1832. Reprint, London: Charles Fox, 1834.

Massie, J. *A Plan for the Establishment of Charity-Houses for Exposed or Deserted Women and Girls, and for Penitent Prostitutes*. London: T. Payne, 1758.

Maurice, F. D., ed. *Lectures to Ladies on Practical Subjects*. 1855. 2nd ed. Cambridge: Macmillan, 1856.

Maurice, Frederick. *The Life of Frederick Denison Maurice: Chiefly Told in His Own Letters*. 2 vols. New York: Scribner, 1884.

M. M. "Cottage Habitations." *The English Woman's Journal* 4 (1859): 73–82.

"A Memoir of Mr. Justice Talfourd, *Law Magazine* n.s. 20 (1854): 323.

Montagu, Barbara. *The Histories of Some of the Penitents in the Magdalen-House, As Supposed to be Related by Themselves*. 2 vols. London: John Rivington and J. Dodsley, 1760.

More, Hannah. *Coelebs in Search of a Wife: Comprehending Observations on Domestic Habits and Manners, Religion and Morals*. 1808. 4th ed. 2 vols. London: T. Cadell and W. Davies, 1809.

————. *Strictures on the Modern System of Female Education*. In *The Works of Hannah More*. Vols. 7–8. London: Cadell and Davies, 1801.

————. *The Works of Hannah More.* 8 vols. London: Cadell and Davies, 1801.

More, Martha. *Mendip Annals.* Edited by Arthur Roberts. 2nd ed. London: James Nisbet, 1859.

Murphy, Arthur. "The Old Maid." In *The Way to Keep Him and Five Other Plays,* edited by John Pike Emery, 243–81. New York: New York University Press, 1956.

My District Visitors. By a Parson. London: Skeffington, 1891.

Nightingale, Florence. *Cassandra and Other Selections from Suggestions for Thought.* 1860. Edited by Mary Poovey. New York: New York University Press, 1992.

————. A 'Note' of Interrogation." *Fraser's Magazine* n. s. 7 (May 1873): 567–77.

Ogle, Newton. *A Sermon Preached at the Anniversary Meeting of the Governors of the Magdalen Charity.* London: Sandby and Faden, 1766.

"On National Economy: Miss Martineau's 'Cousin Marshall.'" Review of *Cousin Marshall,* by Harriet Martineau. *Fraser's Magazine* 6 (1832): 403–13.

Parkes, Bessie Rayner. "Charity as a Portion of the Public Vocation of Women." *The English Woman's Journal* 3 (May 1859): 193–96.

————. *Remarks on the Education of Girls.* London, 1854.

————. "A Review of the Last Six Years." *The English Woman's Journal* (February 1864). Reprinted in *Barbara Leigh Smith Bodichon and the Langham Place Group,* edited by Candida Ann Lacey. New York: Routledge, 1987.

————. "A Year's Experience in Woman's Work." *Transactions of the National Association for the Promotion of Social Science 1860.* London: John W. Parker, 1861.

[Phillips, Lucy F. March]. An Old Maid. *My Life and What Shall I Do With It? A Question for Young Gentlewomen.* London: Longman, Green, Longman, and Roberts, 1860.

Porteus, Beilby. *A Sermon Preached in the Chapel of the Asylum for Female Orphans, at the Anniversary Meeting of the Guardians of that Charity.* London: Harriot Bunce, 1773.

Radcliffe, Ann. *The Mysteries of Udolpho.* 1794. Edited by Bonamy Dobree. Oxford: Oxford University Press, 1970.

Review of *Lectures to Ladies on Practical Subjects,* edited by F. D. Maurice. *Edinburgh Review* 103 (Jan. 1856): 146–53.

[Scott, Sarah]. A Gentleman on his Travels. *A Description of Millenium Hall and the Country Adjacent Together with the Characters of the Inhabitants and such Historical Anecdotes and Reflections as May Excite in the Reader Proper Sentiments of Humanity, and Lead the Mind to Virtue.* 1762. Edited by Jane Spencer. New York: Penguin-Virago, 1986.

————. *The History of Sir George Ellison.* 1766. Lexington: University Press of Kentucky, 1996.

Secker, Thomas. *A Sermon Preached before the Governors of the London Hospital, or, Infirmary, for the Relief of Sick and Diseased Persons, Especially Manufacturers, and Seamen in Merchant-Service, and c. at the Parish-Church of St. Lawrence-Jewry, on Wednesday, February 20, 1754.* London: H. Woodfall, 1754.

Smith, Adam. *Theory of Moral Sentiments.* 1759. Edited by D. D. Raphael and A. L. Mcfie. Oxford: Oxford University Press, 1976; Indianapolis: Liberty Classics, 1982.

Smith, Sydney. Review of *Coelebs in Search of a Wife: Comprehending Observations on Domestic Habits and Manners, Religion and Morals,* by Hannah More. *Edinburgh Review* 14, no. 27 (1809): 145–51.

[Tonna], Charlotte Elizabeth. *Helen Fleetwood.* 1840. *The Works of Charlotte Elizabeth.* Vol. 2. New York: Dodd, 1844.

Trollope, Frances. *Jessie Phillips; a Tale of the Present Day.* London: Henry Colburn, 1844.

————. *The Life and Adventures of Michael Armstrong, the Factory Boy*. 3 vols. London: Henry Colburn, 1840.

Tucker, Josiah. *Hospitals and Infirmaries, Considered as Schools of Christian Education for the Adult Poor; and as Means Conducive towards a National Reformation in the Common People*. London: William Cossley, 1746.

Welch, Saunders. *A Proposal to Render Effectual a Plan to Remove the Nuisance of Common Prostitutes from the Streets of this Metropolis*. London: C. Henderson, 1758.

Work While It is Day. An Appeal to the Women of the United Kingdom (Especially those personally connected with the British Army) on Behalf of our Gallant Soldiers, by One of Themselves. Pamphlet. London: Werthum, Macintosh, and Hunt, n.d.

Yonge, Charlotte M. *The Clever Woman of the Family*. 1865. London: Macmillan, 1889.

————. *The Daisy Chain; or Aspirations: A Family Chronicle*. New York: D. Appleton, 1856.

Secondary Sources

Altick, Richard D. *The English Common Reader*. Chicago: U of Chicago P, 1957. Reprint, 1983.

Andrew, Donna T. *Philanthropy and Police: London Charity in the Eighteenth Century*. Princeton: Princeton University Press, 1989.

Anson, Peter F. *The Call of the Cloister: Religious Communities and Kindred Bodies in the Anglican Communion*. London: SPCK, 1955.

Appleby, Joyce. "Ideology and Theory: The Tension between Political and Economic Liberalism in Seventeenth Century England." *American Historical Review* 81, no. 3 (1976): 499–515.

Ardis, Ann L. *New Women, New Novels: Feminism and Early Modernism*. New Brunswick: Rutgers University Press, 1990.

Armstrong, Nancy. *Desire and Domestic Fiction: A Political History of the Novel*. New York: Oxford University Press, 1987.

Baldick, Chris. *In Frankenstein's Shadow: Myth, Monstrosity, and Nineteenth-Century Writing*. Oxford: Clarendon, 1987.

Barker-Benfield, G. J. *The Culture of Sensibility: Sex and Society in Eighteenth-Century Britain*. Chicago: University of Chicago Press, 1992.

Barrett, Dorothea. *Vocation and Desire: George Eliot's Heroines*. London: Routledge, 1989.

Basch, Francoise. *Relative Creatures: Victorian Women in Society and the Novel*. New York: Schocken, 1974.

Bates, Richard. "The Italian with White Mice in *Middlemarch*." *Notes and Queries* 31, no. 4 (1984): 497.

Beaty, Jerome. "History by Indirection: The Era of Reform in *Middlemarch*." *Victorian Studies* 1, no. 2 (1957): 173–79.

Beer, Gillian. *George Eliot*. Bloomington: Indiana University Press, 1986.

Bell, E. Moberly. *Octavia Hill: A Biography*. London: Constable, 1942.

Bettany, George Thomas. "Thomas Guy." *Dictionary of National Biography*. Vol. 8. 1921. Reprint, Oxford: Oxford University Press, 1967.

Blake, Kathleen. "*Middlemarch* and the Woman Question." In *George Eliot's Middlemarch*, edited by Harold Bloom, 49–70. New York: Chelsea, 1987.

Blau, Peter M. *Exchange and Power in Social Life*. New York: Wiley, 1967.

Bodenheimer, Rosemarie. *The Politics of Story in Victorian Social Fiction*. Ithaca: Cornell University Press, 1988.

Boone, Joseph Allen. *Tradition Counter Tradition: Love and the Form of Fiction*. Chicago: University of Chicago Press, 1987.

Boyd, Nancy. *Three Victorian Women Who Changed Their World: Josephine Butler, Octavia Hill, and Florence Nightingale*. New York: Oxford University Press, 1982.

Bradley, Ian. *The Call to Seriousness*. New York: Macmillan, 1976.

Brantlinger, Patrick. "The Case against Trade Unions in Early Victorian Fiction." *Victorian Studies* 13, no. 1 (1969): 37–52.

———. *The Spirit of Reform: British Literature and Politics, 1832–1867*. Cambridge: Harvard University Press, 1977.

———. "What Is 'Sensational' about the 'Sensation Novel'?" *Nineteenth-Century Literature* 37 (June 1982): 1–28.

Briganti, Chiara. "Gothic Maidens and Sensation Women: Lady Audley's Journey from the Ruined Mansion to the Madhouse." *Victorian Literature and Culture* 19 (1991): 189–211.

Briggs, Asa. *The Age of Improvement, 1783–1867*. London: Longman, 1959. Reissued 1979.

Brown, Ford K. *Fathers of the Victorians: The Age of Wilberforce*. Cambridge: Cambridge University Press, 1961.

Brownstein, Rachel. *Becoming a Heroine: Reading About Women in Novels*. New York: Viking Penguin, 1982.

Burman, Sandra, ed. *Fit Work for Women*. London: Croom Helm, 1979.

Butler, Judith. *Subjects of Desire*. New York: Columbia University Press, 1987.

Carnall, Geoffrey. "Dickens, Mrs. Gaskell, and the Preston Strike." *Victorian Studies* 8, no. 1 (1964): 31–48.

Carretta, Vincent. "Utopia Limited: Sarah Scott's *Millenium Hall* and *The History of Sir George Ellison*." *The Age of Johnson*, A Scholarly Annual 5, edited by Paul J. Korshin, 303–25. New York: AMS, 1992.

Carter, Harry. *A History of the Oxford University Press*. Vol. 1. Oxford: Clarendon, 1975.

Cazamian, Louis François. *The Social Novel in England, 1830–1850: Dickens, Disraeli, Mrs. Gaskell, Kinglsey*. Trans. Martin Fido. London: Routledge and Kegan Paul, 1973.

Chaloner, W. H. "Mrs. Trollope and the Early Factory System." *Victorian Studies* 4 (1960): 159–66.

Chase, Karen. *Middlemarch*. Cambridge: Cambridge University Press, 1991.

Cheal, David. *The Gift Economy*. London: Routledge, 1988.

Climenson, Emily J. *Elizabeth Montagu, The Queen of the Blue-Stockings: Her Correspondence from 1720 to 1761*. London: John Murray, 1906.

Cohen, Monica F. *Professional Domesticity in the Victorian Novel: Women, Work and Home*. Cambridge: Cambridge University Press, 1998.

Colby, Robert Alan. *Fiction with a Purpose: Major and Minor Nineteenth-Century Novels*. Bloomington: Indiana University Press, 1967.

Cole, Lucinda. "(Anti)Feminist Sympathies: The Politics of Relationship in Smith, Wollstonecraft, and More." *ELH* 58, no. 1 (1991): 107–40.

Colloms, Brenda. *Charles Kingsley: The Lion of Eversley*. London: Constable, 1975.

Crittenden, Walter M. Introduction to *A Description of Millenium Hall*, by Sarah Scott. New York: Bookman, 1955.

Dalke, Anne French. "The Shameless Woman Is the Worst of Men: Sexual Aggression in Nineteenth-Century Sensational Novels." *Studies-in-the-Novel* 18 (fall 1986): 291–303.

David, Deirdre. *Fictions of Resolution in Three Victorian Novels:* North and South, Our Mutual Friend, Daniel Deronda. New York: Columbia University Press, 1981.

Davidoff, Leonore, and Catherine Hall. *Family Fortunes: Men and Women of the English Middle Class, 1780–1850.* Chicago: University of Chicago Press, 1987.

Davis, Deanna L. "Feminist Critics and Literary Mothers: Daughters Reading Elizabeth Gaskell." *Signs* 17 (spring 1992): 507–32.

Davison, Lee, et al., eds. "The Reactive State: English Governance and Society, 1689–1750." Introduction to *Stilling the Grumbling Hive: The Response to Social and Economic Problems in England, 1689–1750,* xi–liv. New York: St. Martin's, 1992.

Deegan, Dorothy Yost. *The Stereotype of the Single Woman in American Novels: A Social Study with Implications for the Education of Women.* New York: Columbia University Press, 1951.

Demers, Patricia. *The World of Hannah More.* Lexington: University Press of Kentucky, 1996.

Doyle, Mary Ellen. *The Sympathetic Response: George Eliot's Fictional Rhetoric.* Rutherford: Fairleigh Dickinson University Press, 1981.

Dunne, Linda. "Mothers and Monsters in Sarah Robinson Scott's *Millenium Hall.*" In *Utopian and Science Fiction by Women: Worlds of Difference,* edited by Jane L. Donawerth and Carol A. Kolmerten, 54–72. Syracuse: Syracuse University Press, 1994.

Dutton, H. I., and J. E. King. *"Ten Per Cent and No Surrender": The Preston Strike, 1853–1854.* Cambridge: Cambridge University Press, 1981.

Dyson, A. E. *Dickens'* Bleak House: *A Casebook.* London: Macmillan, 1969.

Edwards, Lee R. *Psyche as Hero: Female Heroism and Fictional Form.* Middletown, Conn.: Wesleyan University Press, 1984.

Elliott, Dorice Williams. "Servants and Hands: Representing the Working Classes in Victorian Factory Novels." *Victorian Literature and Culture* 28, no. 2 (2000): 377–90.

Ellis, Markman. *The Politics of Sensibility: Race, Gender and Commerce in the Sentimental Novel.* Cambridge: Cambridge University Press, 1996.

Engel, Elliott, and Margaret E. King. *The Victorian Novel before Victoria: British Fiction during the Reign of William IV, 1830–37.* London: Macmillan, 1984.

Feltes, N. N. *Modes of Production of Victorian Novels.* Chicago: University of Chicago Press, 1986.

Ford, Charles Howard. *Hannah More: A Critical Biography.* New York: Peter Lang, 1996.

Foster, Shirley. *Victorian Women's Fiction: Marriage, Freedom and the Individual.* London: Croom Helm, 1985.

Foucault, Michel. *Madness and Civilization: A History of Insanity in the Age of Reason.* Trans. Richard Howard. New York: Pantheon, 1965.

Gallagher, Catherine. *The Industrial Reformation of English Fiction: Social Discourse and Narrative Form, 1832–1867.* Chicago: University of Chicago Press, 1985.

Gerard, Jessica. "Lady Bountiful: Women of the Landed Classes and Rural Philanthropy." *Victorian Studies* 30, no. 2 (1987): 183–210.

Gilbert, Pamela K. *Disease, Desire, and the Body in Victorian Women's Popular Novels.* Cambridge: Cambridge University Press, 1997.

Gilbert, Sandra, and Susan Gubar. *The Madwoman in the Attic: The Woman Writer and the*

Nineteenth-Century Literary Imagination. New Haven: Yale University Press, 1979.

Girard, René. *Deceit, Desire, and the Novel: Self and Other in Literary Structure*. Trans. Yvonne Freccero. Baltimore: Johns Hopkins University Press, 1965.

Gray, B. Kirkman. *A History of English Philanthropy*. London: P. S. King, 1905.

Gray, Robert. *The Factory Question and Industrial England, 1830–1860*. Cambridge: Cambridge University Press, 1996.

Greenstein, Susan M. "The Question of Vocation: From *Romola* to *Middlemarch*." *Nineteenth-Century Fiction* 35, no. 4 (1981): 487–505.

Guy, Joshephine M. *The Victorian Social-Problem Novel: The Market, the Individual, and Communal Life*. New York: St. Martin's, 1996.

Haedicke, Susan C. "Doing the Dirty Work: Gendered Visions of Working Class Women in Sarah Daniels' *The Gut Girls* and Israel Horovitz's *North Shore Fish*." *Journal of Dramatic Theory and Criticism* 8 (spring 1994): 77–88.

Haggerty, George E. "'Romantic Friendship' and Patriarchal Narrative in Sarah Scott's *Millenium Hall*." *Genders* 13 (spring 1992): 108–22.

Hall, Catherine. "The Early Formation of Domestic Ideology." In *Fit Work for Women*, edited by Sandra Burman, 15–32. London: Croom Helm, 1979.

Harland, Marion [Mary Virginia Hawes]. *Hannah More*. New York: Putnam's, 1900.

Harrison, Gary. "Wordsworth's 'The Old Cumberland Beggar': The Economy of Charity in Late Eighteenth-Century Britain." *Criticism* 30, no. 1 (1988): 23–42.

Harrison, J. F. C. *A History of the Working Men's College 1854–1954*. London: Routledge, 1954.

Harsh, Constance D. *Subversive Heroines: Feminist Resolutions of Social Crisis in the Condition-of-England Novel*. Ann Arbor: University of Michigan Press, 1994.

Heeney, Brian. *The Women's Movement in the Church of England, 1850–1930*. Oxford: Clarendon, 1988.

Heineman, Helen. *Frances Trollope*. TEAS 370. Boston: Twayne, 1984.

———. *Mrs. Trollope: The Triumphant Feminine in the Nineteenth Century*. Athens: Ohio University Press, 1979.

Hill, Bridget. "A Refuge from Men: The Idea of a Protestant Nunnery." *Past and Present* 117 (Nov. 1987): 107–30.

———. *Women, Work, and Sexual Politics in Eighteenth-Century England*. Oxford: Basil Blackwell, 1989.

———, ed. *Eighteenth-Century Women: An Anthology*. London: George Allen and Unwin, 1984.

Hilton, Boyd. *The Age of Atonement: The Influence of Evangelicalism on Social and Economic Thought, 1795–1865*. Oxford: Clarendon, 1988.

Himmelfarb, Gertrude. *The Idea of Poverty: England in the Early Industrial Age*. New York: Knopf, 1984.

Hobart, Ann. "Harriet Martineau's Political Economy of Everyday Life." *Victorian Studies* 37, no. 2 (1994): 223–51.

Hole, Robert, ed. Introduction to *Selected Writings of Hannah More*. London: William Pickering, 1996.

Holstein, Suzy Clarkson. "A 'Root Deeper Than All Change': The Daughter's Longing in the Victorian Novel." *Victorian Newsletter* 75 (spring 1989): 20–28.

Hopkins, Mary Alden. *Hannah More and Her Circle*. New York: Longmans, 1947.

Horn, Pamela. *The Rise and Fall of the Victorian Servant*. Dublin: Gill and Macmillan, 1975.

Howse, Ernest Marshall. *Saints in Politics: The "Clapham Sect" and the Growth of Freedom*. Toronto: University of Toronto Press, 1952.

Hufton, Olwen. "Women without Men: Widows and Spinsters in Britain and France in the Eighteenth Century." *Journal of Family History* 9 (winter 1984): 355–75.

Hunter, Shelagh. *Harriet Martineau: The Poetics of Moralism*. Brookfield, Vt.: Scolar Press, 1995.

Huskey, Melynda. "No Name: Embodying the Sensation Heroine." *Victorian Newsletter* 82 (fall 1992): 5–13.

Israel, Kali. *Names and Stories: Emilia Dilke and Victorian Culture*. New York: Oxford University Press, 1999.

Jalland, Pat. *Women, Marriage and Politics, 1860–1914*. Oxford: Oxford University Press, 1988.

Johnson, John, and Strickland Gibson. *Print and Privilege at Oxford to the Year 1700*. Oxford: Oxford University Press, 1946.

Johnson, Patricia Ellen. "The Role of the Middle-Class Woman in the Mid-Nineteenth-Century British Industrial Novel." Ph.D. diss., University of Minnesota, 1985.

Johnston, Judith. *Anna Jameson: Victorian, Feminist, Woman of Letters*. Brookfield, Vt.: Scolar Press, 1997.

Jones, Gareth Stedman. *Outcast London: A Study in the Relationship between Classes in Victorian Society*. Oxford: Clarendon Press, 1971.

Jones, M. G. *Hannah More*. Cambridge: Cambridge University Press, 1952.

Jones, Vivien, ed. *Women in the Eighteenth Century: Constructions of Femininity*. London: Routledge, 1990.

Jordan, W. K. *Philanthropy in England, 1480–1660: A Study of the Changing Pattern of English Social Aspirations*. London: G. Allen and Unwin, 1959.

Kaplan, Deborah. "The Woman Worker in Charlotte Elizabeth Tonna's Fiction." *Mosaic* 18 (1985): 51–63.

Judd, Catherine. *Bedside Seductions: Nursing and the Victorian Imagination, 1830–1880*. New York: St. Martin's, 1998.

Kelly, Gary. Introduction to *A Description of Millenium Hall*, by Sarah Scott. Peterborough, Ontario: Broadview, 1995.

Kestner, Joseph A. *Protest and Reform: The British Social Narrative by Women, 1827–1857*. Madison: University of Wisconsin Press, 1985.

Kettle, Arnold. "The Early Victorian Social-Problem Novel." In *From Dickens to Hardy*, edited by Boris Ford. Vol. 6 of The New Pelican Guide to English Literature. Rev. ed. Harmondsworth: Penguin, 1982.

Kovacevic, Ivanka, ed. *Fact into Fiction: English Literature and the Industrial Scene, 1750–1850*. Leicester: Leicester University Press, 1975.

Kovacevic, Ivanka, and Barbara Kanner. "Blue Book into Novel: The Forgotten Industrial Fiction of Charlotte Elizabeth Tonna." *Nineteenth-Century Fiction* 25 (Sept. 1970): 152–73.

Kowaleski-Wallace, Elizabeth. *Their Father's Daughters: Hannah More, Maria Edgeworth, and Patriarchal Complicity*. New York: Oxford University Press, 1991.

Krueger, Christine L. *The Reader's Repentance: Women Preachers, Women Writers, and Nineteenth-Century Social Discourse*. Chicago: University of Chicago Press, 1992.

Kunitz, Stanley J., ed. *British Authors of the Nineteenth Century*. New York: H. W. Wilson, 1936.

Kurata, Marilyn J. "Italians with White Mice Again: *Middlemarch* and *The Woman in White.*" *English Language Notes* 22, no. 4 (1985): 45–47.

Lacey, Candida Ann, ed. *Barbara Leigh Smith Bodichon and the Langham Place Group*. New York: Routledge, 1987.

Langland, Elizabeth. *Nobody's Angels: Middle-class Women and Domestic Ideology in Victorian Culture*. Ithaca: Cornell University Press, 1995.

Lansbury, Coral. *Elizabeth Gaskell: The Novel of Social Crisis*. New York: Barnes and Noble, 1975.

Lanser, Susan Sniader. *Fictions of Authority: Women Writers and Narrative Voice*. Ithaca: Cornell University Press, 1992.

Laqueur, Thomas. *Religion and Respectability: Sunday Schools and Working Class Culture 1780–1850*. New Haven: Yale University Press, 1976.

Larson, Magali Sarfatti. *The Rise of Professionalism*. Berkeley: University of California Press, 1977.

Lean, Garth. *God's Politician: William Wilberforce's Struggle*. London: Darton, Longman and Todd, 1980.

Legates, Marlene. "The Cult of Womanhood in Eighteenth-Century Thought." *Eighteenth-Century Studies* 10, no. 1 (1976): 21–39.

Lewis, Jane. *Women and Social Action in Victorian and Edwardian England*. Hants, England: Edward Elgar, 1991.

Livingston, Paisley. *Models of Desire: René Girard and the Psychology of Mimesis*. Baltimore: Johns Hopkins University Press, 1992.

Lovesey, Oliver. *The Clerical Character in George Eliot's Fiction*. English Literary Studies 52. Victoria, BC: University of Victoria Press, 1991.

Lucas, John. *The Literature of Change: Studies in the Nineteenth-Century Provincial Novel*. New Jersey: Barnes and Noble, 1980.

Macey, J. David, Jr. "Eden Revisited: Re-visions of the Garden in Astell's *Serious Proposal,* Scott's *Millenium Hall,* and Graffigny's *Lettres d'une péruvienne.*" *Eighteenth-Century Fiction* 9 (January 1997): 161–82.

Malcolm, David. "What Is a Pole Doing in *Middlemarch?*" *George Eliot Fellowship Review* 17 (1986): 63–69.

Malmgreen, Gail, ed. *Religion in the Lives of English Women, 1760–1930*. Bloomington: Indiana University Press, 1986.

Markley, Robert. "Sentimentality as Performance: Shaftesbury, Sterne, and the Theatrics of Virtue." In *The New Eighteenth Century: Theory, Politics, English Literature,* edited by Felicity Nussbaum and Laura Brown, 210–30. New York: Methuen, 1987.

Marshall, Dorothy. *The English Poor in the Eighteenth Century*. London: Routledge, 1926. Reissued 1969.

Mathias, Peter. *The Transformation of England*. New York: Columbia University Press, 1979.

Maurice, Emily S., ed. *Octavia Hill: Early Ideals*. London: George Allen and Unwin, 1928.

Mauss, Marcel. *The Gift: Forms and Functions of Exchange in Archaic Societies*. Trans. Ian Cunnison. New York: Norton, 1967.

McCarthy, Kathleen D., ed. *Lady Bountiful Revisited: Women, Philanthropy, and Power*. New Brunswick: Rutgers University Press, 1990.

McKendrick, Neil, John Brewer, and J. H. Plumb. *The Birth of a Consumer Society:*

The Commercialization of Eighteenth-Century England. Bloomington: Indiana University Press, 1982.

Melada, Ivan. *The Captain of Industry in English Fiction 1821–1871*. Albuquerque: University of New Mexico Press, 1970.

Miller, Nancy K. "Emphasis Added: Plots and Plausibilities in Women's Fiction." In *The New Feminist Criticism: Essays on Women, Literature, and Theory*, edited by Elaine Showalter, 339–60. New York: Pantheon, 1985. Originally published in *PMLA* 96, no. 1 (1981): 36–48.

Minogue, Sally. "Gender and Class in *Villette* and *North and South*." In *Problems for Feminist Criticism*, edited by Sally Minogue, 70–108. London: Routledge, 1990.

Mintz, Alan. *George Eliot and the Novel of Vocation*. Cambridge: Harvard University Press, 1978.

Morgan, Susan. *Sisters in Time: Imagining Gender in Nineteenth-Century British Fiction*. New York: Oxford University Press, 1989.

Mullan, John. *Sentiment and Sociability: The Language of Feeling in the Eighteenth Century*. Oxford: Clarendon, 1988.

Myers, Mitzi. "Hannah More's Tracts for the Times: Social Fiction and Female Ideology." In *Fetter'd or Free? British Women Novelists, 1670–1815*, edited by Mary Anne Schofield and Cecilia Macheski, 264–84. Athens: Ohio University Press, 1986.

———. "Reform or Ruin: 'A Revolution in Female Manners.'" In *Studies in Eighteenth-Century Culture*. Vol. 2, edited by Harry C. Payne. Madison: University of Wisconsin Press, 1982.

Nenadic, Stana. "Illegitimacy, Insanity, and Insolvency: Wilkie Collins and the Victorian Nightmares." In *The Arts, Literature, and Society*, edited by Arthur Marwick, 133–62. London: Routledge, 1990.

Nestor, Pauline. *Female Friendships and Communities: Charlotte Brontë, George Eliot, Elizabeth Gaskell*. Oxford: Clarendon, 1985.

Neville-Sington, Pamela. *Fanny Trollope: The Life and Adventures of a Clever Woman*. New York: Viking, 1998.

Newby, Howard. "The Deferential Dialectic." *Comparative Studies in Society and History* 17 (April 1975): 139–64.

Owen, David. *English Philanthropy, 1660–1960*. Cambridge: Belknap Press of Harvard, 1964.

Perkin, Harold. *Origins of Modern English Society*. London: Ark-Doubleday, 1969.

Perry, Ruth. *Women, Letters, and the Novel*. New York: AMS, 1980.

Pocock, J. G. A. "The Mobility of Property and the Rise of Eighteenth-Century Sociology." In *Virtue, Commerce, and History: Essays on Political Thought and History, Chiefly in the Eighteenth Century*, by J. G. A. Pocock, 103–23. Cambridge: Cambridge University Press, 1985.

Pollock, John. *William Wilberforce*. New York: St. Martin's, 1978.

Poovey, Mary. *Making a Social Body: British Cultural Formation, 1830–1864*. Chicago: University of Chicago Press, 1995.

———. *The Proper Lady and the Woman Writer: Ideology as Style in the Works of Mary Wollstonecraft, Mary Shelley, and Jane Austen*. Chicago: University of Chicago Press, 1984.

———. *Uneven Developments: The Ideological Work of Gender in Mid-Victorian England*. Chicago: University of Chicago Press, 1988.

Pope, Norris. *Dickens and Charity*. New York: Columbia University Press, 1978.

Prelinger, Catherine M. "The Female Diaconate in the Anglican Church: What Kind of Ministry for Women?" In *Religion in the Lives of English Women, 1760–1930*, edited by Gail Malmgreen, 161–92. Bloomington: Indiana University Press, 1986.

Prochaska, F. K. *Women and Philanthropy in Nineteenth-Century England*. Oxford: Clarendon, 1980.

Rabb, Melinda Alliker. "Making and Rethinking the Canon: General Introduction and the Case of *Millenium Hall*." *Modern Language Studies* 18, no. 1 (1988): 3–16.

Rabine, Leslie W. *Reading the Romantic Heroine: Text, History, Ideology*. Ann Arbor: University of Michigan Press, 1985.

Rendell, Jane. *The Origins of Modern Feminism: Women in Britain, France, and The United States, 1780–1860*. New York: Schocken, 1984.

Reynolds, Kimberley, and Nicola Humble. *Victorian Heroines: Representations of Femininity in Nineteenth-Century Literature and Art*. New York: New York University Press, 1993.

Richardson, William. "Sentimental Journey of Hannah More: Propagandist and Shaper of Victorian Attitudes." *Revolutionary Worlds* 11–13 (1975): 228–39.

Riley, Denise. *"Am I That Name?" Feminism and the Category of "Women" in History*. London: Macmillan, 1988.

Rizzo, Betty. Introduction to *The History of Sir George Ellison,* by Sarah Scott. Lexington: University Press of Kentucky, 1996.

Rodgers, Betsy. *Cloak of Charity: Studies in Eighteenth-Century Philanthropy*. London: Methuen, 1949.

Rosman, Doreen M. *Evangelicals and Culture*. London: Croom Helm, 1984.

Rousseau, G. S. "Nerves, Spirits and Fibres: Towards the Origin of Sensibility." In *Studies in the Eighteenth Century*. Vol. 3, edited by R. F. Brissenden, 137–52. Canberra: Australian National University Press, 1975.

Russell, Anthony. *The Clerical Profession*. London: SPCK, 1980.

Sanders, Valerie. *Eve's Renegades: Victorian Anti-Feminist Women Novelists*. New York: St. Martin's, 1996.

———. *Reason over Passion: Harriet Martineau and the Victorian Novel*. New York: St. Martin's, 1986.

Schneewind, J. B. "Philosophical Ideas of Charity: Some Historical Reflections." *Giving: Western Ideas of Philanthropy,* edited by J. B. Schneewind, 54–75. Bloomington: Indiana University Press, 1996.

Schnorrenberg, Barbara Brandon. "A Paradise Like Eve's: Three Eighteenth Century English Female Utopias." *Women's Studies* 9, no. 3 (1982): 262–73.

Schor, Hilary M. *Scheherazade in the Marketplace: Elizabeth Gaskell and the Victorian Novel*. New York: Oxford University Press, 1992.

Shrivastava, Dr. K. C. *Women Novelists: Their Contribution to the Proletarian Novel in the Victorian Age*. Salzburg Studies in English Literature: Romantic Reassessment. Edited by James Hogg. Salzburg, Austria: Institut für Anglistik und Amerikanistik, 1985.

Skinner, Gillian. *Sensibility and Economics in the Novel, 1740–1800: The Price of a Tear*. Houndsmills, Hampshire: Macmillan, 1999.

Smith, Johanna M. "Philanthropic Community in *Millenium Hall* and the York Ladies Committee." *The Eighteenth Century: Theory and Interpretation* 36 (autumn 1995): 266–82.

Smith, Olivia. *The Politics of Language 1791–1819.* Oxford: Clarendon, 1984.

Spencer, Jane. Introduction to *A Description of Millenium Hall,* by Sarah Scott. New York: Penguin-Virago, 1986.

Spinney, G. H. "Cheap Repository Tracts: Hazard and Marshall Edition." *The Library,* 4th series, 20 (1939): 295–340.

Stoddard, Eve Walsh. "The Politics of Sentiment: Sarah Scott's *Millenium Hall." Transactions of the Eighth International Congress on the Enlightenment, #2. Studies on Voltaire and the Eighteenth Century* 304 (1992): 795–98.

Stoneman, Patsy. *Elizabeth Gaskell.* Bloomington: Indiana University Press, 1987.

Sturrock, June. *"Heaven and Home": Charlotte M. Yonge's Domestic Fiction and the Victorian Debate over Women.* English Literary Studies 66. Victoria, BC: University of Victoria Press, 1995.

Summers, Anne. "A Home from Home—Women's Philanthropic Work in the Nineteenth Century." In *Fit Work for Women,* edited by Sandra Burman, 33–46. London: Croom Helm, 1979.

Sutherland, John. *The Stanford Companion to Victorian Fiction.* Stanford: Stanford University Press, 1989.

———. "Wilkie Collins and the Origins of the Sensation Novel." *Dickens Studies Annual* 20 (1991): 243–58.

Sutherland, Kathryn. "Hannah More's Counter-Revolutionary Feminism." In *Revolution in Writing: British Literary Responses to the French Revolution,* edited by Kelvin Everest, 27–63. Philadelphia: Open University Press, 1991.

Terry, R. C. *Victorian Popular Fiction, 1860–80.* London: Macmillan, 1983.

Thomas, Gillian. *Harriet Martineau.* TEAS 404. Boston: Twayne, 1985.

Thomson, Patricia. *The Victorian Heroine: A Changing Ideal 1837–1873.* London: Oxford University Press, 1956.

Tobin, Beth Fowkes. *Superintending the Poor: Charitable Ladies and Paternal Landlords in British Fiction, 1770–1860.* New Haven: Yale University Press, 1993.

Todd, Janet. *Sensibility: An Introduction.* London: Methuen, 1986.

———. *The Sign of Angellica: Women, Writing, and Fiction 1660–1800.* London: Virago, 1989.

Tromp, Marlene. *The Private Rod : Marital Violence, Sensation, and the Law in Victorian Britain.* Charlottesville: University Press of Virginia, 2000.

Tromp, Marlene, Pamela K. Gilbert, and Aeron Haynie, eds. *Beyond Sensation: Mary Elizabeth Braddon in Context.* Albany: State University of New York Press, 2000.

Valenze, Deborah M. *The First Industrial Woman.* New York: Oxford University Press, 1995.

Vicinus, Martha. *Independent Women: Work and Community for Single Women, 1850–1920.* Chicago: University of Chicago Press, 1985.

Wagner, Peter. "The Discourse on Sex—Or Sex as Discourse: Eighteenth-Century Medical and Paramedical Erotica." In *Sexual Underworlds of the Enlightenment,* edited by G. S. Rousseau and Roy Porter, 46–68. Chapel Hill: University of North Carolina Press, 1989.

Webb, Igor. *From Custom to Capital: The English Novel and the Industrial Revolution.* Ithaca: Cornell University Press, 1981.

Weinstein, Philip M. *The Semantics of Desire: Changing Models of Identity from Dickens to Joyce.* Princeton: Princeton University Press, 1984.

Williams, Raymond. *Culture and Society 1780–1950*. 1958. Reprint, New York: Penguin, 1976.

Wood, H. G. *Frederick Denison Maurice*. Cambridge: Cambridge University Press, 1950.

Yeazell, Ruth Bernard. *Fictions of Modesty: Women and Courtship in the English Novel*. Chicago: University of Chicago Press, 1991.

———. "Why Political Novels Have Heroines: *Sybil, Mary Barton,* and *Felix Holt*." *Novel* 18 (winter 1985): 126–44.

Yeo, Eileen Janes. *The Contest for Social Science: Relations and Representations of Gender and Class*. London: River Orams Press, 1996.

Zlotnick, Susan. *Women, Writing, and the Industrial Revolution*. Baltimore: Johns Hopkins University Press, 1998.

Index

Victorian Literature and Culture Series

CHRISTINA ROSSETTI *The Letters of Christina Rossetti,* vols. 1–3, Edited by Antony H. Harrison

BARBARA LEAH HARMAN *The Feminine Political Novel in Victorian England*

JOHN RUSKIN *The Genius of John Ruskin: Selections from His Writings,* Edited by John D. Rosenberg

ANTONY H. HARRISON *Victorian Poets and the Politics of Culture: Discourse and Ideology*

JUDITH STODDART *Ruskin's Culture Wars:* Fors Clavigera *and the Crisis of Victorian Liberalism*

LINDA K. HUGHES AND MICHAEL LUND *Victorian Publishing and Mrs. Gaskell's Work*

LINDA H. PETERSON *Traditions of Victorian Women's Autobiography: The Poetics and Politics of Life Writing*

GAIL TURLEY HOUSTON *Royalties: The Queen and Victorian Writers*

LAURA C. BERRY *The Child, the State, and the Victorian Novel*

BARBARA J. BLACK *On Exhibit: Victorians and Their Museums*

ANNETTE R. FEDERICO *Idol of Suburbia: Marie Corelli and Late-Victorian Literary Culture*

TALIA SCHAFFER *The Forgotten Female Aesthetes: Literary Culture in Late-Victorian England*

JULIA F. SAVILLE *A Queer Chivalry: The Homoerotic Asceticism of Gerard Manley Hopkins*

VICTOR SHEA AND WILLIAM WHITLA, EDITORS *Essays and Reviews: The 1860 Text and Its Reading*

MARLENE TROMP *The Private Rod: Marital Violence, Sensation, and the Law in Victorian Britain*

DORICE WILLIAMS ELLIOTT *The Angel out of the House: Philanthropy and Gender in Nineteenth-Century England*